MUSEUMS AND SOCIAL JUSTICE

MAURA REILLY

WITH A CONTRIBUTION BY LIISA-RÁVNÁ FINBOG

MUSEUMS AND SOCIAL JUSTICE

TOWARDS RECKONING AND CHANGE

WITH 19 ILLUSTRATIONS

T&H

Frontispiece: Carrie Mae Weems, *Museum Island*, 2008, from the *Museum Series*, 2006–present © Carrie Mae Weems. Courtesy of the artist and Gladstone Gallery, New York, Fraenkel Gallery, San Francisco, and Galerie Barbara Thumm, Berlin.

First published in the United Kingdom in 2026 by
Thames & Hudson Ltd, 6–24 Britannia Street, London WC1X 9JD

First published in the United States of America in 2026 by
Thames & Hudson Inc., 500 Fifth Avenue, New York, New York 10110

Cover designed by Callin Mackintosh

EU Authorized Representative: Interart S.A.R.L.
19 rue Charles Auray, 93500 Pantin, Paris, France
productsafety@thameshudson.co.uk
interart.fr

A CIP catalogue record for this book is available from the British Library

Library of Congress Control Number 2024943967

ISBN 978-0-500-02459-1
01

Printed and bound in Türkiye

MIX
Paper | Supporting responsible forestry
FSC® C136333

INTRODUCTION

Museums are modern European inventions that trace their origins to the private collections of the Renaissance era—assemblages curated primarily by elite white male collectors who accrued wealth and status through imperial ventures. The royal, aristocratic and private "cabinets of curiosity" (*Wunderkammern*) of the 16th to 18th centuries serve as the historical precursors to our art, natural history, anthropology, and ethnographic museums. These early museological forms were inextricably linked to colonial enterprise, often functioning as symbolic repositories of conquest, dominance, and cultural appropriation.[1]

From the 15th century onward, all Western European nations participated in colonial expansion. At its height, just before the outbreak of World War I, European imperial powers collectively controlled approximately 84% of the world's landmass.[2] This expansive domination was rationalized through prevailing ideologies of racial hierarchy, which framed colonial rule as the natural ascendancy of so-called "superior" races over those deemed "inferior." In some instances, colonialists justified their unscrupulous collecting or "serial kleptomania" (as scholar Clémentine Deliss has described it) by arguing that these so-called "barbaric," "primitive" races would soon be wiped out, and that any cultural heritage that was not European or American needed to be preserved for posterity.[3] As scholar Rolando Vázquez argues in "The Museum, Decoloniality, and the End of the Contemporary": "With this Eurocentric, colonialist mindset the 'Other' was racialized, animalized, impoverished, de-sexualized, or hyper-sexualized; the Other was made sub-human and the male/white/western-self became the norm of the human."[4] From their inception, museums have reflected this Euro-American-centric, white, male view of the world that has validated racist and sexist stereotypes, and that has explicitly ranked the worlds' cultures, placing the most economically and racially privileged on top. Museums' classificatory and geographic delineations, cataloguing, and exhibition displays serve to substantiate these fictions.

In the wake of women's, civil, and LGBTQ+ rights movements in the 1970s, and with the development of the theory of "new museology" in the 1980s, many art institutions sought to shift away from the traditional role of the museum as an elite, Euro-American-centric ivory tower of culture toward a model that is more ethical and civic-minded.[5] Since then, museums have transformed themselves from static repositories of objects into dynamic spaces that actively engage with the myriad communities they serve. Today, many museums are embracing decolonial, anti-racist agendas, producing exhibitions and programs *with* and *for* their diverse stakeholders, so that all audiences (no matter their race, ethnicity, religion, sexuality, gender, ability, and so on) feel not only welcome, but represented. As museums strive to become agents of change, the concepts of multivocality, participation, collaboration, relevance, decolonization, community engagement, and ethics are increasingly understood as critical to the future and survival of museums.

Indeed, in more recent years, the roles and functions of art institutions have shifted so dramatically that in August 2022, after considerable debate and turmoil, the International Council of Museums (ICOM)—the world's preeminent professional art organization, which represents over 40,000 members from 20,000 museums globally—saw fit to propose a new definition. "A museum," they wrote,

> is a not-for-profit, permanent institution in the service of society that researches, collects, conserves, interprets, and exhibits tangible and intangible heritage. Open to the public, accessible and inclusive, museums foster diversity and sustainability. They operate and communicate ethically, professionally, and with the participation of communities, offering varied experiences for education, enjoyment, reflection, and knowledge sharing.[6]

While the museum's conventional functions—namely to "research, collect, conserve, interpret, and exhibit tangible and intangible heritage"—remain foundational, the updated definition incorporates language aligned with contemporary discourse on the civic responsibilities of museums. Terms such as "diversity," "sustainability," "accessibility," and "inclusivity" signal a shift toward more progressive and socially engaged understandings of institutional purpose.[7] Importantly, the new definition also suggests that a museum should operate "ethically," although neither the statement nor committee offered further guidance. This leaves institutions to determine for themselves: What does it mean for a museum to "communicate and operate ethically?" What is an ethical museum?

Some traditionalists complained the new definition was too "woke," while others in the art world felt that ICOM's definition did not go far enough toward acknowledging museums' complicated histories of privileging white, male, heteronormative, and Euro-American-centric paradigms. While not every museum professional agreed on the new definition, all acknowledged that it was long overdue. (Prior to 2022, ICOM's definition of a museum was last updated in 2007.) The new definition reflects a museum world in the midst of a cultural reckoning. Since 2007, the sector has been plagued by accusations of systemic racism and toxic philanthropy, while calls for repatriation of colonial-era objects have been an almost daily occurrence. Even climate change is an issue being played out in museums, as campaigners repeatedly glue themselves to canonical artworks in major institutions to call attention to the planet's environmental emergency, while demonstrators protest institutional funding by major polluters.

Shortly after war broke out in Gaza in October 2023, museums faced increased pressure to comment on the conflict. Over the next year, dozens of pro-Palestinian demonstrations at museums in the U.S. and Europe, as well as increased anti-Semitism and Islamophobia around the world, raised the stakes. While museums globally have unequivocally rallied around politically potent topics like the war in Ukraine and the murder of George Floyd, the subject of the Israel-Hamas war has been extremely fraught. Some museums have taken a clear stance by canceling exhibitions or censoring artists who have expressed support for Palestine (such as the Barbican Centre, London; the Eskenazi Museum of Art, Bloomington, Indiana; or the Museo del Barrio, New York),[8] many more have been reluctant to make a public statement, including the Metropolitan, Whitney, and British Museums, even after recent pro-ceasefire demonstrations calling for one. In divisive political situations such as these, *any* stance taken is bound to garner criticism.

For a museum to take a political position can jeopardize funding—individual donors who disagree with what they perceive to be the museum's position can simply withdraw their support. In June 2024, for instance, a major donor at the Palais de Tokyo, a contemporary art museum in Paris, resigned from the museum's board, stating publicly that she refused to support an institution that was "anti-capitalist," "anti-Semitic," and "Islamo-leftist."[9] Similarly, a 2024 article in the *Chronicle of Philanthropy* reported on the loss of funding for many nonprofits in the U.S. who were vocal about the war in Gaza. Organizations committed to racial equity were also facing what one expert calls a "funding cliff," as promises made in 2020 dry up.[10]

While I firmly believe that museums should be activist spaces and forums for dialogue, where pressing and even controversial ideas can be explored in curatorial activist exhibitions and programming, I don't agree that museums have to make big, sweeping, public declarations in support of one cause or another. As public charities and nonprofit organizations, in the U.S., at least, museums are obligated to be nonpartisan, or they run the risk of losing their tax-free status. Some may argue that it's a complete exaggeration to say that if a museum takes a political position, it will jeopardize its nonprofit status, but in the U.S. it is a real concern. In 2024, a legislative bill passed the U.S. House of Representatives, with bipartisan support, that would grant the U.S. Treasury sole authority to designate any charity as supporting terrorism, thereby automatically revoking its nonprofit status.[11] Introduced in November 2024, amid numerous protests against the war in Gaza, the bill has been called "a new legislative offensive against organizations advocating for Palestinian rights."[12] The supporters of the bill have expressed concern that tax-exempt charities are providing funding for pro-Palestinian causes, including the student groups who have demonstrated across U.S. university campuses. While the bill is, ostensibly, a measure to fight the financing of terrorism, many fear that the unilateral power afforded the Treasury could extend to other conservative agendas, like anti-LGBTQ+ and anti-DEI crusades, or be used to target any nonprofit whose mission is perceived to oppose the administration's policies—all a widespread effort to persecute those who are believed to be Donald Trump's political enemies. The bill might not become law (as of the time of writing, it still awaits a vote in the U.S. Senate), but the threat it represents is very real—and one that many public charities across the globe are no doubt facing.

In the U.K., in 2021, for instance, the heads of multiple government-funded historical societies signed an open letter contesting the government's right to deny funding to charities it deemed "too political."[13] Similarly, in 2024, Arts Council England (ACE) was involved in a controversy over its new guidance for National Portfolio Organisations (NPOs), which initially suggested that charities avoid "artistic and creative output that might be deemed controversial, activity that might be considered to be overtly political or activist."[14] After a public outcry across the culture sector, ACE revised its guidelines in support of freedom of expression.

On the continent, too, museums and politics make for a complicated mix. In 2022, the Museum Watch Governance Management Project report (published by ICOM) found that, among a broad range of institutions surveyed in Central and Southeast Europe, museum governance has been continually subject to increased levels of "influence and interference via politicians."[15] Alt-right nationalist governments in countries like Poland, Hungary, and Turkey have been known to interfere politically in the operations of museums. Although not the primary focus of the ICOM report, the U.K. has not been exempt from concerns regarding political interference in museum governance: in 2022, the government was accused of breaching impartiality rules by appointing senior figures with ties to the Conservative Party to the boards of public institutions, such as the British Museum and the Victoria and Albert Museum (V&A).[16]

As I write this, and as the world ventures forth into an increasingly conservative era, with far-right, authoritarian politicians in office throughout the U.S. and Europe, I worry about the survival of museums, especially as we watch the slashing of arts budgets and canceling of exhibitions by conservative politicians. With the prospect of a humanity in peril (with a climate catastrophe that will make the planet unlivable, perpetual wars, and nuclear armament), and the eroding of human rights on a daily basis (for women and queer people, BIPOC, immigrants, and refugees, especially), what role will museums play in the future? If arts and culture are no longer a priority for governments, and if citizens don't insist on our right to access and enjoy them, will there be arts funding in the future? Will all social justice exhibitions be censored and/or funding withdrawn? What is for certain is that our planet, our societies, and our cultures are rapidly changing, and it will be incumbent upon museums to embrace the changes ahead.

As the book's title, *Museums and Social Justice*, implies, this text will explore multiple social justice concerns—among them decolonization; indigenization; restitution and repatriation; systemic racism, sexism, ableism, lesbo-homo-trans-phobia; and toxic philanthropy. Chapter 1, "Decolonizing Museums: Enacting Epistemic Disobedience," takes Walter Mignolo's definition of decolonization as its guiding principle. For him, and other scholars, decolonization is intersectional: it requires de-linking from multiple forms of oppression. The chapter examines curatorial projects and artistic interventions that embody this definition and that enact aesthetic and epistemic disobedience, including projects by Clémentine Deliss, Okwui Enwezor, Sarah Farrar, and others, as well as those by Fred Wilson, Pedro Lasch, Amalia Mesa-Bains, and Yuki Kihara. I examine the Pitt Rivers Museum's new strategic direction as a case study in decolonizing an institution. I argue that the process of decolonizing a museum requires that institutions embody its principles structurally and not just as token gestures.

In Chapter 2,"'We Were Here First': Indigenizing Museums," Sámi scholar Liisa-Rávná Finbog and I explore the museological process of indigenization. We argue that to indigenize a museum is a different venture than to decolonize, insofar as the latter always centers the colonizer, while to indigenize is to center Indigenous knowledge, values, and ways of being. As examples of an indigenizing museum practice, we examine the groundbreaking exhibition at the Nordnorsk Kunstmuseum (Northern Norway Art Museum; NNKM) in 2017—in which the local and regional Sámi communities were offered the entire museum footprint to display artworks and objects—and the Sámi Pavilion at the 59th Venice Biennale in 2022. In this chapter, we also address the importance of repatriation and restitution as part of the process of indigenizing museums and discuss the feminist practice of rematriation of illegally acquired objects.

One of the most pressing dilemmas in the world of art and culture today concerns the return of property taken without consent. Throughout history, conquerors, colonialists, archaeologists, generals, and dictators have stolen or illegally acquired objects and artworks, often from communities subjugated by colonial powers. The descendants of those communities are now seeking the return of these objects of cultural significance from the museums and private collections, mainly in the U.S. and Europe, in which they are housed. Currently, the controversy rages on over objects and art taken from Benin and the Congo, as well as Greece's famed Parthenon Marbles and works stolen by the Nazi regime. Chapter 3,"'Give It All Back': Reconciling with Cultural Heritage," examines the need for an ethical approach to the subject of restitution and repatriation in which the power dynamics are flipped. After offering up a short history of International Conventions on Heritage Protection, I explore the subject of the Benin Bronzes and Native American Graves Protection and Repatriation Act (NAGPRA), and take a close look at the British Museum, the Victoria and Albert Museum, and the Metropolitan Museum of Art's stances on repatriation claims.

Recent reports from Artnet, the American Association of Museum Directors (AAMD), Williams College, Freelands Foundation, and Arts Council England (ACE) demonstrate that equality in the art world is still far from reach.[17] BIPOC are still broadly discriminated against as artists and art workers. While women are underrepresented in exhibitions and permanent collections, they occupy most staff positions in museums, but are paid far less than their male counterparts, especially at the executive level. In Chapter 4, "Whose Museum Is It? Inclusion and Exclusion in Museums," I examine the impact of the #MeToo and Black Lives Matter movements on museums and investigate the ways in which continued systemic sexism, racism, and ableism within our institutions lead to lack of representation in their collections and exhibitions, and the exclusion of museumgoers.

Many museums fail to adequately represent the LGBTQ+ community in their collections and exhibition programs, and they fail to account for these communities as audiences, all of which is representative of an institutionalized lesbo-homo-trans-phobia. Along with a number of significant group exhibitions focused on LGBTQ+ artists that have taken place since the 1970s, several museums have made concerted efforts to address gaps in representation by mining their collections for queer content, a curatorial process known as "queering the museum." In Chapter 5, "Prizing Open the Museum's Closets: Queering the Museum," I analyze artist Jo Darbyshire's curated exhibition, *The Gay Museum* (2003) at the Western Australian Museum, Perth, as an early example of this increasingly common museological practice. Next, I offer an overview of two permanent collection exhibitions—one at the National Museum in Warsaw (NMW), Poland, and another at the Birmingham Museum & Art Gallery, both in 2010. Finally, I analyze the exhibition *Queer* (National Gallery of Victoria, Melbourne, 2021), curated by a team of LGBTQ+ curators, as a stellar example of a museological initiative to queer a museum.

"Toxic philanthropy," "blood money," and "art-washing" are the latest terms being used to describe private philanthropy and patronage in the art world, which is enduring a series of scandals that have called into question the ethics of the boards that govern them and the patrons who support them financially. Chapter 6, "How Bloody Is Too Bloody? Toxic Philanthropy and the Corporatization of Museums," examines some of these scandals that have unfolded around donors and board members of major institutions, including the Sacklers (owners of Purdue Pharma), as well as individuals like Leon Black, Rebekah Mercer, and Warren Kanders. Turning to corporate social responsibility and tax-exempt lobbying, I delve into the questionable philanthropic practices of British Petroleum and Airbnb. I argue that the current conflicts we're seeing around museum philanthropy are tied directly to the corporatization of museums, which commenced in the 1980s and continues today. The for-profit mindset inherent to corporations has trickled down into every facet of museums. Ultimately, I argue that de-corporatization is mandatory if museums are to become ethical, democratic institutions.

In the end, there are innumerable issues museums currently face, too many to explore in a single book. There are new developments almost daily: objects and artworks are being returned to source communities; new patrons and corporations are being singled out for toxic philanthropic practices; accusations of white supremacy abound; and the work of decolonizing museums continues. There is no way in which a book like this can be comprehensive; nor can it be fully up-do-date with all the rapid-fire developments outlined daily in global media outlets. (For instance, as this book was being written, there were numerous demonstrations occurring at National Trust locations in the U.K. in protest against its banking relationship with Barclays, which is the largest funder of fossil fuels in Europe.[18]) To fully present the complexities of museums today would also necessitate the integration of different scholarly voices, as mine is just one among many on these subjects. As a white, U.S.-born, queer woman whose scholarship is defined by my activist principles, my perspective differs radically from individuals from different backgrounds and identities. I encourage others to join the continuing conversation.

CHAPTER 1
DECOLONIZING MUSEUMS: ENACTING EPISTEMIC DISOBEDIENCE

INTRODUCTION

The history of the colonial era cannot be disconnected from the history of genocide, enslavement, plundering, extractivism (the extraction of natural resources, like minerals and gems), capitalism, sexual exploitation, a superimposition of strict heteropatriarchal gender roles, a construction of the (racial) Other as epistemologically irrelevant, and a firm belief that those from Euro-America are intellectually and culturally superior to those from colonized communities. As institutions founded during the colonial era, when explorers, archaeologists, and other oppressors "acquired" objects for display in their private residences as "cabinets of curiosity," or for public display as symbols of conquest, museums came to embody these same principles. Racism, sexism, heteropatriarchy, Euro-American-centrism (which in this context will primarily refer to Europe, as well as the U.S. and Canada)—these have been the cornerstone of museums since their founding. Discrimination is built into their DNA.

If we accept that museums are intrinsically colonial constructs that are inherently exclusionary, we must ask if decolonizing them is even possible—and, if it is not, then what is the best way forward? Must museums be destroyed and rebuilt, as curator Dan Hicks of the Pitt Rivers Museum suggests? Must museums be abandoned altogether, as scholar Walter Mignolo would advise? Must they be reconceptualized? Absolutely. While museums cannot undo history, they are of course capable of self-reflexivity. The colonial bones might run too deep, and the sacrifices needed too large, but it does not mean museums are not obligated to try, or that some good might not come of institutions' thoughtful engagement with their troubled pasts. Given the significant public trust vested in art institutions, the museum sector bears a critical responsibility to avoid reproducing the harmful ideologies of its colonial past. Museums are thus ethically obligated to pursue decolonizing efforts with intention and rigor. Through such transformative work, these institutions hold the potential to shift from being "sites of colonial harm into sites of healing, empowerment, and revitalization."[1]

Scholars from the Global South, including Walter Mignolo, Aníbal Quijano, María Lugones, and Rolando Vázquez, are at the forefront of theorizing a broader, intersectional definition of the term "decolonization," which can be implemented in the context of the museum sector.[2] For them, unlearning Euro-American systems of knowledge is to begin the process of decolonization. They argue that decolonization is about an "epistemic de-linking" from Euro-American-centric, settler colonial knowledge production, which is characterized by white supremacy more broadly, but also by sexism, ableism, heteropatriarchy, classism, and other forms of oppression.[3] (Epistemic means "systems of knowledge"; de-linking, in this context, means "learning to unlearn."[4]) Decolonial theorists from the Global South argue that the achievements of the Renaissance in Europe, indeed the Enlightenment itself, would have been impossible without the exploitation and subjugation of Other(ed) countries and peoples. As such, for them, Euro-American-centrism in and of itself dismisses Indigenous ways of being and thinking and instead reinforces whiteness through processes of racialization and the enforcement of the modern/colonial order (which in truth is also, at best, epistemic ignorance).[5] In art history this is evident in the white, male Euro-American-centrism of our traditional canon and the positing of all Other art (which is to say, all art produced by the majority of the world) as inferior. Art historians and museums have become the definers and gatekeepers of what is deemed beautiful and the sublime. Mignolo would call this a colonization of aesthesis.[6] To decolonize aesthesis, then, Mignolo advocates for "epistemic disobedience," or de-linking from Euro-American-centrism.[7] It is this theory of "epistemic disobedience," and its enactment within museums, that forms the throughline in this chapter.

There are myriad definitions of decolonization—from those put forth by Eve Tuck, K. Wayne Yang, Wanda Nanibush, and Shaheen Kasmani to Amy Lonetree, Linda Tuhiwai Smith, and Decolonize This Place (DTP)—but it is Mignolo's that resonates most for me, as its implementation within a museum setting is visibly actionable, as will be evident in the case studies below.[8] What all of the scholarly definitions of decolonization have in common is that the process involves an overhaul of entire systems of knowledge, or episteme. Each of the scholars looking to define decolonization call for a constant questioning of one's own location in what Mignolo calls the "colonial matrix of power."[9] Most agree that to decolonize involves a centering of Indigenous ways of being and knowing; while others, as is explored in Chapter 2, believe the verb "to indigenize" more accurately reflects that desire. All definitions agree that successful repatriation and restitution efforts are critical to decolonizing a museum, because unless there is a sound reason to do otherwise, erroneously acquired objects should be returned, as will be explored in detail in Chapters 2 and 3. Ultimately, all definitions converge on the understanding that decolonization is a protracted, difficult, and inherently incomplete process.[10]

To decolonize is no small task, but many museums and curators today are making strides toward doing so. The following case studies examine some of the ways in which institutions, curators, and artists are embracing the call to decolonize by enacting aesthetic and epistemic disobedience.

WELTKULTUREN MUSEUM, FRANKFURT (2010–15)

From 2010 to 2015, the ethnographic Weltkulturen Museum (or Museum of World Cultures) in Frankfurt became a laboratory for a radical institution-wide, decolonial vision enacted by its then director Clémentine Deliss. As described in her book *The Metabolic Museum* (2020), she transformed a museum that was, in her words, an "emporium of old dusty objects" into one conceived as a metabolism, a living, dynamic, and transformative system rather than a static repository of objects.[11] She described the museum's collections as "reservoirs of memories," "as banks of stored code, as strata of symbolism, desire, and ingenuity" whose value is suspended—all awaiting emancipation.[12] Starting from the premise that "the very notion of 'ethnos' is inherently racist,"[13] Deliss sought to "breathe presence back into the artifacts, restore consciousness to their unfinished status, and help to heal the disposition of the institution."[14] She observes that when long-forgotten objects are recognized as "agents," the process of "remediation"—or healing—can begin.[15] As she explains: "To remediate also implies to remedy a deficient situation, for example, the ambivalent resonance of the colonial past."[16]

To revitalize the historically outdated institution, Deliss undertook a critical recontextualization of the museum's collections, re-presenting objects in ways that foregrounded their colonial entanglements. For instance, she introduced into public view previously unexhibited materials, such as photographs of female genitalia taken in Africa in the late 1950s, as well as hundreds of photographs of migrant workers from a Sumatran tobacco plantation in the 1890s, which were taken by the museum's founding director, the German physician Bernhard Hagen.[17] Accompanied by interpretive wall texts, these displays illuminated the role such images played in the production of racial hierarchies within medical and anthropological discourses of the 19th and 20th centuries.[18] Exhibition galleries were reconfigured to incorporate tables and additional seating, promoting prolonged looking and dialogical exchange. New participatory structures emerged, including "Friends of the Museum," an amateur club of anthropology enthusiasts, and public programs oriented around provenance debates were presented.[19] Additionally, a gastro-anthropologist was engaged to prepare meals and run an evening class called "The World of the Spoon," which focused on culinary practices from non-Euro-American traditions. This extended the museum's decolonial ambitions into the sensory and social realm.[20]

Deliss invited artists, scientists, writers, curators, and musicians for one-month residencies to respond to the thousands of artifacts taken from Africa during Germany's colonial expeditions, now housed in the permanent collection. Residents included the German artist Antje Majewski, Belgian curator Dieter Roelstraete, Ghanian artist and filmmaker John Akomfrah, Senegalese painter and activist El Hadji Sy, German writer and anthropologist Hans-Jürgen Heinrichs, Nigerian artist Otobong Nkanga, German filmmaker Werner Herzog, Mexican curator Pablo León de la Barra, and American musician DJ Spooky, among many others.[21] The residents were encouraged to mine the collection and to produce exhibitions, lectures, films, musical compositions, or other original programs based on their contemplations. For example, the English writer and artist Tom McCarthy engaged directly with the museum's archives in the development of his novel *Satin Island* (2015), centering the narrative around an ethnographer protagonist and incorporating museum staff as fictionalized characters. He metaphorically described the museum's storage facility as a "giant sarcophagus" housing hidden, internalized histories.[22] Similarly, the German Pop Art pioneer Thomas Bayrle contributed to the project by exhibiting a series of works on paper by his father, Alf Bayrle—gouaches and drawings produced during a 1930s collecting expedition to Ethiopia—which were displayed in dialogue with stone steles held in the museum's collection for nearly a century.[23] In another intervention, New Zealand artist Luke Willis Thompson used his allocated production budget to facilitate the repatriation of the ancestral remains of a Muslim immigrant, thereby redirecting institutional resources toward reparative justice.[24]

With each artistic intervention and curatorial innovation introduced by resident collaborators, and with each successive exhibition, the museum's eclectic and historically anachronistic objects were imbued with renewed contemporary significance.[25] Deliss's was a refreshing decolonial vision for a 21st-century ethnographic museum—but one that was short-lived. After five years at the helm, she was dismissed without cause. It is possible that her decolonial, post-ethnographic vision was perceived as too radical, encountering resistance from institutional custodians of the collection as well as from more traditional scholars within the field of anthropology.

POSTWAR: ART BETWEEN THE PACIFIC AND THE ATLANTIC 1945–1965 (2016–17)

In the context of museums, to decolonize involves "resisting the reproduction of colonial taxonomies" and "vindicating radical multiplicity."[26] The process begins with a fundamental reconceptualization of modernism as more vigorously diverse because it is always already linked with European imperialism and Euro-American-centrism. Art history as a discipline must be reconsidered, then, in favor of a transcultural or global approach to objects and history. The exhibition *Postwar: Art Between the Pacific and the Atlantic 1945–1965*, curated by Okwui Enwezor, Ulrich Wilmes, and Katie Seigel, at the Haus der Kunst, Munich from 2016 to 2017, undertook such an approach by proposing a new, global history of post–World War II art—or, more precisely, an exhibition that proposed plural modernisms. As typically told in the U.S. and Europe, the history of post–World War II art follows a progression of loose art historical "isms" geographically aligned with Euro-America—from Abstract Expressionism and Pop to Minimalism and Conceptualism. With few exceptions, the artists that exemplify these movements are white, heterosexual, male, and Euro-American. As it has been replicated by every major museum in Europe and the U.S., this trajectory of Euro-American post–World War II art has been reified. But the *Postwar* exhibition, which included 350 works by 218 artists from 65 countries, demonstrated that these movements were taking place all over the world, simultaneously, albeit as differently called art movements. As a result, artists from Brazil's Neo-Concretism movement were shown alongside Japan's Gutai avant-gardists, while figures little known in Europe and the U.S.—such as Malangatana Ngwenya, Hervé Télémaque, and Avinash Chandra—were placed on equal footing with canonical names like Willem de Kooning, Carl Andre, and Andy Warhol. Similarly, celebrated artists like Henry Moore and Joseph Beuys appeared beside lesser-known figures such as Andrzej Wróblewski and Fateh al-Moudarres.[27] By exposing these blind spots in art history, the curators did not seek to construct a new, unified narrative to replace the Euro-American canon, but rather to unsettle its dominance. Their goal was to present, in Enwezor's words, a "multivalent network of relationships and differences, affiliations and cultural solidarities, singularities and multiplicities," in an attempt to "shrug off" the burden of "canonical" art history, and to let it "fall, gracefully, by the wayside."[28] The exhibition, and its 800-page catalogue, effectively "tore a hole in the continuum of art history," according to *ARTnews*.[29] The exhibition revealed that the narrow historical emphasis on postwar art of Europe and the U.S. failed to capture the full scope of the "wild, weird, and groundbreaking" art produced from 1945 to 1965.[30] *Postwar* made clear that a global vision of art history is possible and that such exhibitions can function as a form of aesthetic and epistemic disobedience that replaces or displaces white Euro-American-centric art historical discourses with multivocal perspectives.

However, a global art history is not without its critics.[31] Cultural theorist Joaquín Barriendos Rodríguez critiques the concept of global art—often equated with the free circulation of artworks within a globalized market—as a manifestation of the coloniality of power.[32] He argues that the presentation and collection of art from around the world may, in fact, replicate colonial extractivist logics by appropriating and commodifying the cultural productions of others for the enrichment of dominant institutions.[33] This puts museums into a difficult position. As art historian Marie-Laure Allain Bonilla explains, "Museums are caught in a paradox: on the one hand, the need to make their functions and policies evolve towards a geopolitical revisionism informed by postcolonial and decolonial perspectives; on the other, the risk of imposing a new geo-aesthetical expression of the Western model."[34] Regardless, with such endeavors as *Postwar*, curators can query the "heroic history of Franco-American modernism," which art historian Tim Barringer argues, "lives on as a zombie ideology among museum goers."[35] Curators can help erase distinctions between high and low art; they can disrupt the assumption of history as a linear progression—one that continues to locate historical agency solely with white, male Euro-Americans while excluding vast constituencies of Others.[36] Importantly, as was the case with *Postwar*, curators can dismiss center/periphery, East/West, Black/white, male/female, and other binaries, promoting instead a plurality of voices, including non-Euro-American artists as equal players rather than token inclusions. This latter style of curating—replacing binaries with pluralities—has been termed "exhibition-as-polylogue."[37] Utilizing this curatorial strategy, as I have argued in *Curatorial Activism* (2018), time can be perceived as not long but wide; vision is no longer singular, belonging to a monolithic, dominant community, but kaleidoscopic. This curatorial strategy—polyvocality mixed with transculturality—is, I posit, the most transformative in relation to the canon and the most effective tool in decolonizing aesthesis and in de-linking from Euro-American-centrism.

TŪRANGAWAEWAE: ART AND NEW ZEALAND (2018–21)

The *Tūrangawaewae: Art and New Zealand* exhibition at the Museum of New Zealand / Te Papa Tongarewa (2018–21), organized by a multicultural curatorial consortium led by Sarah Farrar, is a stellar example of decolonial curation.[38] It could have been a linear, historic trajectory of art in New Zealand produced by white colonialists, told by white settlers, from early portraits by William Beetham or Gottfried Lindauer and mid-20th-century works by Colin McCahon to contemporary works by Dane Mitchell and Simon Denny. Instead, the bilingual (in Māori and English) rotating permanent collection exhibition presented over one hundred artworks in an ahistorical, heterogenous fashion utilizing a curatorial strategy of "relational studies" or "exhibition-as-polylogue."[39] This was first evident in its introductory room, "Toi Whenua / Beginnings," where contemporary works were de-hierarchized; known and lesser-known artists hung beside works by unknown creators. The history of art in New Zealand has typically involved the story of primarily Pākehā (white New Zealander) artists, a narrative that begins with the European arrival in New Zealand in 1769. Not so here.

Tūrangawaewae (which translates roughly as "a place to stand"[40]) was a mash-up of historic and contemporary Māori, Pacific Islander, Papua New Guinean, and Pākehā artists—all presented on equal footing. In fact, it could be argued that the art of Māori artists was given preference throughout the exhibition. For example, the exhibition granted pride of place to key works that foreground Indigenous perspectives and artistic genealogies. Centrally positioned in the first gallery was *Haumia, Rangitiina, Tiinia* (1980), a sculptural installation by contemporary Māori artist Arnold Manaaki Wilson. Elevated on a square white plinth, Wilson's three imposing painted *pou*—figurative representations of atua (deities)—recall *pou whenua*, traditional Māori boundary markers.[41] Their strategic placement interrupts the viewer's line of sight to the adjoining gallery, compelling an embodied engagement with the work before passage is possible. Complementing the presence of Wilson's sculpture, the first gallery also featured three contemporary appliqué tapa (barkcloth) works by Ömie artists Sarah Ugibari (b. 1919) and Brenda Kesi (b. 1937), which were set in dialogue with two earlier examples of Papua New Guinean tapa created by unnamed artists.[42]

The next room, titled "Ngā Tai Whakarongorua / Encounters," featured a dense salon-style hang of historical portraits by mostly white male artists of multi-race subjects, including many portraits of Māori. Yet flanking this long wall were two powerful works that functioned to offset that dominance. Installed within the left-hand wall was an inset display case featuring *Te Umukohukohu*, a *pūtātara*—a traditional trumpet crafted from carved wood and a conch shell—with a documented provenance extending back to the 17th century.[43] As curator Sarah Farrar describes this piece: "A treasured taonga, Te Umukohukohu ... is a musical instrument, a symbol of power and status, and an object of resistance: pūtātara were to signal warning and Te Umukohukohu is documented to have been used in 1867, when Te Whenuanui was active in the New Zealand Wars."[44] The presence of the *taonga* disrupted conventional art historical narratives that locate the origins of cultural significance in Aotearoa New Zealand with European arrival.
The inclusion of the *pūtātara* functioned as a deliberate curatorial intervention, foregrounding the longstanding presence and cultural sovereignty of Māori prior to colonization. On the opposite wall, a compelling counterpoint was offered by a portrait of an unnamed young Māori woman, whose gaze was directed across the gallery toward the historical portraits—an evocative gesture that appeared to symbolically interrogate the entangled histories of encounter among Māori, Pacific peoples, and Europeans. (Notably, the salon-style installation also featured two portrait-sized framed mirrors, strategically placed by the curators to implicate viewers directly—inviting them to reflect on their own positionality within these historical narratives.)[45]

The *Tūrangawaewae: Art and New Zealand* exhibition at Te Papa proved that an institution with an encyclopedic collection can engage in aesthetic and epistemic disobedience. However, their innovative decolonial project was one temporary exhibition among many in the institution, the majority of which adhere to Eurocentric museology. So, how does one decolonize an *entire* so-called "universal" museum like Te Papa—or the Met or the British Museum for that matter—that claims to represent the "whole world"? Individual exhibitions like *Tūrangawaewae* are important, of course. But can these museums truly de-link from their Euro-American-centric underpinnings, when they continue to adhere to strict classifications like geographic locations (Chinese art, American art) and historical periods (Ancient art, Contemporary art)? Can one decolonize by simply inserting contemporary artists beside historic objects? Will that suffice when the existing collections are inherently colonial enterprises? Curatorial interventions like *Tūrangawaewae* can still make a difference, because they remind us that misbehaviors and disobedience *within* the museum itself can undermine racist and sexist ideologies.

REFRAMING PICTON (2020–22)

In 2020, in the midst of Black Lives Matter protests, which reached a new intensity in response to the murder of George Floyd, the National Museum of Wales in Cardiff removed an 1812 portrait of Welsh slave owner Sir Thomas Picton by Sir Martin Archer Shee from their Hall of Heroes. Historically, Picton has been celebrated as a hero who died at the Battle of Waterloo, but as governor of Trinidad in the 1790s and early 1800s, he was known to have abused the people he enslaved, for which he later stood trial in London. He was convicted, but the decision was eventually overturned, given his connections.[46] The portrait was removed from view at National Museum Cardiff as part of a youth-led initiative called "Reframing Picton" that was sponsored by the museum and conducted in collaboration with a community partner, the Sub-Sahara Advisory Panel (SSAP). The painting, which had been on view for a century, was moved to storage, and artists with Trinidadian roots were commissioned to "reinterpret" Picton's life and legacy in the Caribbean, according to a press release from the museum. Trinidadian and Tobagonian multidisciplinary artist Gesiye and Laku Neg (Black Yard), a U.K.-based collective of artists of Trinidadian heritage that shares African diaspora stories through the arts, were chosen to collaborate on the new monuments. The museum also chose to replace Picton's portrait temporarily in the Hall of Heroes with a portrait from 1937 depicting a young working-class Welsh man named William Lloyd, who likely dug ditches in coal mines, as painted by artist Albert Houthuesen. It is a heroic portrait of an everyday, working man.

Two years after the museum's removal of the Picton painting, they presented an exhibition using the initiative's title, "Reframing Picton," within which they featured the new commissions by artist Gesiye and Laku Neg alongside the portrait of Picton. Rather than hung on the wall, the historic portrait was displayed at floor level in a wooden travel frame. The exhibition's aim was "to give a voice to those most affected by Picton's actions, and to those who live with the legacy today," according to the museum.[47] The new commissions by Gesiye and Laku Neg "explore narratives of ancestry, healing, transformation and empowerment," and aim "to challenge colonial narratives that have traditionally existed in the National Museum Cardiff's galleries by centering Black consciousness, experiences, and voices."[48] Gesiye's work, *The Wound Is a Portal*, comprised a series of portraits and a short film that investigated tattooing as a cathartic and embodied practice through which participants engaged with intergenerational trauma rooted in their relationship to the land.[49] Laku Neg's *Spirited* was an immersive installation comprising woven newspaper, a metal sculpture resembling gallows, three videos, a soundscape, and found objects. It aimed to offer "reimaginings and re-creations of a period in which Trinidadian and Welsh history overlap."[50] Their commission undertook a re-presentation of Luisa, Thisbe, and Present—three named individuals who suffered under Picton's brutal regime in Trinidad—foregrounding narratives that had previously been excluded from the museum's interpretation of the portrait.[51] The exhibition also featured artifacts and documents related to the 1806 Picton trial, and the 18th-century anti-slavery movement in Britain.

One of the expressed goals of the exhibition, according to the museum's and SSAP's press release, was "to create healthy ways of addressing trauma," and to encourage visitors to listen and learn from past injustices.[52] Importantly, they hoped that the exhibition would function as "a site of conscience rather than indoctrination." As Fadhili Maghiya, director of the SSAP, said: "For the longest time Picton has been celebrated in Wales, now, for the first-time communities that were historically exploited and abused by the likes of Picton have a reason to celebrate .... Our stories, told through beautiful and affirmative pieces of art, celebrate our resilience and remembering our heritage and history, our side of the story."[53] In the end, *Reframing Picton* fundamentally shifted the ways in which we engage with history. Insofar as the act of decolonization is an act of decentering the colonial, *Reframing Picton* functioned as curatorial/epistemic disobedience within the walls of the National Museum Cardiff.

INVISIBLE INVENTORIES: QUESTIONING KENYAN COLLECTIONS IN WESTERN MUSEUMS (2021)

According to a database compiled by the Invisible Inventories Programme (IIP), a collective of Kenyan and European scholars, archivists, and artists, at least 32,000 objects looted from Kenya by colonialists currently reside in over thirty European and North American collections. The exhibition *Invisible Inventories: Questioning Kenyan Collections in Western Museums*, which premiered in 2021 at the Nairobi National Museum, followed by the Rautenstrauch-Joest-Museum in Cologne and the Weltkulturen Museum in Frankfurt, used the database as curatorial fodder. The exhibition was a collaborative project by the IIP, the SHIFT collective (Germany/France), Njoki Ngumi (a filmmaker and member of "The Nest" collective, Kenya), and the Goethe-Institut in Nairobi, and sought to spotlight art and artifacts that had been forcibly removed by Europeans from Kenya during a series of colonial occupations (1895–1963). The exhibition aimed to make the database visible, highlighting the deep sense of loss experienced by communities who are deprived of their heritage. Thus, many of the exhibition cases were empty, like "altars to the absence of phantom objects."[54] Positioned above each empty display case was an illustration suggesting the type of object it may once have contained, such as ornamental items, armor, garments, or ritual artifacts.[55]

The exhibition also included extended wall labels with photographs that detailed the historical accounts of many of the looted objects. One such label recounted the story of the Ngadji, a sacred drum belonging to the Pokomo people, which was stolen by a Norwegian wood trader and is currently held in the British Museum. The label noted that the drum has remained in storage for over a century without ever being publicly displayed. Other labels drew attention to the widespread presence of ancestral remains in European and American institutions, including the head of Koitalel Arap Samoei, the spiritual leader of the Nandi people. As the label emphasized, his soul is believed to be unable to rest without the performance of specific burial rites, which are contingent upon the return of his remains. The exhibition also included Vigango—totemic effigies created by the Mijikenda peoples to commemorate deceased family members.[56] These sacred objects serve not only to honor the dead but also to sustain intergenerational ties, reinforcing lineage and ensuring the spiritual and material wellbeing of the living.[57] The exhibition presented profiles of some white imperialists known for their cold-blooded brutality, such as Colonel Richard Meinertzhagen, a British soldier and intelligence officer who was posted to British East Africa in 1902. Meinertzhagen was reported to have been particularly violent, in one instance leading an expedition that resulted in the slaughter of over 1,500 Kenyans (and 33 British). (Incidentally, Meinertzhagen was also responsible for the execution and decapitation of Koitalel Arap Samoei, the revered leader of the Nandi people, whose severed head was subsequently sent to London for purported scientific study.[58])

The exhibition also included works by contemporary artists addressing the legacies of loss. One such piece, titled *31,302*, dated 2021, produced by Jim Chuchu and Njoki Ngumi, comprised thousands of shipping labels strung together, each inscribed with information about a Kenyan artifact held in an institution abroad. One of the SHIFT Collective's contributions to the exhibition was a *Kanga*, a Swahili cloth made for women, with a message that read: "Anadaiwa hata kope si zake" (That person is so deep in debt even their eyelashes are not their own). In another contemporary work, the SHIFT Collective produced a sound installation that explored the complex and contested narratives surrounding the so-called Man-Eaters of Tsavo—two iconic lions whose lethal attacks temporarily disrupted British imperial expansion during the construction of the Kenya-Uganda Railway at the turn of the twentieth century. Since 1925, the preserved remains of these lions have been displayed as taxidermy specimens at the Field Museum in Chicago.[59] Many Kenyans regard them as national treasures that should be returned to Kenya.

While the exhibition showcased just how many objects had been looted and in which institutions they currently reside, the organizers also hoped to open the conversation regarding the repatriation of all material culture, art, and artifacts removed from Kenya during colonial times. This curatorial project was in and of itself decolonial—and most certainly "de-linked" the treasures from their Euro-American host institutions, at least temporarily.

SLAVERY AND THE BANK (2022–24)

In 2020, as Black Lives Matter protests intensified in the U.K., the Bank of England removed from display eight paintings and two busts of former governors and directors who, it had been revealed, once collectively owned 4,920 enslaved people.[60] The revelation came from a database being compiled by the University College London's Centre for the Study of the Legacies of British Slavery, which also contained documentation of the bank's ownership of a plantation in Grenada and involvement in the West Indian slave trade. Following these revelations, the bank appointed a researcher to document its connections to the transatlantic trade in enslaved people and committed to presenting an exhibition at the Bank of England Museum to explore that part of its history. The show *Slavery and the Bank*, organized by the bank's curator, Jennifer Adam, in consultation with the Bank of England Ethnic Minority Network, opened in April 2022, without the contested portraits on display, and ran through February 2024 (Fig. 1).

The exhibition was structured chronologically, beginning with the founding of the East India Company in 1600 and extending through to the imperial expansions on the African continent in the early 20th century.[61] One of the exhibition's principal aims was to explore the bank's involvement in the business of slavery as well as its financial connections to British institutions that benefited from those profits. For instance, one panel at the entrance to the exhibition featured a large reproduction of a portrait by Lorenzo da Castro of Sir Robert Clayton (1629–1707). Clayton was the governor of the Bank of England from 1702 to 1707 and served on the board of, and was a major investor in, the Royal African Company, a London-based corporation that trafficked and enslaved innumerable African people (from the 1670s through the 1750s).[62] He also owned a plantation in Bermuda. Some of the immense wealth he acquired from his investments in these endeavors was donated to charitable organizations, like Christ's Hospital and St. Thomas' Hospital, both in London, on whose boards he sat for many years.

The exhibition's displays explained the bank's role in slavery compensation, as well. Following the abolition of slavery by the British government in 1833, a total of £20 million was allocated in compensation to slave owners. Although the bank did not provide the funds directly, it played an administrative role in overseeing the disbursement of payments on behalf of the government.[63] In another display, visitors were invited to handle a gold ingot once extracted by enslaved Africans in Brazil; while another features a painted portrait by Godfrey Kneller of Humphry Morice (1671–1731), former governor of the Bank of England, who amassed a fortune trading and transporting enslaved people from West Africa to the Caribbean.

At the heart of the exhibition's narrative was a large panel devoted to the 599 enslaved people at the bank's Grenada plantations, which the bank took possession of after a bankruptcy case in the 1770s. The first names of the enslaved men, women, and children who lived and worked at the Grenada plantation are listed on the panel—Michele, Babie, Luke—which hangs above a facsimile visitors can flip through of the "inventory" from the plantation, where people are catalogued alongside different forms of property like buildings, stock, and land. The facsimile also records the value assigned to each person in British pounds, ranging from £30 to £330.

Some of the panels presented information that proposed challenging questions for the visitors. In one display, for instance, which explored how the Royal African Company and the East India Company transported gold mined in Ghana to London, the panel's text asked if gold contains traces of slavery. In another display devoted to the Clapham Sect, a provocative question is posed as to whether we should celebrate abolitionists. It explains that while the Sect's members were evangelical reformers dedicated to abolition, they were also later involved in the indenturing of former slaves into apprenticeships.[64]

The Bank of England's historical analysis of its links to slavery—as displayed in the exhibition—is part of broader, recent assessments by many of Britain's financial institutions, including Barclays and Lloyds Banking Group. Michael Taylor, author of the book *The Interest* (2020), has explained that most U.K. banks of a similar age would have had some involvement in the slave trade.[65] For Britain, the "world's leading slave power," the transatlantic trade in enslaved people was vital to its prosperity, according to Taylor.[66] British financial institutions offered long-term commercial credit to plantations in the colonies for the purpose of purchasing slaves and investors, while the banks got richer and richer, with that money trickling down into philanthropic endeavors, the building of country estates, and into bank accounts that, it can be assumed, continue to support many of Britain's elite families.[67]

While a temporary exhibition can never repair harm done, for the Bank of England to present the exhibition *Slavery and the Bank* is a step towards reconciling with historical injustices, if for no other reason than for its transparency and acknowledgment of the horrific legacy of its complicity in the trade of enslaved people.

DECOLONIAL ARTISTIC INTERVENTIONS

Exposing institutional biases is often difficult for those working from *inside* museums. It has frequently been artists involved in the process of institutional critique, working with permanent collections, that have enacted some of the most interesting examples of epistemic de-linkings from Euro-American-centric, settler colonial knowledge production. The most renowned of these museological interventions is Fred Wilson's *Mining the Museum* (1992–93) in which the artist rearranged objects from the permanent collection of the Maryland Historical Society into jarring juxtapositions. For example, with *Metalwork, 1793–1880*, he placed iron slave shackles with a grouping of decorative silver tableware to draw attention to the historical treatment of African American peoples, while (ostensibly) white slave owners sipped tea from expensive silverware. In another juxtaposition, *Modes of Transport, 1770–1910*, Wilson installed a mask of the Ku Klux Klan with a baby carriage.

As a whole, in highlighting the unheard and unseen voices of African Americans in the museum collection, Wilson's project was a devastating indictment of institutionalized racism and a prime example of decolonial artistic praxis.[68]

In a similar example of decolonial artistic intervention, an installation by Pedro Lasch called *Black Mirror/Espejo Negro* (2008–9) was first commissioned by the Nasher Museum of Art, Duke University, to accompany its blockbuster exhibition *El Greco to Velázquez* in 2008. For his intervention, Lasch selected sixteen figures from the museum's permanent collection of pre-Columbian art and placed them on pedestals with their backs turned to the viewer. In front of the figures hung large, rectangular black mirrors, reflecting the fronts of the sculptures. In one grouping, an ancient statue of the Aztec goddess Coatlicue was combined with Velázquez's *Las Meninas* (1656, Fig. 3); in another, a Mesoamerican statue from circa 1000 BCE was juxtaposed with a 17th-century painting by José de Ribera, titled *La mujer barbuda* (1631). Standing within Lasch's installation, the museumgoer viewed colonial-era paintings, and their own face and body, all visible on a single mirrored plane. The reflections collapsed past and present, allowing for the perception of co-temporality, embodying what Walter Mignolo refers to as a "modernity/coloniality union."[69] As Mignolo explains, the black mirrors "act as go-betweens between the present and the absent, the visible and the invisible, the colonizer and the colonized."[70] In this configuration, the Spaniards depicted in the paintings are no longer positioned as the observers but become the observed—thereby inverting the colonial gaze and destabilizing the traditional power dynamic between colonizer and colonized. Mignolo called this installation "an act of aesthetic, epistemic, and political disobedience," which reminds viewers that modernity's "darker side" is coloniality.[71]

Amalia Mesa-Bains's *New World Wunderkammer* (2013–14, Fig. 2) is an example of a decolonial museological intervention that employs *Wunderkammern*, or cabinets of curiosities—early precursors of the museum itself.[72] For the large-scale installation, she worked with the collection of the Fowler Museum at the University of California at Los Angeles (UCLA) to create a wall-sized sculpture inclusive of three cabinets of curiosities representing Africa, the Indigenous Americas, and *mestizaje* (descendants of Europeans, Indigenous Americans, and Africans). The site-specific installation with altar-like components featured seventy-five objects from the museum's collection alongside some of the artist's personal belongings. Mesa-Bains claims that with the *Wunderkammer* she sought to "invert older intercultural power relationships"[73] and to "restore spiritual meaning" to objects that had been forcibly removed from their places of origin and to recontextualize them within the "themes of memory, struggle, loss, and wonder."[74] Her goal was to reframe objects that were once collected for purposes such as scientific study or as curiosities of the "exotic," offering them new interpretations. In creating a space "for wonder, beauty, and healing that are at the same time political remembrances of injustice, sorrow, and death,"[75] hers was a *taking back* of and a de-linking from the princely *Kunstkammern* of the Enlightenment period in a sustained effort to reconstruct the past.

The practices of Wilson, Lasch, and Mesa-Bains select and recontextualize objects from existing museum collections in order to advance a decolonial agenda. Yuki Kihara's *Culture for Sale* (2012–14) enacted epistemic disobedience within the museum itself, in this instance at the Wellington City Gallery in New Zealand. During a trip to Germany to investigate archives related to the German occupation of Samoa (1900–1914), the artist discovered that there were several groups of Samoans—including men, women, and children—that had been forcibly exhibited in human zoos, which was a popular form of exotic entertainment at the time. Conceptually informed by the forced Samoan participation in the human zoos in Germany, *Culture for Sale* was a live public performance and video installation that featured Samoan dancers who were instructed to perform briefly when they were paid money by the audience. The video installation echoes the performance in that the audience was able to pay-per-view the footage of the performance by inserting a 20-cent coin into a slot machine. While the installation-performance educated viewers on the mistreatment of Samoans, it also explored the commercialization of Samoan culture in the wake of the fiftieth anniversary of Samoa's independence in 2012. Ultimately, Kihara's *Culture for Sale* was an epistemic de-linking from Eurocentric, settler colonial knowledge production, which is characterized by white supremacy.

Museological interventions like these by Wilson, Lasch, Mesa-Bains, and Kihara prove that a decolonial approach to art making is possible. Theirs are acts of epistemic and aesthetic disobedience that put form and action to decoloniality.

A DIRECTOR'S DECOLONIAL VISION: PITT RIVERS MUSEUM, OXFORD

As with the ethnographic Weltkulturen Museum mentioned above, how does a large archaeological and anthropological museum like the Pitt Rivers, with 500,000 artifacts in its collection, reconcile with its colonialist past? That was the question posed by the museum's director Laura Van Broekhoven, who, over a period of four years from 2017 to 2020, led the pioneering Internal Review of Displays and Programming from an Ethical Perspective, which involved both internal staff and external stakeholders, including Oxford students, local residents, refugees, and immigrants. The review provided a plan for reckoning with the complicated issue of a museum's display of objects acquired either under duress or legally during the period of British expansionism.

The report also addressed decolonization, a process defined by the Museums Association as "not simply the relocation of a statue or an object; it is a long-term process that seeks to recognize the integral role of Empire in [British] museums—from their creation to the present day. Decolonization requires a reappraisal of our institutions and their history and an effort to address colonial structures and approaches to all areas of museum work."[76] The Pitt Rivers's decolonial strategy is one that "embraces hope, reconciliation and redress and focuses on co-curatorial approaches to bring new voices into the Museum and ensure public engagement is led by socially engaged work with communities."[77]

There were some exhibition cases that the report identified as in need of immediate review, including those that displayed ancestral bodily remains and objects with questionable provenance or of sacred importance to source communities. In analyzing the wall labels, they also identified derogatory and racist language, all of which was immediately rewritten.

One important outcome of the internal review was the decision in 2020 to remove 120 ancestral remains that had been on display for decades, including a mummy and a shrunken head. As Broekhoven explains apropos the removal from display of remains in 2020: "Our audience research has shown that visitors often saw the Museum's displays of human remains as a testament to other cultures being 'savage', 'primitive' or 'gruesome.'"[78] In a case displaying ancestral remains, called "Treatment of Dead Enemies," visitors now discover an educational label about the museum's collections of ancestral remains in general, and their plans to restitute or repatriate those remains. Visitors are now also offered an explanation as to why the remains were taken off display, with one reason being that they "formed part of problematic past academic practices of physical anthropology and race science, and how those are linked to racist ideas about superiority and inferiority."[79] While the museum still stewards about 3,000 bodily remains, the Pitt Rivers staff is proactively reaching out to and conversing with the source communities to determine how best to meet their needs. These conversations will no doubt result in the repatriation of many ancestral remains.

Pitt Rivers has also recently installed new educational material that offers visitors insights into the way the museum initially formed its collections. Displays now explain how some of the historic labels have obscured the deeper understanding of other cultures and therefore offer very limited insight into complex historical processes that reinforce racist stereotypes. The new didactic materials and multimedia components, like podcasts and films, present fresh interpretations that offer visitors the opportunity to engage further with myriad stories about objects in the collections, told through the voices of local residents from Kenya, Zimbabwe, Hong Kong, and Oxford, as well as of artists and Indigenous leaders.

The implementation of the Internal Review of Displays and Programming from an Ethical Perspective's recommendations is now embedded into the museum's strategic plan with the institution acknowledging that the changes will be part of a long-term program of curatorial work that will engage many stakeholders and, according to Broekhoven, will "stretch out over years, probably decades to come."[80]

The Pitt Rivers's thoughtful approach to decolonization is noteworthy and is clearly fueled by an ethics of care. Under Broekhoven's leadership, with the establishment of an internal review, removal of emotionally harmful objects, efforts towards repatriation and restitution, new curatorial models, and fresh interpretation, the institution has become a world leader in how best to tackle the difficult process of decolonizing a museum.

CONCLUSION

In 2019, the Pitt Rivers's director Laura Van Broekhoven wrote that "The work of decolonizing needs to be done and translated into practice, structure and budgeting for it to be effective."[81] Decolonizing a museum requires that institutions not pay lip service to the process but that they embody its principles structurally. Indeed, as museums continue to enact decolonial initiatives, one must ask if substantive change is even possible without a complete reconfiguration of the inner workings of the museum itself—again, an institution that is always already a colonial construct. Exhibitions and interventions are, by their nature, temporary. Without substantive structural transformation, do decolonizing initiatives not risk being perceived as tokenistic—or worse, as symbolic gestures that serve primarily to reassure institutions of their own progressive intentions, rather than effecting meaningful democratization of the museum?

The decolonial shift is not just about rethinking content; that shift must also decenter a museum's authority. Or, as the activist group Decolonize This Place argues, "decolonization should be a simultaneous decentering of institutional authority and intensification of accountability."[82] This might entail the establishment in museums of "decolonizing commissions," which would write decolonization plans and then continually assess progress, holding the institution accountable. It might also entail newly written collection and deaccessioning policies that address restitution and repatriation head-on. One avenue for advancing structural transformation within museums involves the development and implementation of more inclusive hiring policies, recognizing that the legacies of colonialism are also evident in institutional staffing practices. A survey conducted by the Mellon Foundation revealed that leadership positions within art museums remain disproportionately occupied by non-Hispanic white individuals, underscoring persistent inequities in representation at the executive level.[83] As art historian Steven Nelson explains, "There is a pipeline problem. Museums are perceived as being for people of privilege."[84]

New hiring policies with recruitment plans to diversify will go a long way. As public institutions, museums should implement transparency of compensation and benefits across the museum to ensure equity. The account ChangeTheMuseum on Instagram, which reports instances of injustice in museums around the U.S. as they occur, has demonstrated the degree to which foundational issues remain, especially as pertains to unequal pay structures where a director might make seven figures while their staff is barely making a livable wage. The recent wave of unionizations in dozens of museums across the U.S. is hardly surprising.

Revised organizational structures have the potential to signal a substantive commitment to lateral, rather than hierarchical, models of leadership—models that actively resist the reproduction of entrenched social and racial hierarchies. A compelling example can be found in the recent organizational chart of the Oakland Museum of California, colloquially referred to as "the flower" within the institution.[85] This model features six cross-functional and cross-disciplinary centers, each dedicated to enhancing visitor experience and fostering participatory community engagement. As a decolonial approach to institutional governance, it offers an alternative framework for museum collaboration—one that genuinely centers the public within the institution's operational logic and, importantly, redistributes and decentralizes power.

But it is not just about equal pay, shared authority, and lateral management. To decolonize, museum governance needs an overhaul too—as many recent protests have demonstrated—and as explored in detail in Chapter 6. From Warren Kanders and Leon Black to Rebekah Mercer and the Sackler family (owners of Purdue Pharma), the museum world needs an evaluation of their board-vetting procedures, as well as new fundraising plans that allow them to sustain themselves financially without being dependent on corporations—like British Petroleum—dogged by reports of unethical business practices.

As is no doubt evident, decolonizing a museum is not an easy process. Nor can it ever be fully realized. It will take more than land acknowledgments and welcome ceremonies and globalized exhibitions representing a plurality of voices. It will take more than one-off exhibitions and interventions. It will require more than an epistemic de-linking from Euro-American-centric, settler colonial knowledge production on the part of curators and artists. It will take more than newly reconfigured permanent collection displays. It will not be enough to repatriate objects to their rightful owners or to rewrite didactic labels. It will require *all* these things, and more, to begin the process of decolonizing a museum. And there will be pushback. As Tuck and Yang have warned us, "Settler colonialism and its decolonization implicates and unsettles everyone"[86] because it demands the deeply unsettling task of confronting our own complicities and silences.

While the continual process of decolonizing a museum may seem Herculean at times, and it is, this is clearly a moment for hope and optimism. Artists and curators are enacting aesthetic and epistemic disobedience, as we've explored, and institutions are making public commitments to, and steps toward, decolonization. Moreover, the International Slavery Museum (Liverpool), the National Museum of African American History and Culture (Washington, D.C.), the Legacy Museum and the National Memorial for Peace and Justice (Montgomery, Alabama), and the new Museum of West African Art MWAA (Benin City, Nigeria) are all new institutions that from their origins have sought to intentionally de-link the legacy of Euro-American-centric, settler colonial knowledge production and the racial hierarchies of slavery and subjugation. Although the concept of the museum remains inextricably linked to its colonial origins, these newly established institutions—deliberately conceived from the outset to engage in the ongoing and essential work of decolonization—represent a promising beginning.

CHAPTER 2
"WE WERE HERE FIRST": INDIGENIZING MUSEUMS

WITH LIISA-RÁVNÁ FINBOG

INTRODUCTION: *THERE IS NO*

On the morning of Friday February 15, 2017, visitors to Sjøgata 1 in the city of Tromsø, Norway, would have witnessed the opening of the Sámi Dáiddamusea X (Sámi Art Museum; SDMX) in what had previously been the site of the Nordnorsk Kunstmuseum (Northern Norway Art Museum; NNKM). Seemingly overnight, the building had been transformed into a museum dedicated to the art of the Sámi, the Indigenous people who for centuries have been subjected to broad discrimination by the dominant Nordic cultures. The Sámi's homeland, Sápmi, is today divided by the colonially imposed borders of Norway, Sweden, Finland, and Russia.

Both the exterior and interior of the museum now featured a bold new logo—a prominent "X" against a contrasting background.[1] A quick google search would have further distinguished the old NNKM from the new SDMX, as the former's website automatically redirected to the latter's. On social media platforms, the SDMX appeared as if it had always been there. Meanwhile, NNKM's presence was muted, and its digital existence erased. In addition, a new administrative profile was created, with the well-known Sámi performance and installation artist Marita Isobel Solberg announced as the new institution's director and curator—a move that not only reinforced the reality of SDMX, but also distanced it from the NNKM and its director, Jérémie McGowan. Throughout the building, visitor information and directions were printed, in bold black, in the North Sámi language,[2] a language that had seldom been seen in non-Indigenous Norwegian museums. Later the same day (February 15), SDMX launched its inaugural exhibition, *There Is No*, to a large crowd—visitors were welcomed, for the very first time, by a Sámi director speaking in both Norwegian and North Sámi. However, it was soon revealed that the "new museum" and its exhibition were, in fact, temporary works of performative art designed to draw attention precisely to the *absence* of a museum dedicated to Sámi art. The SDMX vanished from view just two months after its installation.

The initiative was developed jointly by the NNKM and the Sámi museum RiddoDuottarMuseat (RDM)—a consolidated association comprising four museums and an art collection in Karosjok, Norway. It was devised principally as a call for action with respect to Sámi art: the performance was never intended to be *an actual* "Sámi Dáiddamusea," but rather a *possible* Sámi art museum—an imagining of possibilities and strategies, and a questioning of institutional negligence and responsibilities.

As McGowan has framed it, the exhibit was "a solidarity and advocacy project supporting the RDM and the claims to realise the Sámi dáiddamusea"—hence the exhibition's title, *There Is No.*[3] In this sense, *SDMX* emerged as a utopian, self-reflective, short-term project that recognized that the museum as an institution of art had been ignoring large constituencies and core members of its community. Despite the good intentions, today the NNKM occupies Sjøgata 1, and the bold "X" of the *SDMX* only survives in press releases and as a graphic design element on various memorabilia—designed and distributed in a persistent ongoing effort to call attention to the continued lack of a Sámi art museum.

The *SMDX* and *There Is No* were bold experiments aimed at broadening both the profile and the assumed social role of the NNKM. For an institution that had rarely presented as its main focus the complex artistry of Sámi *dáiddarat*, *There Is No* was unquestionably a game changer. It featured works from more than sixty Sámi artists, including trailblazers such as John Savio (1902–1938), Iver Jåks (1932–2007), Synnøve Persen (b. 1950), Britta Marakatt-Labba (b. 1951), and other members of the Mázejoavku (Máze Group) and onward to artists of today's generation such as Joar Nango (b. 1979) and Hanne Grieg Hermansen (b. 1984). The works—jointly selected and curated by NNKM and the Sámi director of RDM, Anne May Olli, thus highlighting the museum's intention to share authority with Indigenous experts—were brought in from the RDM's collection of Sámi art. The collection in question, currently the largest in the world, consists of around 1,500 works and continues to grow through a purchase committee whose members serve two-year terms, and are elected by the Sámi Parliament on the Norwegian side of the border.

Sámi aesthetic practices are constituted in complex cultural contexts and within specific material and social circumstances. As has happened innumerable times across the globe and throughout history, when colonizers have encountered Indigenous cultures that they do not understand, these multiple and diverse practices, which Sámi people have collectively called *duodji*, were robbed of their context. Over time, and despite the inherent complexity of the term, *duodji* has come to be known simply as "craft." Because of the dominating culture's aesthetic view, it has therefore not been afforded the same status or significance as "art"—at least, not in the institutional landscape in which the NNKM has situated itself and, regrettably, continues to situate itself.

Historically, the material expressions created by *duodji* have been defined by non-Indigenous scholars as "primitive" or "ethnographic" artifacts—as with Indigenous aesthetics worldwide, the aesthetic practices and creations of non-Euro-American and Indigenous people have been imported into a non-Indigenous system of classification.[4] The complex and multilayered expressions of Sámi aesthetics have been forced into a normative and limiting framework.[5] In the 1960s and '70s, fraught with political tensions and embedded in discourses of sovereignty and land rights, this distinction between Sámi aesthetic practitioners and the colonial concept of what constitutes "art" seemingly reached an impasse. At this time, however, a growing number of newly graduated Sámi artists (including those who went on to form the Máze Group), trained in art schools in the West, began to critique the present state of the art world. Though their primary education was in non-Sámi art expressions, they were keen to define their creative practice in Sámi terms.[6] The debates these artists instigated eventually led to the introduction of a new term. Borrowing from the Finnish *taidde*, meaning "art," *dáidda* became an equivalent term in the Sámi language, conceptualized to embody a Sámi perspective on aesthetics, without stripping works of their cultural context.[7] Taking its initial cue from these long-standing ideas within and around Sámi artistic practice, the exhibition title *There Is No* referred to a "series of dynamic and vibrant manifestations of cultural expression that strategically resist, extend and challenge established ways of thinking in mainstream art history. There is no set of rules for Sámi art. There is no fixed definition of Sámi art. There is no limitation on Sámi artists. There is no."[8]

The *Sámi Dáiddamusea X* and *There Is No* have been described as performances with an intent to decolonize.[9] We will take this argument a step further by suggesting that the performances were, in fact, an attempt to *indigenize the museum*. We use the term "indigenize" rather than "decolonize" purposely because we view the two initiatives as entirely separate yet related museological processes. The phrase "decolonization" has been used more frequently than "indigenization" in scholarly circles, but unlike most scholars, we do not use the terms interchangeably. Many scholars, including Amy Lonetree, Eve Tuck, K. Wayne Yang, Puwai Cairns and Kwame Opoku, argue for the urgent need to decolonize museums—while we applaud the intent of this initiative, we disagree with the terminology. In the pages that follow, using the Sámi Dáiddamusea and other relevant case studies, we suggest that, oftentimes, when scholars call for decolonization, they are, in fact, calling for indigenization. This is far from a simple matter of semantics, and our aim is to clarify the very different effects of the two processes.

Whereas to decolonize is a process of deconstructing colonial ideologies and the centrality of Euro-American-centric thinking and values, to indigenize is much more—it is a process that seeks to insert Indigenous ways of being (ontology), of knowing (epistemology), and of doing (axiology), prioritizing Indigenous methodologies for both theory and practice.[10]

TO DECOLONIZE OR TO INDIGENIZE —THAT IS THE QUESTION

In his doctoral work, artist and curator Brook Garru Andrew asks: "Is it enough to invite Indigenous peoples to work within the institutional paradigm, or does more work need to be done such as rejecting European models of working and terminologies and allowing First Nations peoples to set and lead the entire agenda?"[11] These questions are fundamental in discourses that center on decolonization and indigenization.

The act of decolonization is a process of deconstruction. That is, it seeks to address the inherent bias against non-Indigenous epistemologies and ontologies, but it does not necessarily work to dismantle these fundamental Euro-American prejudices, even if certain aspects of Indigenous knowledges and practices have been incorporated into museological presentations.[12] We suggest that the act of decolonization is an act of de-centering the colonial—whether that be ideologies, practices, or imaginaries. It is a process that continues to be embedded within the colonial structures that perpetuate the existing, inherently colonial, conditions of institutions (or academia), making it a highly problematic term as it continues to "polarise an already polarised debate, on the terms set by colonialism."[13]

To indigenize, on the other hand, is the continued process of recognizing the colonial legacy in institutions and ideological frameworks; acting to dismantle them; and, as an extension of that, clearing the way for non-Euro-American epistemologies and ontologies to be, not merely inserted, but actually embedded as a fundamental basis for theory and practice. As curator Kimberley Moulton reminds us: "There is strength in challenging the status quo, rejecting the pattern that our art, bodies and culture are only noticed when recognised by the white centre."[14] Decolonization, we argue, still requires being "recognized by the white center." At the same time, the lived reality of Indigenous people is that recognition by the white center is not needed, because, as Moulton further argues, the ways of being and understanding of "our First peoples" surpass this. "And we do not need to be defined within this canon as we can never fit within something that is constructed from our exclusion."[15]

It is in the wake of this understanding that the act of indigenization becomes pertinent. In her now canonical book, *Decolonizing Museums* (which, according to our definition, would be titled *Indigenizing Museums*), scholar Amy Lonetree argues that museums must begin by "telling the hard truths of colonization and the genocidal acts committed against Indigenous people."[16] Because museums are "painful institutions for native people" and intimately tied to the colonization process, they must "honor Indigenous knowledge and worldviews, challenge the stereotypical representations of Native people produced in the past, and serve as sites of 'knowledge making and remembering' for their own communities and the general public."[17] It is incumbent upon museums, she argues, to become "sites of conscience" that, in embracing truth-telling as a strategic priority, can promote healing and understanding. Based on Lonetree, and our own understanding and experience, to indigenize is a processual conceptualization of acts and intentions, constantly moving, evolving, and shifting between layers and contexts.

That is not to say that how we understand and use "decolonization" and "indigenization" is an established canon within our fields. On the contrary, decolonial scholars disagree on the fundamental definition of decolonization and many use it interchangeably with indigenization. For example, scholars Eve Tuck and K. Wayne Yang argue that "decolonization" is very much linked with indigeneity and efforts of sovereignty in postcolonial nations. In their view, "decolonization" is always already about the repatriation and restitution of Indigenous land to Indigenous people.[18] (This is why we believe that when Tuck and Yang use the term "decolonization," it would be more accurately termed "indigenization.") For scholars Walter Mignolo and others from the Global South, including Aníbal Quijano, María Lugones, and Rolando Vázquez, "decolonization" is characterized by white supremacy more broadly, but also by sexism, ableism, heteropatriarchy, classism, and other forms of colonial oppression.[19] While Mignolo et al. admit that an emphasis on indigeneity is critical to the process insofar as colonization always concerns land, they contend that ultimately decolonization is about an "epistemic delinking" from Eurocentric settler colonial knowledge production, in all its manifestations.[20] It is this broader, more intersectional definition of decolonization that we adhere to and that works as a counterpoint to our definition of indigenization.

Like Tuck and Yang, curator Puwai Cairns contends that decolonization is another insidious form of colonization because the colonizer always remains the principal figure in a process that should center on the colonized. It is for this reason that she is not comfortable using the term. Cairns prefers the term “māorification.”[21] As Moana Jackson explains, to māorify a museum is “to recentre Māori voices in an act of restoring *mana motuhake* (independent thought and autonomy) and [to] privilege the various ways that Māori perceive knowledge and knowledge sharing.”[22] In this context, to māorify, as in “to indigenize,” is to create more space and opportunity for Indigenous people to tell their stories on their own terms, as opposed to being spoken about in the third person. In a museum setting, māorification would recognize the “unique kinship bonds that exist between objects, people, and our histories—and the obligations that come with this recognition.”[23] Māorifying a museum, then, would mean organizing exhibitions (featuring Indigenous and/or non-Indigenous objects) that respect that there are many different worldviews and that incorporate Māori ways of being (ontology), of knowing (epistemology), and of doing (axiology).

In a similar vein, several scholars have discussed indigenization as the Indigenous equivalent of decolonization, arguing that whereas the latter directly impacts from within institutions, the former is more an act that originates and impacts from the outside. For example, artist and scholar Lisa Hilli maintains that “decolonization is an inside job,” and that instead they would prefer to look to their own languages and practice, pointing to how the words *pasin way blo yumi* mean “Indigenous ways, or Indigenizing” and that “it translates to our ways, our cultural ways.”[24] Scholar and curator Stephen Gilchrist makes a distinction between a curatorial practice that privileges philosophies of decolonization over indigenization. For him, the former is “about *undoing* something that invariably feels like you are forever playing catch up”; whereas indigenization is “about *doing*; manifesting, instantiating, and running our own race on our own terms.”[25] He sees indigenization as a process that *opens up* versus forecloses pathways to Indigenous ways of seeing, knowing, and being. He proposes that indigenization be understood variously as “a form of declaration, protest, continuation, maintenance, renewal and memorial” and, as such, requires a methodology of *relearning* versus unlearning.[26]

Sámi scholars such as Aile Aikio and Liisa-Rávná Finbog also embed the act of indigenization, as a Sámi alternative to decolonization, in their own language, preferring the term *sámáidahttin* (sámification) to "decolonization."[27] The term "sámification" first appeared as a concept in a Sámi-led evaluation of Reform 97, the comprehensive Norwegian school reform undertaken in 1997.[28] Defining the need for more educational exercises with an emphasis on Sámi cultural sensitivity and ways of thinking, the authors of the evaluation called for the sámification of pedagogical methods and the curriculum. The term *sámáidahttin* was reasserted in 2009 as the act of sámification by Asta Balto—a Sámi elder and educator whose contribution to the development of a Sámi pedagogy is unrivaled—and Liv Østmo, a Sámi social scientist and one of the founders of the Sámi University of Applied Sciences (Sámi allaskuvlla) in Kautokeino, Finnmark county, Norway. Balto and Østmo stated that *sámáidahttin* was a process that combatted Eurocentric and Western norms of education, institutions, and perspectives through a return to Sámi values and norms.[29] Balto, in her earliest development of the term, defined *sámáidahttin* as a collective process that reflects the collective character of Sámi knowledge production.[30] More recently, the concept has been adapted and applied according to context and need—for example, in museological settings, where it has been defined as "developing Sámi-based museum work and adopting Sámi thinking as the starting point of preservation, examination and presentation of cultural heritage."[31] Applied more broadly as indigenization, the term "sámification" has been defined by Finbog as the initiation of a process "whereby the significance and application of Indigenous knowledge is asserted into academia, but from a place of Indigenous sovereignty, and centered in Indigenous values, practices, and knowledge systems."[32]

In sum, whether situated in Māori, Sámi, Samoan, or other Indigenous practices, to indigenize is to initiate a process that moves beyond decolonization, aiming not only to reveal the impact of colonization, but to develop practices that envision a pre-colonial era. To indigenize a museum, then, is to cede authority, power, and control to Indigenous peoples. Each situation is different insofar as there is no one monolithic definition of Indigenous culture or Indigenous knowledge.[33] Definitions and strategies will therefore depend on the people with whom one is in communication; they will be localized and specific to place and context. To indigenize a museum is to make its institutional objectives and operational practices more responsive to the needs of Indigenous people, and supportive of Indigenous sovereignty and self-determination.

REMATRIATION: INDIGENIZING COLLECTIONS

Whether forcefully taken, traded under pressure, or secretly looted, the removal of material culture (artworks, significant objects, tools, records) from their Indigenous source communities has had a tremendous impact on those communities, with devastating consequences. Indigenous objects are often vital components of both layered and complex social relationships within their source communities. These objects have fundamental associations with cosmological belief systems, ritual practices, symbolic values, and epistemological roles and functions, and in many cases are used to uphold and maintain religious practices, invoke core values or social conduct, and aid in the transference of knowledge.[34] It is within this framework that repatriation and restitution to Indigenous source communities should be understood and facilitated. Over the past decade, museums have worked to improve and transform their relationship to source communities by offering increased access to their collections. In this shift towards a more ethically sustainable practice, many museums are striving to acknowledge their imperial and colonial connections by positioning themselves as institutions that promote social equality, raise awareness of social and political issues, and give voice to previously silenced groups.[35] The ongoing debate on repatriation and restitution is a reflection of this process.[36] Repatriation and restitution are distinct processes, as discussed in further detail in Chapter 3. Repatriation occurs when, following the request of a government, cultural objects are returned to the nation or state from which those objects were unethically taken. Restitution is the return of such objects to an individual or community.

That tangible property, illegally or dubiously acquired, should be returned to source communities is without question. This should be done immediately when legal dictates demand it (for example, as in the Native American Graves Protection and Repatriation Act of 1990 in the U.S.), but also when source communities insist upon it. In 2018, Senegalese academic and writer Felwine Sarr and French art historian Bénédicte Savoy presented a report, commissioned by President Emmanuel Macron of France, on African cultural heritage in French museums. The scholars highlighted that the displacement that the former French colonies had experienced was not simply a matter of objects being taken. What had also been removed were "reserves of energy, creative resources, reservoirs of potentials, forces engendering alternative figures and forms of the real, forces of germination; and this loss is incommensurable."[37] This loss, they continued, had over time created a "syndrome of incompleteness" that had silenced or erased the memory of the objects in their source communities.[38] The process of silencing implied by the words "syndrome of incompleteness" is only exacerbated by the fact that the objects in question have not been made available to their source communities,[39] which means that many of the significances, values, and stories embedded in the objects have similarly been silenced or lost altogether. In response to this, multiple Indigenous and non-Indigenous scholars have argued for the necessity of repatriation and restitution.[40]

Furthermore, as Sarr and Savoy outline in their report, repatriation and restitution need to expand beyond the simple return of objects.[41] It is imperative that museums take a human rights-based approach to repatriation and restitution, but also that they assume liability on such matters, relinquishing control of objects that belong to other communities or people. Institutions can begin this process in a number of ways: by reconceiving themselves as custodians and *not owners* of objects; by reversing the current imbalance in power relations with source communities whereby the latter become judge and jury, rather than the opposite; by committing not to acquire additional works with dubious provenance; and by honestly evaluating their collections and making them publicly accessible, for instance, in online databases. Above all, institutions should approach the question of returns with an ethics of care in which the aggrieved parties are shown respect, compassion, and empathy.

The need for museums to rethink how they view repatriation and restitution is made all the more urgent by the fact that most older Indigenous objects—since they are under the current (albeit contested) ownership of museums—are physically and spiritually removed from their source communities. The provenance of some objects is, of course, not always known—at least, not as far as a person, family, or even a specific community or area is concerned. However, this does not mean that museums should be absolved from their responsibilities. On the contrary, initiatives that seek to find the provenance of collections should be put in motion. Examples of this include the Berlin-based Museum Europäischer Kulturen (Museum of European Cultures), an institution dedicated to preserving European culture that in December 2022 began an extensive provenance research project on their Sámi collection; the Deutscher Museumsbund's (German Museums Association) commitment in 2019 to begin a complete digital, accessible, nationwide inventory of objects from colonial contexts; and the 2017 policy of the Museum of Us in San Diego to seek guidance from Indigenous communities about the treatment of the 8,000 or so ancestral remains in their collection.

Furthermore, museums should always consult with Indigenous communities or people about how best to reconcile with their pilfered collections—ultimately, decisions about how the items should be handled rests with the source communities themselves. This can and should include, at the very least, a shift in ownership—such as a long-term loan of the object in question to its source community—but preferably a return. Lonetree argues for the repatriation and restitution of ancestral remains, sacred objects, and objects of cultural patrimony, as one would perhaps expect; however, she also underlines that "righting the wrongs is only the beginning."[42] As well as the repatriation and restitution of Indigenous objects, she calls for conversation, dialogue, and respect—or, in our terms, she calls for *rematriation*. In many cases—for example, in the latest work on rematriation from a Sámi perspective[43]—rematriation does not necessarily demand the return of physical objects.[44] It is more important that communities have full access and the possibility to reassert such objects within their everyday life. Broadly speaking, then, while repatriation and restitution deal with the return of objects, rematriation, as, Liisa-Rávná Finbog has written, "deals with every aspect of objects—tangible as well as intangible—being re-inserted into society."[45]

Working from the premise that Indigenous worlds are most often about relationships[46]—a nexus of interconnected relationships between and to people, land, water, animals, other-than-human beings and spirits and/or entities—we find it is the interactions that result from these interconnected relationships that create the worlds in which we live and, by extension, the communities to which we belong. Over generations, this Indigenous perspective has made way for societies that are based on a system of kinship that honors the value and importance of all within an interconnected creation of existence.[47] Colonization destroyed these relations, alienating people from land and place, as well as all other beings that inhabited the space.

Philosopher Ailton Krenak cites this alienation as vital to the capitalist project, as it is only when humans no longer recognize the land, waters, and animals as kin that they feel comfortable imposing their dominion over them.[48] So, while objects remain important agents within a system of kinship in Indigenous communities,[49] when they are adapted into the objects-based epistemology of museology, they are reinterpreted into passive material, which subjects them to the dominion of museums.[50] This is why, when we work to indigenize museums, repatriation and restitution alone are not enough. Indeed, the act of rematriation—understood as restoring "a living culture to its rightful place on Mother Earth," in order "to restore a people to a spiritual way of life, in sacred relationship with their ancestral lands, without external interference"[51]—must be included in the discussion. While we believe that the repatriation and restitution of tangible and intangible heritage should be mandatory for all museums, we also believe that the process of rematriation is of equal value.

Initially a word meant to inspire the importance of healing within Indigenous communities, "rematriation" can be connected to the reforging of relations that were broken by colonization—for example, those between source communities and objects. For scholar Robin R. R. Gray, rematriation—insofar as it concerns matrilineal kinship structures—is the antithesis of repatriation. As she explains, repatriation is "derived from the Latin root word *patr-*, referring to the father or the patriline," which, she argues, "assumes that the nation is patriarchal, or that 'the state is a man.'"[52] Repatriation, then, is about control, nationhood, property, and ownership. Or, as scholar Aileen Moreton-Robinson argues, repatriation is one cog in the wheel of settler logic that operationalizes the "possessive logics" that underpin "patriarchal white sovereignty."[53] Rejecting this possessiveness, multiple Indigenous artists, curators, scholars, and practitioners are centering their practices in rematriation.

The collaboration between Sámi artist Outi Pieski and Finnish archaeologist Eeva-Kristiina Nylander (formerly Harlin) is an excellent example of rematriation. Their work focused on the female apparel of the *ládjogáhpir* (hornhat), which is a part of Sámi women's regalia in specific communities but was banned by Christian priests in the 19th century, precisely because the hornhat is connected to female sexuality and what Pieski terms "gender power," which was perceived as threatening. Pieski and Nylander have worked to return *eana eannážan* ("to our mother earth") in order to restore the balance of relations within the world's system of kinship (Fig. 5).[54] Working to embrace and reassert the symbolic meanings and values housed in the hat, Pieski and Nylander initiated a series of workshops that would encourage people to relearn and revitalize the making of the hats. They defined these workshops as examples of "craftivism," which they explained as a process of reappropriation of museum objects through crafting them anew.[55]

To clarify the terminology here, we recognize the ontological ambivalence of the term "craft." In a Euro-American context, it has been strongly linked to the Arts and Crafts movement in England in the second half of the 19th century, as well as with 1970s feminist artistic practice, both of which sought to break down the barrier between the fine and decorative arts to celebrate aesthetic practices that have traditionally been defined as "women's work" (embroidery and crochet, for example). Conversely, "craft" has also been used strategically to devalue specific Indigenous practices, which in turn has helped to create an implied and colonially imposed hierarchy, placing the latter below non-Indigenous "fine art," which is typically understood to include oil paintings, sculptures, and architectural monuments produced by European, and predominantly white males.[56] Nevertheless, the introduction of the term "craftivism" is pointed as it aligns with a specific form of activism through a specific medium. Liisa-Rávná Finbog likens craftivism to *duodjebádji* in that both are "safe spaces" that encourage participants to share their stories and relearn the making of specific Indigenous objects.[57] As described here, "craftivism" or "duodjebádji" are actually specific methods that have been established in Sámi communities, beginning in the 1970s and '80s when repatriation and restitution were believed to be impossible. The hope was that in reproducing the objects, the makers could bring cultural heritage home to its originating source communities.[58] This reinforces our argument, above, that while repatriation and restitution demand a physical return, rematriation may happen without one, but nevertheless be equally valid.

The interventionist museological projects by artist Rosanna Raymond also embody the practice of rematriation. In the late 2000s and again in the early 2010s, as an artist of Samoan and Māori descent, Raymond was invited by several museums in the U.K.—including the Wellcome Collection in London and the Ethnography Museum at University College London (UCL)—to consecrate Indigenous objects in their collections. In 2010, she was asked by curators at the Wellcome Collection to assist in installing a *poutokomanawa*, sometimes called a *pou*, a sacred Māori carved figure (an object traditionally used as a post in a Māori meeting house), which they had borrowed from UCL for an exhibition entitled *Skin* (2010). Raymond requested that the *taonga* (treasure) be readorned with earrings made of barkcloth, shell, and shark teeth, which she made specifically for the figure. As she explains: "By readorning him, I intended to help him regain his *mana* [magical power] and activate his *mauri* [the spark of life that sustains existence and form] as a way of connecting past and present. This process was rendered through the *whakanoa* [to make free from restrictions] or blessing which the *pou* was a part of along with myself, the artist George Nuku, and members of the Ngati Ranana (a U.K.-based Māori community)."[59]

In the ceremony, which was centered on the belief that the Polynesian body is a vessel for the ancestor, Raymond's aim was to activate the *va*, a Samoan term for space, which would bring the *pou* into the present, thus binding past with present. Once removed from the spatial confines of its storage box at the museum, the *pou* can then produce new narratives and histories—that is, the *pou* is restored and respirited and can carry his message into the future. Following the *va* ceremony, Raymond read a poem she had written for the *pou*; the Ngati Ranana then greeted the sacred object and welcomed him into the gallery.

In 2012, Raymond was invited to UCL to conduct a blessing ceremony for the same *poutokomanawa*. During this ceremony, the figure was given permission to leave his home in order to go on loan to the Horniman Museum, London, as part of its exhibition *The Body Adorned: Dressing the World City*. Upon return of the object to UCL in 2013, Raymond also facilitated a ceremony to welcome the object back into the Ethnography Collection, to thank him for his work as a cultural ambassador and return him to rest in the collection storage. In both ceremonies, Raymond did not request the object be returned to Polynesia, but that it be respected and activated. In Raymond's eyes, the *va* ceremony is a process of "spiritual repatriation"; for us, it is an example of rematriation.[60]

TRUTH-TELLING AND STORYTELLING: INDIGENIZING EXHIBITIONS

From the earliest antecedents of the museum in 17th-century Europe, consisting of the exotic memorabilia brought home by "explorers," scholars, and nobles from what they perceived to be the far corners of the world, to the scientific collections of matter and ethnographia, museums have preserved, displayed, and disseminated material culture.[61] While this has created a modus operandi built upon the act of narrativization, creating histories supported by objects, it has also enabled Europe and America to categorize, label, and organize the world. As sociologist and philosopher Jean Baudrillard notes, "Not only do objects help us master the world, by virtue of their being inserted into practical sets, they also help us, by virtue of being inserted into mental sets, to establish dominion."[62] Museums thus continue to exist within a discourse of dominion, where winners and losers are strictly organized within a hierarchy that mimics the world of Euro-American privilege and rationality. It is here, in these institutional spaces that reify Euro-American privilege, that we face what scholar Rauna Kuokkanen defines as an "epistemic ignorance," which refers to the ways in which intellectual traditions, other than the dominant Western European ones, are excluded. The challenge is not simply to recognize this exclusion in practice, but to actively reject it. Or more to the point, the challenge is not simply to decolonize, but *to actively indigenize* collections and exhibitions.

Truth- and storytelling are essential to any approach to indigenization. According to scholar and activist Larissa Behrendt, storytelling is "a transformative practice" as well as "an act of sovereignty" that ensures the reassertion of "our stories on our land," which in turn asserts Indigenous "ownership."[63] The narrative quality of museum practice thus needs to be shifted to create space for Indigenous people to tell their own stories—to reassess, when needed, and rewrite history to include their truth. This means that museums must facilitate for and engage with truth-telling. Lonetree argues that museums must begin telling "the hard truths" of colonization—the only way museums can begin to initiate decolonization is if they truthfully address the history and legacy of colonialism in their collections, exhibitions, and programs.[64] Further, it is not enough that museums simply acknowledge that the history of Indigenous peoples has been authored from outside Indigenous communities—until recently, most Indigenous exhibitions have been curated by non-Indigenous individuals. Institutions must be willing to take a step back, making room for Indigenous people and other source communities to assume authority, present their lived experience, tell their own stories, and choose how collections may, or indeed may not, be used in support of this process. This is to indigenize.

Following Lonetree's suggestion, as well as examples set by Te Papa Tongarewa, New Zealand and the National Gallery of Canada, many museums have begun to bring Indigenous perspectives into decision-making by means of conversation, dialogue, collaboration, and/or in the hiring of Indigenous curators. (Indeed, Australian museums have made a public commitment to hire at least one Indigenous curator at every major museum by 2029.[65]) Collectively, then, there seems to be a growing understanding within institutions themselves that to indigenize in a museum setting necessarily demands, as a bare minimum, the sharing of authority and power with Indigenous curators and collaborators for the documentation and interpretation of Indigenous art and culture. It also entails the inclusion of the work and perspectives of Indigenous artists, practitioners (of various aesthetic practices, that might not be privileged by a colonial aesthetic, such as weaving and beading), storytellers, historians, anthropologists, archaeologists, singers, performers, and other content experts throughout planning processes—whether exhibition and public programming, or otherwise. This is particularly pressing if we consider the implications of "epistemic ignorance" within museums.

Museum curators and scholars are invariably trained within fiercely traditional Euro-American academic contexts. If emphasis is shifted to Indigenous epistemologies, the focus changes immeasurably. Art, for example, along with other aesthetic practices, often forms part of extremely complex and dynamic knowledge systems. When these aesthetic practices are devalued through "epistemic ignorance," it is often the Indigenous peoples' own aesthetics (not the dominating culture's) that are diminished in value. In turn, Indigenous academics that are trained in their own academic traditions are rarely afforded the same status and authority as their Euro-American counterparts.

RIDDODUOTTARMUSEAT (RDM) NORWAY

This Euro-American-centrism must be challenged if we are ever to reach the ethical and human rights-based statutes that so many of today's museums claim to be grounded in. The RDM offers a good example. Admittedly, it is a Sámi museum and thus an Indigenous institution. However, because it is obliged to conform to the International Council of Museums (ICOM) statutes to be eligible for public funding, its fundamental structure mimics the structure of a Euro-American museum. Nevertheless, its practice is to indigenize—its current permanent exhibition display, for example, is a journey of discovery in a unique blend of a Sámi epistemology realized in material culture and disseminated to a broader audience.[66] The exhibition has been heavily criticized, defined as outdated, not intended to be interactive, and portraying Sámi culture as both static and exotic—a pale imitation of the typical ethnographic genre.[67] From a purely museological point of view, the exhibition may indeed seem to reflect the critics' claims; if understood from a Sámi perspective, it exists as a highly sophisticated, interactive exhibition. That is, what may be misread as a typical ethnographic display, with clusters of objects arranged by chronology and typography, is in fact a display with clusters that are categorized and arranged according to a Sámi understanding of seasonal activities and general practices. One cluster, for example, consists of objects typical of early spring, while another is associated with the practice of *duodji*. These thematic clusters and their epistemological basis, however, are not explained in the exhibition. The museum's curators made a conscious decision, with a Sámi audience in mind, to celebrate and showcase Sámi culture. In so doing, they integrated Sámi knowledge into the curation. Non-Sámi visitors are encouraged to take advantage of the Sámi guides the museum employs—only then are they able to experience the exhibition in a similar way to someone with a lived Sámi experience. This approach ensures that the source community retains the authority to represent their story as they see fit, and that Sámi ontologies and epistemologies are central to the exhibition, even though it takes place within the context of a Western institution.

This is not to say that we would advocate for indigenization as something that can only be achieved by Indigenous curators. The implementation of Indigenous epistemologies and ontologies nevertheless requires not only theoretical knowledge, but also the actual practice of such theory in the form of lived experience. This may include, as Lonetree argues, the use of Indigenous curators and practitioners in all phases of producing an exhibition. Failure to do so can result in multiple complications, as was the case at the Walker Art Center in Minneapolis in 2017, when a sculpture by artist Sam Durant was commissioned without input from the local Dakota tribe.

Durant's installation, which was exhibited on sacred Dakota land, drew inspiration from the gallows that were built for seven major executions in U.S. history, including the largest mass execution ever to take place in the U.S. in which, in 1862, thirty-eight Dakota men were hanged in Mankato, Minnesota. The Dakota people demanded the destruction of the sculpture, arguing that the work trivialized a traumatizing chapter in the community's history. After considerable mediation between the Dakota community, the artist, and the museum, the issue was resolved. It was decided that the steel from the sculpture would be recycled and that the wood, given to the Dakota people, would be ceremonially buried under the direction of the elders of the community. The case of the Walker Art Center serves as a painful reminder of how Indigenous people, even today, are not considered the owners of their own past and history. Furthermore, as we see it, this is a powerful example of why truth-telling needs to be accompanied by storytelling—Durant's piece was an act of truth-telling, but because it was not accompanied by storytelling, a deeply traumatic and complex narrative was (once again) shared on behalf of an Indigenous community, without their input.

Another example of a museum adopting a truth-telling stance is an exhibition at the Zimmerli Art Museum (New Brunswick, New Jersey), entitled *Indigenous Identities: Here, Now & Always* (2025). The prominent Indigenous American artist-curator Jaune Quick-to-See Smith was invited by Maura Reilly to curate a large exhibition of the work of ninety-eight contemporary Indigenous American artists, of which almost every element was entirely Indigenous-led. This is to say that the curator, book designer, editor, authors, curatorial assistant, and lecturers were all Indigeneous Americans. The Zimmerli relinquished control and granted full authority to Smith, who stated that until then she had never been given absolute reign over an entire exhibition project. The intent to indigenize the museum was evident, in that it constituted an effort to insert Indigenous ways of being (ontology), of knowing (epistemology), and of doing (axiology), prioritizing Indigenous methodologies for both theory and practice. This was an implicit acknowledgment that when organizing exhibitions of Indigenous art or planning to install artwork on Indigenous land, it is incumbent upon museums to consult with Indigenous individuals or communities.

INDIGENIZATION STRATEGIES

It would nevertheless be remiss to stop there. Establishing true indigenization is not simply a case of inviting Indigenous people in as guests for fleeting moments to curate, give advice (on advisory boards), or interact with objects and collections. This level of inclusion merely replicates the asymmetrical power relations between institutions and source communities. In 1997, scholar James Clifford famously conceptualized these one-way relationships as the markers of "contact zones," or spaces of colonial encounters (in a museological setting).[68]

In addition to group exhibitions organized by Indigenous guest curators, in-house (non-Indigenous) curators working *within* non-Indigenous institutions can develop a series of indigenizing strategies. Not only can they organize solo and group exhibitions dedicated to Indigenous artists, but they can choose to indigenize their permanent collections. One high-profile example of this is New York's Metropolitan Museum of Art's (the Met) exhibition *Art of Native America: The Charles and Valerie Diker Collection* in 2018, organized by the Met's Curator of American Art, Sylvia Yount. It featured 116 major works representing the achievements of more than 50 Native American communities across North America (ranging in date from the 2nd century to the early 20th century). This was the first time the museum exhibited Indigenous American objects in the American Wing—previously, they had been "ghettoized" in their own "Native" section, the sort of space First Nations Australian artist Richard Bell (Figs. 4, 7) refers to as the "darkies' corner."[69] To view Indigenous American works—among them a jar by the Hopi-Tewa ceramicist Nampeyo; a painted shield by the Hunkpapa Lakota master Joseph No Two Horns, from the Standing Rock reservation in the Dakotas—alongside the (mostly) white male heroes of 20th-century art, such as John Singer Sargent, Gilbert Stuart, and John Trumbell, felt like a game changer and was undoubtedly groundbreaking art historically.

It should be stated collectors Charles and Valerie Diker gifted their significant collection to the Met with the stipulation that they could only be exhibited within the museum's American Wing. Nevertheless, this was a huge step for the Met, and allowed for the meaningful curatorial juxtapositions discussed above. But no sooner had they opened their exhibition doors than they were criticized by the Association on American Indian Affairs (AAIA) for not consulting tribal representatives or performing due diligence on specific objects. The advocacy group took particular issue with the fact that the Met had called the Indigenous objects "art," when they were meant as "ceremonial or funerary objects."[70] The advocacy group demanded that the promised gifts, which they argued "could only have ended up in a private collection through trafficking and looting," be returned to their respective communities.[71] Even if the AAIA had no legal grounds to ask for promised gifts back from private collectors, the group had good reason to criticize the Met. The Native American Graves Protection and Repatriation Act (NAGPRA), enacted in 1990, mandates that museums receiving federal funding—including institutions such as the Metropolitan Museum of Art—conduct comprehensive inventories of their holdings of Native American cultural artifacts and ancestral remains, and recognize the rights of Indigenous communities to reclaim and repatriate those materials.[72] The Met has been painfully slow to respond to this law, as have most U.S. museums. What this incident demonstrates is that working with Indigenous source communities in advance of an exhibition is an essential component in the process of indigenization, as is the dialogue that is precipitated by any missteps. (In 2020, two years after the *Art of Native America: The Charles and Valerie Diker Collection* exhibition—and possibly in response to the highly public criticism it received—the Met hired Patricia Marroquin Norby, their first full-time Indigenous curator.[73])

While the intent to indigenize may start with conceiving of projects and exhibitions, and the hiring of permanent and tenured Indigenous staff, there is no guarantee it will actually have a significant impact on institutional structures. This is evident, for example, in the case of *Sámi Dáiddamuse X* and *There Is No*. The idea and execution began with NNKM director Jérémie McGowan and RDM director Anne May Olli. While this was initially, by all accounts, a successful project, the later controversies surrounding McGowan's dismissal from NNKM demonstrated that well-intentioned initiatives do not necessarily result in structural change. In late March of 2020, shock waves ran through the Norwegian art scene as it became clear that McGowan had been asked by the museum board to leave his position immediately. No reason was given for his abrupt dismissal; and, in fact, only recently before that dismissal, his tenure as director had been extended by two years. It was a controversial decision, underlined by the fact that most of the museum staff published a letter in support of their director and that some members of the board resigned in protest. The controversies were exacerbated by the fact that McGowan later went on record stating that his dismissal was due to his pro-Sámi sympathies. This has subsequently been denied by the remainder of the board. So, while NNKM achieved fame in discourses of indigenization with the pioneering production of *SDMX*, it also became infamous the way it curbed McGowan's intent, supported by the local Sámi communities, to indigenize the institution.

NORDIC PAVILION, 59TH VENICE BIENNALE, 2022

In 2022, the Nordic Pavilion (of Norway, Sweden, and Finland) at the 59th International Art Exhibition of the Venice Biennale was transformed into a Sámi space of art and sovereignty. It proved to be one of the most significant Sámi exhibitions of all time. The pavilion had a strong political profile, and press communications from the curatorial team highlighted that: "The official Nordic contribution to Biennale Arte 2022, comes at a critical time in the history of the Nordic region, where Truth and Reconciliation Commissions addressing Nordic colonialism have started in Norway, Finland and Sweden; when the Sámi are making restitution claims for their art and artifacts and at a time when the Arctic is experiencing unprecedented consequences of the climate crisis."[74] The exhibition was jointly curated by Sámi scholar Finbog, Sámi Nature Guardian and *duojár* Beaska Niillas, the then-director of the Office for Contemporary Art, Norway (OCA) and commissioner, Katya Gárcia-Antón; the contributing Sámi artists were Máret Anne Sara, Anders Sunna, and Paulina Feodoroff.

The project was initiated in the spirit of sharing authority and truth- and storytelling, embedding Sámi ways of being (ontology), knowing (epistemology), and doing (axiology) to create a Sámi methodological framework. While the various works of installation (Sara), paintings (Sunna), and performance (Feodoroff) addressed the political reality of the Sámi and their history—considering not only the colonial harm experienced by the Sámi but also questioning the continuity and impact of violence in the present day—they did so through Sámi values and traditions of narrativization. Despite the success of the collaboration, and its positive reception globally, it also acted as a reminder: The Sámi Pavilion was conceived of as a celebration of Sámi sovereignty, and yet, as has been remarked by Jérémie McGowan, it is also a glaring illustration that the Sámi people do not have the funding or an institution of art to themselves commission Sámi curators and artists, nor do they have the representation and facilities necessary to repeat the Sámi Pavilion at the next Biennale.[75]

McGowan's remarks reflect some of the institutional difficulties that were experienced by the Sámi exhibition in the Nordic Pavilion. The Venice Biennale is an institution unto itself and has strict regulations that all pavilions must adhere to, principally that each pavilion represents a "nation-state." The Indigenous status of the Sámi people and the pavilion were especially impacted by this regulation. In line with the intent to express the sovereignty of the Sámi people as a nation, the curators attempted to have the brass letters that spell out the names of Norway, Sweden, and Finland that were attached to the outside of the pavilion replaced with "Sápmi." This was denied because the Biennale did not recognize Sápmi as a nation-state and could therefore not allow it to appear on the Nordic Pavilion. The next suggestion, to simply remove the three countries' names from the wall, leaving it blank instead, was also denied. Eventually, the artists and the curatorial collective erected a tablet made from birch in order to cover the names of the colonial nations whose borders divide the Sámi homeland (Fig. 6). Despite the project's intent to indigenize the Nordic Pavilion, the inherent European and colonial mindset of the Venice Biennale proved to be an insurmountable obstacle at that time. Again, while the act of indigenization may be pursued by individual curators and groups, it must include the unswerving support of the institutional structures themselves. Without this, exhibitions and projects run the risk of becoming merely performative, highlighting the processes of indigenization but without any real commitment.

One could argue that temporary exhibitions of Indigenous art in non-Indigenous settings (such as the NNKM and the Met) are equally performative insofar as they are temporary endeavors that do not necessarily result in broad institutional change and may indeed be simply tokenistic. However, we would argue that museums should still commit to this practice because they are a first step in an attempt to indigenize museums. From *Sakahàn: International Indigenous Art* at the National Gallery of Canada, organized in 2013 by First Nations curator Greg Hill, to *Hearts of Our People: Native Women Artists*, an exhibition organized by non-Indigenous curator Jill Ahlberg Yohe and Indigenous artist-curator Teri Greeves, which traveled the U.S. from 2019 to 2021, temporary exhibitions at non-Indigenous institutions that are dedicated to Indigenous art make invaluable contributions to the museum field—not least because in their presentation of a diverse selection of contemporary Indigenous practitioners, they raise awareness, consciousness, and offer visibility to those communities who have been traditionally overlooked or silenced altogether.

However, in organizing exhibitions of Indigenous art, museums must be wary of monolithic definitions—that is, not all Indigenous people are alike or share the same values and sensibilities. While each community may share a commitment to honoring their ancestors and to supporting future generations, there is no consensus on how to achieve this.[76] As Chickasaw curator heather ahtone explains: "We have to work really hard through the challenges that emerge when you have matrilineal and patrilineal cultures, when you have people who come from the stars and people who come from the Earth. When you have histories of tribes that have not been kind to one another. We each carry our individual and cultural histories into play in everything we do. So, you can imagine the challenge of drawing a consensus for the emotionally and culturally sensitive tasks that we manage."[77] We believe it would make more sense to embed multiplicities within the framework of museums, rather than any one definitive strategy. Each exhibition, dissemination program, and so forth must be related to the materiality of that exhibition. For example, if the exhibition deals with one specific tribe, then the methodological framework for that exhibition comes from the knowledge of and from that tribe. Curators should also keep in mind that although there are local specificities, it might also be the case that they are working with communities who all connect with an overall concept. The philosophy of gift-giving, for instance, is found in multiple communities across the world. And though it is commonly based in the understanding of the world as relational, and that the gift acknowledges that relationality, the process of gift-giving is done differently and employs different terminologies depending on the Indigenous community. Emphasizing the differences between Indigenous communities is critical to the indigenizing process in museums, as is community-curated exhibition development. As Amy Lonetree explains, museums need to shift from being "strictly curator-controlled sites to more inclusive and collaborative spaces"—centering collectivity and dialogue.[78] The notion of collectivity is a fundamental basis in the structuring of many Indigenous societies. As has been pointed out by scholar Shawn Wilson, Indigenous ways of knowing rest in the fundamental belief that knowledge is relational; it "is shared with all creation."[79] It is no surprise, then, that Indigenous museums, in particular, have embraced this practice of inclusiveness and collaboration. It is also important "to move away from object-based presentations that focus on the functions and uses of objects according to ethnographic categories," Lonetree explains.[80] It is critical that exhibitions highlight the relationships the objects have to contemporary Indigenous communities. As curator Trudy Nicks has acknowledged, "Museums now accept that many contemporary Indigenous groups see objects as living entities .... [and] the significance of objects is no longer restricted to past contexts of manufacture, use, and collecting, but now takes into account the demonstrated meanings they may have for indigenous communities in the present and for the future."[81] Thematic exhibitions developed in consultation with Indigenous community advisory boards are preferable. This will ensure objects are chosen to illuminate specific themes critical to those communities, including the importance of land, family, elders, education, language, and sovereignty. Central to these presentations, Lonetree explains, is the display of objects "in ways that convey both their historic and contemporary resonances"; equally important is the highlighting of "survivance," which emphasizes Indigenous survival within a colonial context.[82]

Presenting a clear and coherent understanding of colonialism and its ongoing effects should be another goal—otherwise, the public fails to grasp the history of genocidal acts committed against Indigenous people. Above all, the primary function of an indigenizing museum practice must address what Lonetree calls "historical unresolved grief."[83] In the end, museums should strive to become "sovereign spaces" for Indigenous communities, where, as Puwai Cairns explains, "Māori can be Māori, tell Māori stories with all their complications and contradictions, Māori storytellers and historians telling stories to Māori, inclusively and without apology."[84]

CONCLUSION

To indigenize a museum is not simply a matter of changing content or relinquishing control and sharing authority—it must also involve a shift in the logic of the conversation between museum and Indigenous communities. The goal should not be merely to find a singular anchor within established museological practices in the frameworks created via non-Indigenous academia, which is founded on Euro-American-centric perspectives. On the contrary, to truly indigenize demands the acknowledgment and honoring of many dynamic layers of multiple realities (ontologies). In this, we do not mean to claim that the goal is to replace one system with another; it is not about replacing one singularity with another. Nor is it our intent to argue that a merging of multiple systems is the best solution. Instead, we believe that indigenizing must encourage the weaving together of many different systems of knowledge and practices, so that we are left with a synergic core of multiplicities offering myriad perspectives and understandings, while maintaining the distinctiveness and diversity of many, localized ways of being, knowing, and doing. Museums should be sites of collectivity, understanding, and dialogue across borders of time and place—the museum setting itself, its structure, and its public commitments should also strive to foreground Indigenous knowledges and practices.

In settler colonial contexts, within the colonial structures that imperialism has enforced overall, and where all land is unquestionably Indigenous, this process can begin, quite simply, with land acknowledgments and welcome ceremonies. At museums in Australia, New Zealand, and Canada, and some museums in the United States, for example, it is customary to recognize the traditional owners of the land on which people gather, and at each public event—like an exhibition opening or a lecture—a land acknowledgment is read aloud. Indeed, in some cases, a computer user cannot enter a museum website without first acknowledging traditional landowners, as is the case with the Museum of Contemporary Art Australia, Sydney, and other institutions from the Global South. The basic idea behind a land acknowledgment is that non-Indigenous settler communities recognize Indigenous people and their homelands within the borders that make up the colonial nations of the world. This, at least in theory, resists the erasure of Indigenous histories and presence on the land, commemorating the kinship between Indigenous people and their ancestral homelands.

One could argue that a land acknowledgment runs the risk of becoming just another example of performative allyship, nothing more than an empty gesture that sidesteps the problematic issues caused by colonialism that affect Indigenous communities. At the same time, in many Indigenous contexts and certainly in the Sámi context, how often are non-Indigenous people surprised when told how far Indigenous homelands reach? How often, for example, is Sámi visibility, both in history and the present, silenced and erased? A land acknowledgment, if nothing else, highlights the fact that Norway, Finland, Sweden, and Russia (as well as many other nations) are nations born from colonialism and spreads the knowledge of Sápmi (and other Indigenous homelands) as more than an abstract idea. (Thus, as we write this essay in New Jersey, we acknowledge that we are living and working on occupied Lenni-Lenape land that was seized by the Dutch through force in the 17th century;[85] and in Finland, whose establishment rests on the dissolvement of Sámi systems of land tenure and the erasure of the *siida* as clan-based territories that make up Sápmi, the Sámi homeland.)

In addition to land acknowledgments, museums in Australia, New Zealand, and Canada also perform "Welcome to Country" ceremonies, in which the traditional owners "welcome" all audiences onto their land, typically accompanied by music and/or dance performances. In so doing, these institutions facilitate an assertion of protocols, which means that they help enact rules and guidelines that cater to the specific needs and cultural demands of the perspectives of those involved. In this way, multiple ontological realities are simultaneously enacted. Unfortunately, to our knowledge, neither of these practices—land acknowledgments or welcome to country ceremonies—has been broadly enacted at U.S. or Scandinavian museums. In fact, land acknowledgments have only just recently been appropriated in the context of the Global North, and as yet are only practiced at a handful of institutions. Also not visible in the Euro-American context are "cultural sensitivity warnings," which are meant to alert Indigenous people that galleries or websites contain images, voices, or names of deceased individuals in photographs, film, audio recordings or printed material. These warnings recognize that many traditional Indigenous populations avoid referring to or depicting the deceased as a mark of respect. We would recommend that these three practices be enacted in an effort towards indigenizing museums.

In addition to land acknowledgments, welcome to country ceremonies, and cultural sensitivity warnings, some museums have made specific commitments to adopt indigenization policies at the structural level. The Abbe Museum in Bar Harbor, Maine, a museum of Wabanaki art, history, and culture, was arguably the first museum in the U.S. to embrace an institutional position of indigenization, written into its bylaws in 2015; it was followed by the San Diego Museum of Us in 2017. (These institutions' plans use the term "decolonization"; we would use "indigenization" to describe the same set of actions.)[86] Other museums and organizations are also developing strategic plans that foreground indigeneity. For example, the Australian Museums and Galleries Association published a ten-year *Indigenous Roadmap* (2019–29) in 2019 which aims to enhance Indigenous engagement in museums across Australia.[87] Its ultimate goals are for all museums to have an Indigenous curator, senior leadership representation, policies for interpreting Indigenous materials, statements of reflection, collection inventories, and reconciliation action plans (frameworks that give organizations an outline for how to work toward reconciliation).[88] The action plans as set forth by the Australian Museums and Galleries Association include goals such as "increasing Indigenous employment, setting procurement targets, increasing staff cultural awareness, celebrations of Indigenous events, and community education."[89] It remains to be seen how successful the museums will be in this endeavor, but it is a valiant effort on the part of hundreds of museums in Australia to reckon with colonization.

The shameful reality is that most museums continue to serve as painful reminders of violence, dispossession, and trauma. An indigenized museum would foster community wellbeing and empowerment, serving as a site of restorative justice and a vehicle for repairing the harms of colonization.

That said, we will close this chapter by cautioning against any museum believing that their process of indigenizing could ever be finished. To indigenize is a processual initiative that continuously seeks to identify and resolve the problematic issues within museological institutions. As such, it does not end, but continues to be a chosen practice. More to the point, to indigenize becomes a choice made daily by institutions to better themselves and thus the services they provide to their communities—all of their communities, not simply those that have historically benefited from the implementation of imperialism and the consequent process of colonization.

CHAPTER 3
“GIVE IT ALL BACK”: RECONCILING WITH CULTURAL HERITAGE

INTRODUCTION

In November 2017, during a trip to Burkina Faso, French President Emmanuel Macron made a landmark pledge to ensure "the temporary or permanent restitution of African heritage to Africa" within the next five years.[1] Citing colonization as "a crime against humanity, a true example of barbarism," he promised to commission a report on the subject that would offer guidance to the French government moving forward.[2] The 95-page report, "The Restitution of African Cultural Heritage: Toward a New Relational Ethics," was published in November 2018 and authored by two academics, the Senegalese economist Felwine Sarr and the French art historian Bénédicte Savoy.[3] In the report, Sarr and Savoy revealed that 90% of Africa's cultural heritage is housed in major European and American museums, with France alone possessing over 90,000 objects from sub-Saharan Africa in its public collections, most of them housed in the Musée du quai Branly – Jacques Chirac in Paris, a museum devoted to the art of Africa, Asia, Oceania, and the Americas with approximately 350,000 objects in its permanent collection.[4] It opened in 2006 to some controversy—a complex saga of politics, architecture, and the attempt to create a museum that was part art, part anthropology.[5]

The Sarr-Savoy report recommended the permanent restitution and repatriation of all objects "taken by force or presumed to be acquired through inequitable conditions" by the military, scientific expeditions, or colonial administrators during France's rule in Africa, spanning from the late 19th century to 1960.[6] The authors rejected the idea of long-term loans, advocating instead for the unconditional return of all artifacts and ancestral remains, and called on institutions to abandon "political prudence and museum anxiety."[7] Ultimately, the report called for a change to France's Heritage Code to address the ongoing question of inalienability—a law dating from 1566, *L'édit de Moulins*, which prevents monarchs and French institutions from transferring cultural objects or other inherited assets, *la règle de l'inâlienabilité*.[8] Given the strictness of the code, a new French law has been required each time an individual object is returned to its country or community of origin. (As will be discussed below, in 2023–25, following the Sarr-Savoy report and mounting international demands for restitution and repatriation, the French government has begun to ease the restrictions of the Heritage Code to enable the return of ancestral remains, artworks looted during the Nazi occupation, and treasures taken during the colonial era that remain in French collections.)

Upon publication of the Sarr-Savoy report, Macron immediately announced that the Musée du quai Branly would permanently return twenty-six objects from the Royal Palaces of Abomey to the modern-day Republic of Benin—Nigeria's neighbor to the west—which had been looted by French colonial forces in 1892.[9] He also promised that a sword belonging to a 19th-century Islamic ruler would be returned to Senegal. These transfers were unanimously approved by the French legislature two years later, in December 2020. The legislation associated with these returns made clear that this approval pertained only to the specific repatriation requests from Benin and Senegal; future requests would be independently reviewed and would require additional legislation.[10]

BENIN BRONZES

The highly publicized Sarr-Savoy report and Macron's subsequent promise to restitute artifacts to Africa sent shock waves through European and U.S. museums with colonial-era collections. While there had been growing demands for the repatriation of cultural artifacts in France for decades, Macron's commissioned report and promise signaled a step change. Bénédicte Savoy called Macron's speech in Burkina Faso “a revolution ... In two minutes and 33 seconds ... Macron swept aside several decades of official French museum policy.”[11] In the aftermath, museums across Europe and the U.S. began quickly making public statements and developing new policies in an effort to address increased public pressure and incoming calls from colonized countries.

The thousands of objects forcefully removed from Benin City (in what is now Nigeria) by the British during a particularly violent military expedition in 1897 became the lightning rod in these debates. Indeed, mention of the pilfered treasures has been a regular occurrence in the art press since 2018, when Nigeria announced its plans to build the Museum of West African Art (MWAA) in Benin City to house the returning treasures, designed by Ghanaian-British architect David Adjaye.[12] The first building in the vast complex opened in November

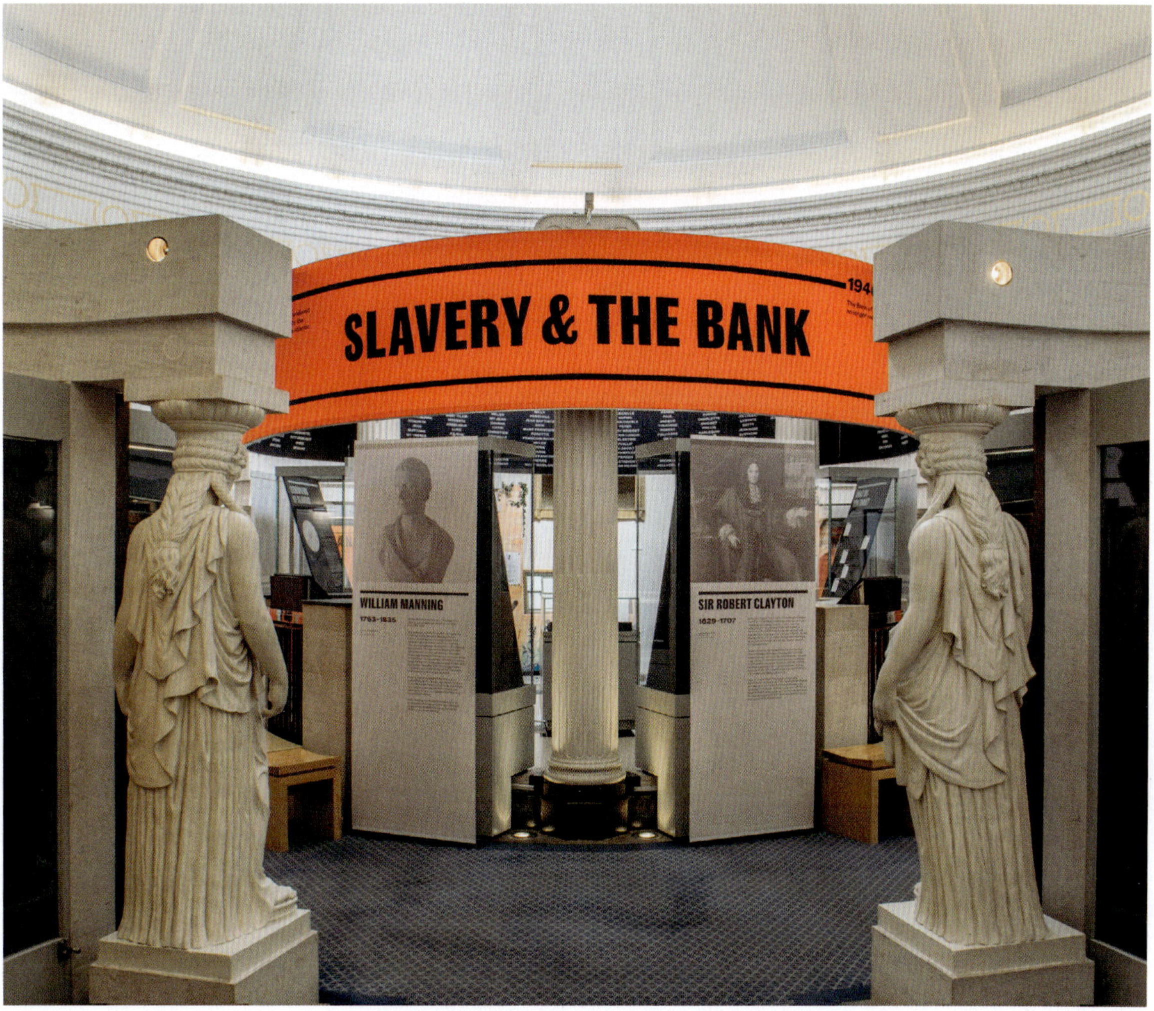

1 *Slavery and the Bank*, exhibition installation, Bank of England Museum, London, 2022–24.

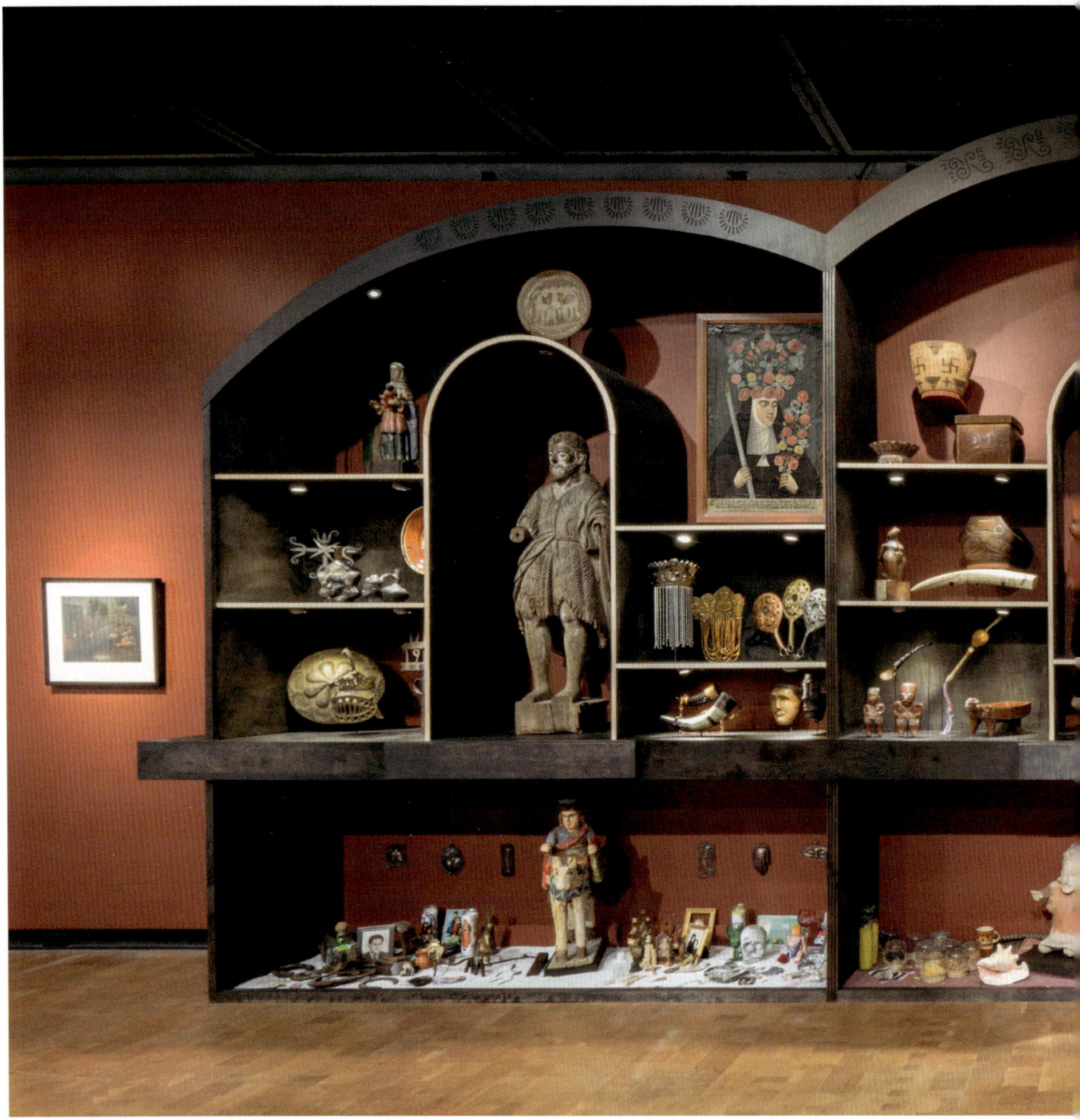

2 Amalia Mesa-Bains,
New World Wunderkammer,
2013–14.

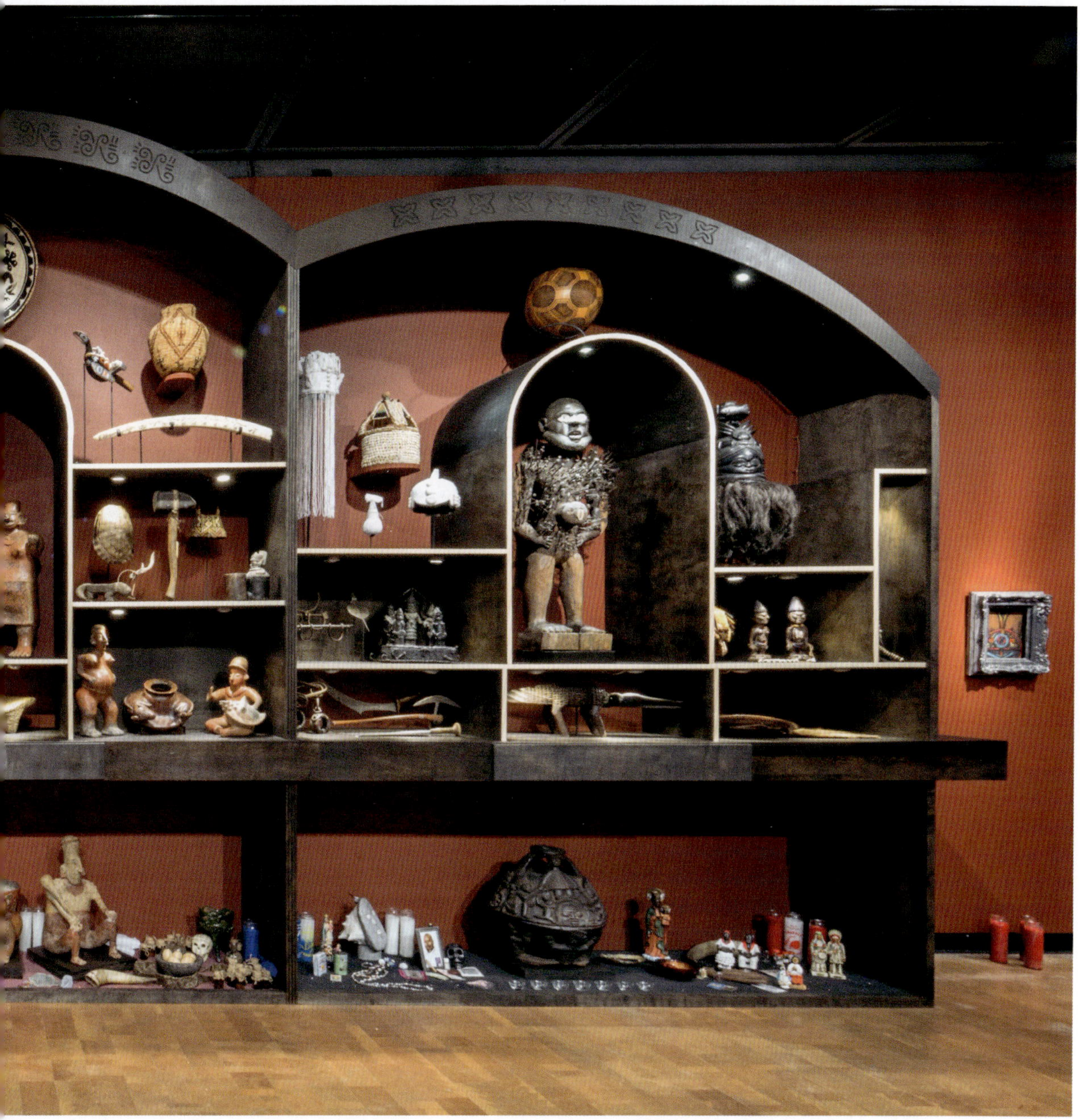

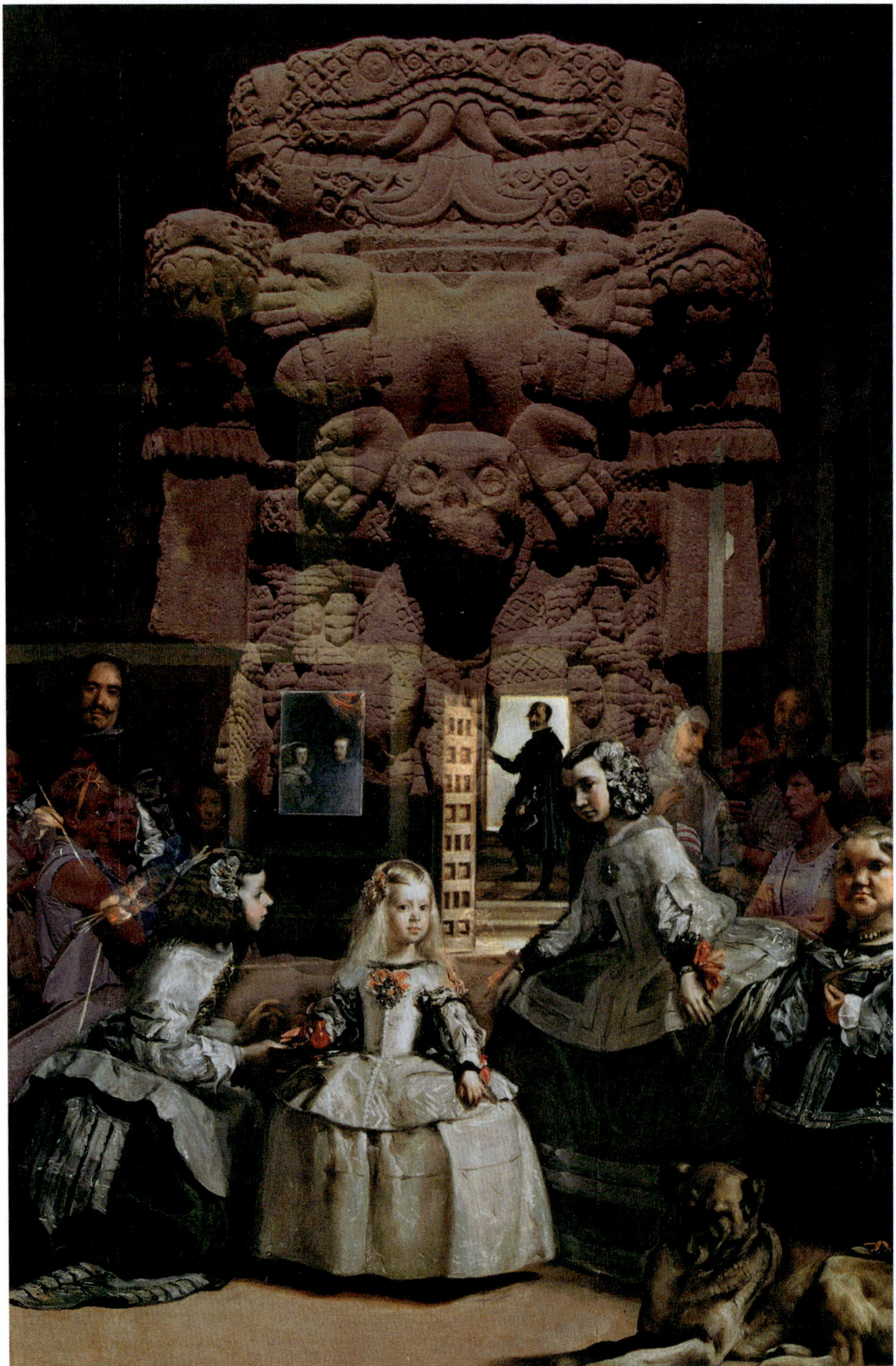

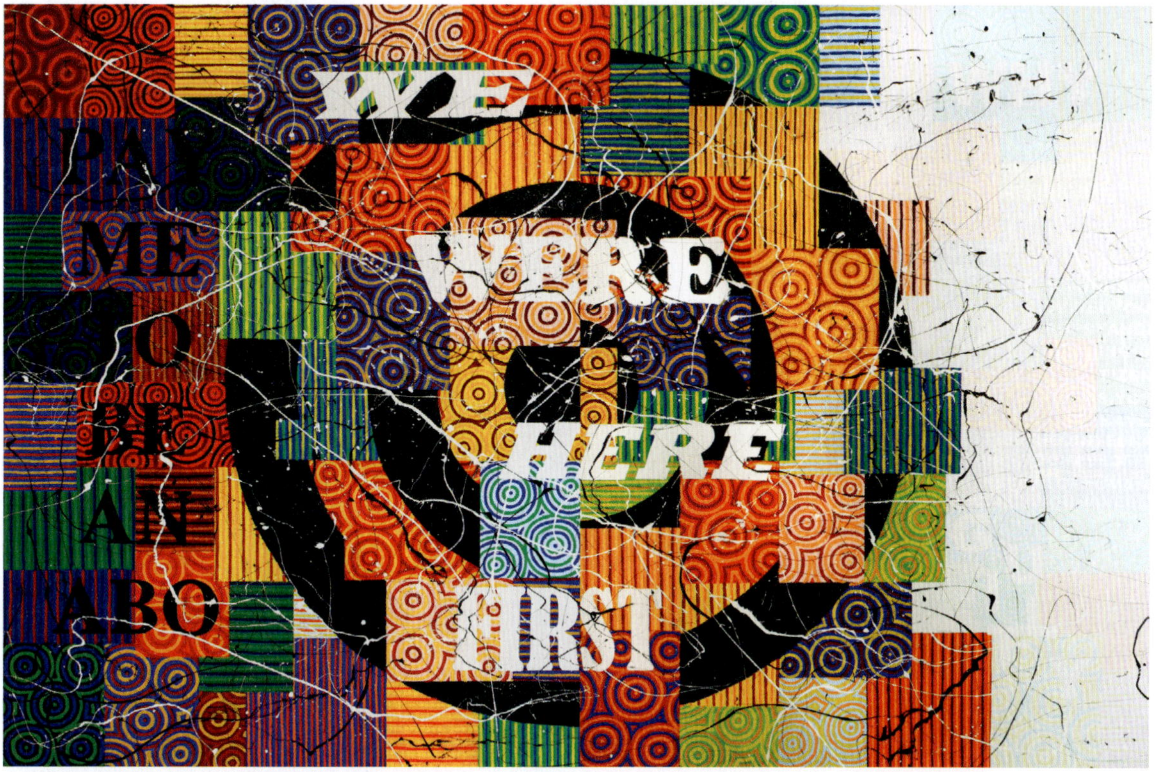

3 Pedro Lasch, *Coatlicue and Las Meninas*, 2008, from the *Black Mirror/Espejo Negro* series, 2007–present. Simulation of installation at Museo del Prado, Madrid, and Museo Nacional de Antropología, Mexico City.

4 Richard Bell, *We Were Here First*, 2007.

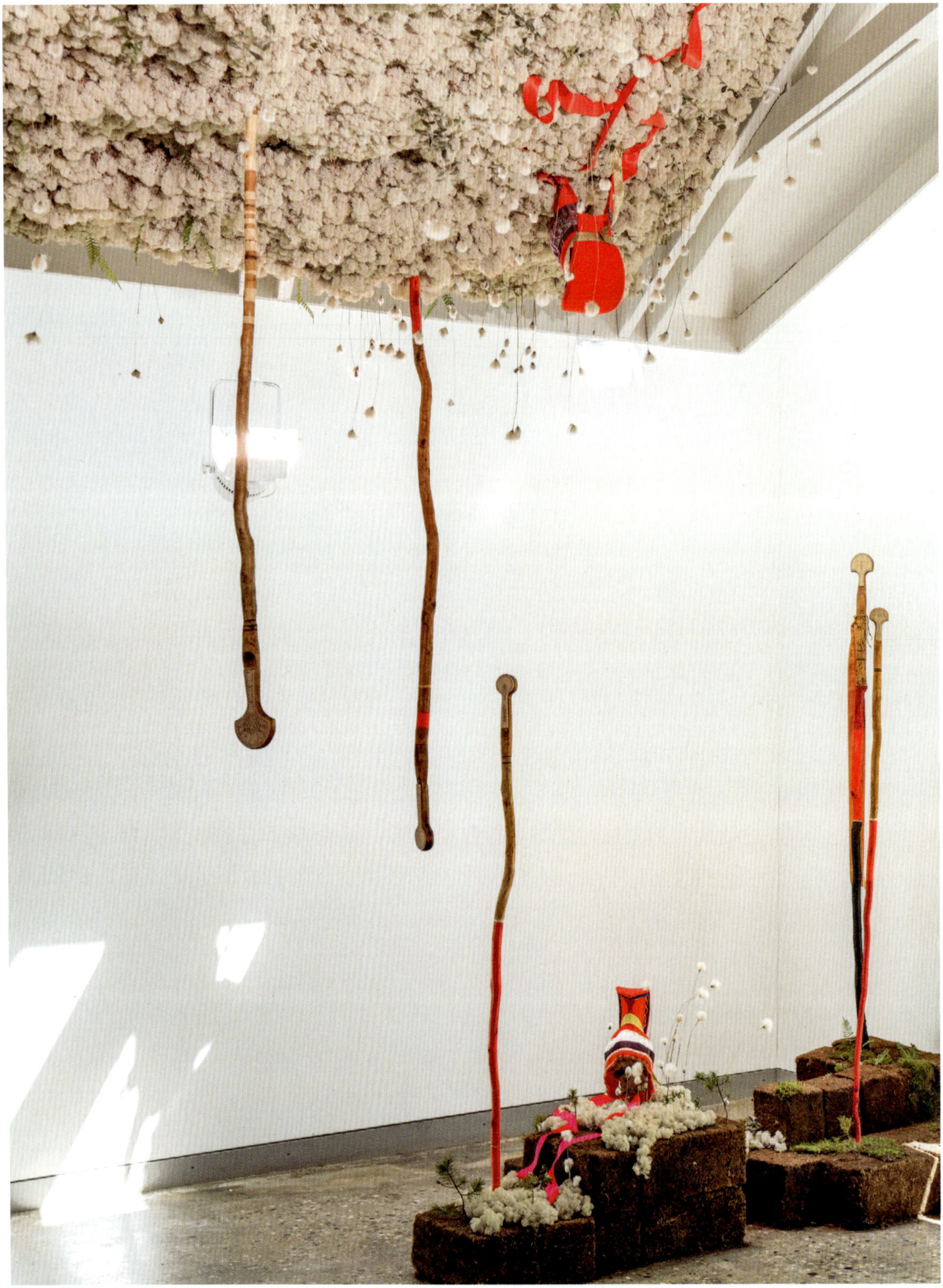

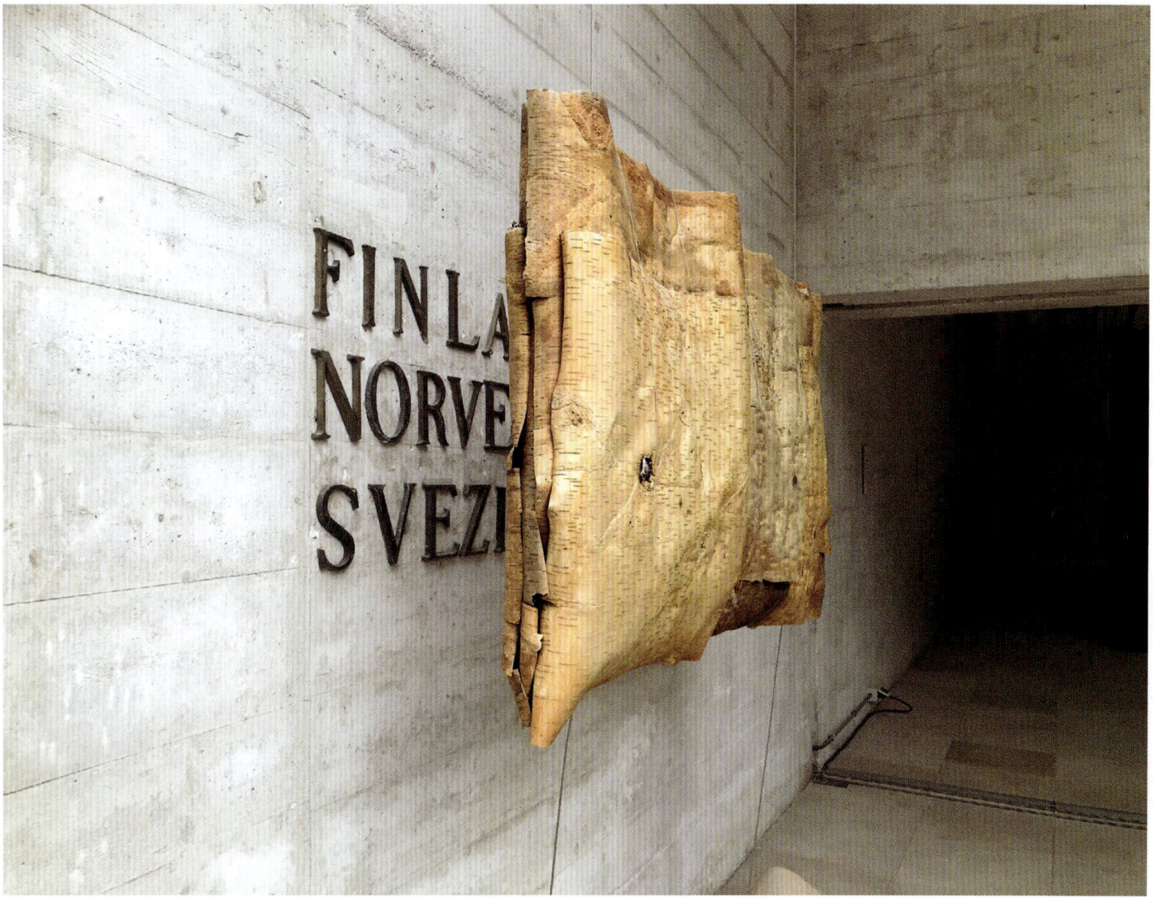

5 Outi Pieski, *Ovdavázzit—Forewalkers*, Alvar Aalto Pavilion at the 58th Venice Biennale, 2019.

6 Tablet made of birch panels and sinews, crafted by the curatorial collective, artists, and other helpers associated with the Sámi Pavilion at the 59th Venice Biennale, 2022. The panel obscures from view the words "Finland," "Norway," and "Sweden."

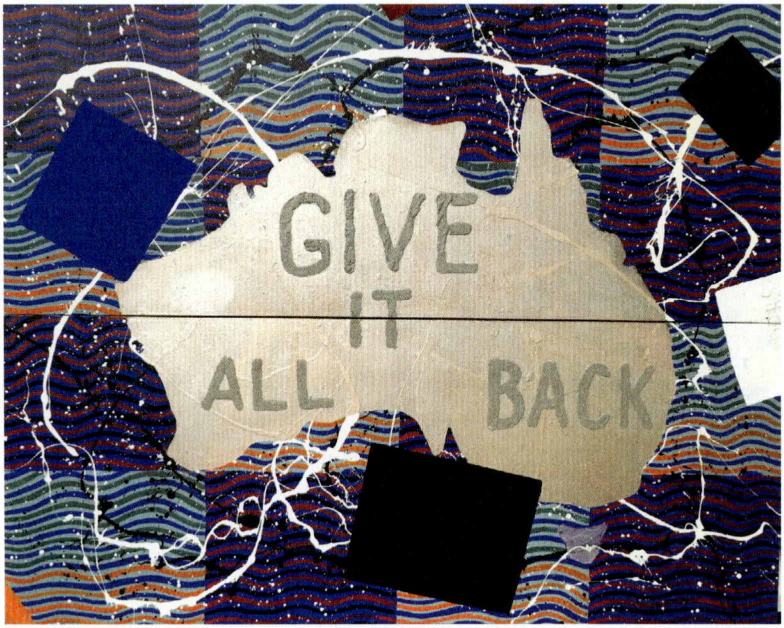

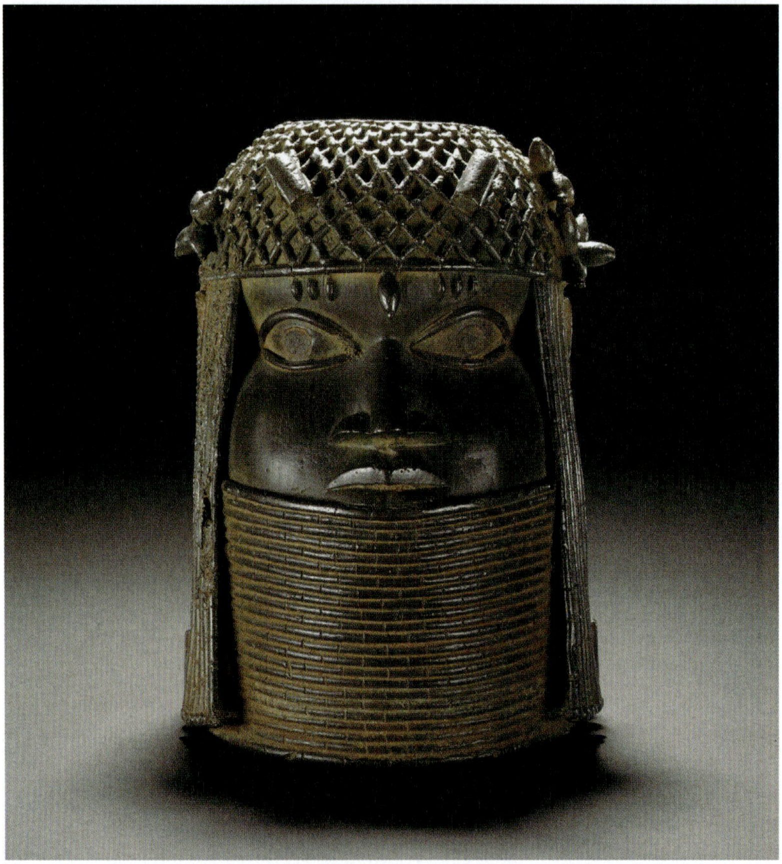

7 Richard Bell, *Whole Lot*, 2002.

8 Commemorative head of an Oba (king), lost-wax cast in brass, Benin City, 1550–1650.

2024, but the remainder of the master plan will roll out in the next few years. Specifically, it is the thousands of objects looted from Benin City that are collectively referred to as the "Benin Bronzes," despite the fact that not all objects are bronze. The large stash of looted objects includes figurines, sculptures of Obas (heads of state), elephant tusks, and ivory masks, among other treasures.

In his 2020 book, *The Brutish Museum: The Benin Bronzes, Colonial Violence and Cultural Restitution*, Dan Hicks, Curator of World Archeology at the Pitt Rivers Museum at Oxford University, compiled a list of the 161 institutions worldwide that have "acquired" Benin Bronzes specifically as a result of the British raid of Benin City.[13] Hicks's list includes many beloved museums, including, among others, the Metropolitan Museum of Art (New York), the Smithsonian's National Museum of African Art (Washington, D.C.), the Victoria and Albert Museum (London), the Vatican Museums (Rome), the Australian Museum (Sydney), and, of course, the British Museum (London), which has the largest contingent of Benin Bronzes in the world (900 works, see Fig. 8), followed by the Ethnological Museum in the new Humboldt Forum in Berlin, which has the second-largest collection (440 works in their collection are directly linked to the 1897 raid). One of the biggest issues for Hicks, of course, is that whereas many non-African institutions hold Benin Bronzes, only nine Nigerian museums steward objects that have been repatriated from the original stash of looted treasures, according to Hicks's count.

Since it gained independence in 1960, Nigeria has repeatedly called for the repatriation of the objects plundered by British troops from Benin City. The resistance to repatriation of the objects to Nigeria has been fierce, but those calling for the return of these culturally significant objects are not without allies. Since 2007, the Benin Dialogue Group (BDG), a network of European museums that have Benin Bronzes in their collections, has been instrumental in ensuring museums address the issue head-on. The BDG commitment has resulted in numerous conversations with museums worldwide, some of whom have agreed permanently to return artifacts unethically acquired from Benin City to Nigeria. Institutions with some of the smallest numbers of objects were the first to agree to the returns, including Jesus College at the University of Cambridge, Horniman Museum & Gardens (London), National Museum of Ireland (Dublin), National Museum of World Cultures (Amsterdam), and the University of Aberdeen, the latter being the first institution in Europe to commit to restituting a Benin Bronze in March 2021. Since then, under increased international pressure, the Metropolitan[14] and Smithsonian museums,[15] among others, have repatriated treasures to the Nigerian government. In July 2022, the German government restituted to Nigeria 1,100 Benin Bronzes that had been housed in German museums.[16] A Nigerian official, Lai Mohammed, described the step as "the single largest known repatriation of artefacts in the world," and encouraged others to follow Germany's example.[17] According to the agreement between the two countries, while many of the objects have already been repatriated, Nigerian authorities are currently in the process of determining whether they would like those that remain in Germany to be returned to Nigeria, or to remain on view in German museums as cultural ambassadors for Nigeria.[18]

While hundreds of Benin Bronzes have now been repatriated, the process has faced complications. When the Museum of Archaeology and Anthropology at the University of Cambridge pledged to return 116 artifacts to Nigeria in 2022, the process was paused over opposing claims to ownership. The current Oba (head of state) of Benin City, Ewuare II, and the Nigerian government were conflicted about who should receive the returning treasures. Another stumbling block occurred when, in March 2023, the country's outgoing president, Muhammadu Buhari, recognized the Oba as the guardian of the bronzes.[19] Former legal advisor at the United Nations office in Vienna and scholar Kwame Opoku agreed with the decision, explaining that the "Benin bronzes ... were made for the Oba of Benin City by a guild of bronze casters he employed and that the sculptures were displayed in the Royal Museum in the Palace in Benin City."[20] Nigerian officials agreed, and in April 2023, officially transferred ownership of the Benin Bronzes to the Oba, including those already repatriated and those yet to be repatriated. In February 2025, the 2023 presidential decree was overturned, assigning the responsibility of retrieving and housing the artifacts with the National Commission for Museums and Monuments (NCMM).[21] With the NCMM officially in charge, its head, Olugbile Holloway, confirmed the Oba's support for the commission's role in displaying, conserving, and repatriating the artifacts. In February 2026, the University of Cambridge and NCMM announced that the legal title of the 116 artifacts has been transferred to Nigeria, with physical returns scheduled for 2027.[22]

ARGUMENTS AGAINST RETURNS

Since 2018, which is to say the year that Nigeria announced its much-publicized plans to build the MWAA, museums have offered innumerable excuses for not returning the cultural artifacts to Nigeria. These excuses are not new; they have been used for decades as a bid to avert restitutions and repatriations. The most frequently cited justification against claims to restitution is the "rescue" argument, which contends that the objects would not have been adequately preserved were it not for the interventions of wealthier nations, and that they have helped to safeguard the cultural heritage. The British Museum, for instance, claims that Lord Elgin's "removal" of the marbles from the Parthenon saved them from destruction, arguing at the time that they were not, in their opinion, being adequately preserved. The rescue argument also suggests that the communities from whom the objects were "acquired" would soon be extinct, so colonialists justified the theft by arguing that they wanted to preserve the objects for posterity. Objects were considered representatives of a "vanishing race" that needed urgent documentation and scientific research (such was the excuse employed by grave robbers of Indigenous American ancestral remains who sought to argue "scientifically" for the racial superiority of whites, a concept fundamental to white supremacist ideology).

The rescue argument also implies that certain museums are better capable of caring for objects than the source communities, which is infantilizing to originating nations and communities. Given the recent scandals at the British Museum and the Metropolitan—which involved staff theft of thousands of objects and the exposure of thousands of illegally acquired antiquities, respectively—the argument that European and American museums are better custodians of others' property is ludicrous. Other museums using the "care" argument have insisted that communities or nations requesting objects' return must build institutions to properly steward the looted objects before they'll consider restitution or repatriation. Of course, there are many museums in Egypt, Greece, and Nigeria, for example, with state-of-the-art facilities more than capable of taking care of the returned heritage.[23] In cases of repatriation to countries that may have the cultural, but not the financial resources or latest technologies to direct to the care of these objects, Euro-American institutions would be wise to question the assumption that they be the arbiters, on a global scale, of where these objects are permanently housed. Institutions operating from a position of financial privilege ought to pursue alternative solutions, some of which are discussed further in this chapter under "Recommendations."

Sometimes, the conversation about the return of cultural property goes to the extreme, with museums arguing that if they return all of the looted objects then it will wipe out their collections. The goal with restitution and repatriation is not to empty museums, as some conservatives fear. Instead, Bénédicte Savoy suggests that the goal is a "rebalancing of the geography."[24] As she explains in a 2018 interview, the international distribution of African heritage is currently "extremely imbalanced" in museums: "European museums have almost everything, and African museums have almost nothing."[25] Of the more than 350,000 objects in the collection of the Musée du quai Branly, Paris, for example, only some 3,500 are on view at any given time.[26] If the museum were to return even 1,000 objects to rightful owners, then, it would hardly diminish its permanent collection holdings. Moreover, according to a British Museum fact sheet, of the 8 million collection objects, just 1% are currently on display.[27] Of that 1%, about only a hundred of the 900 objects stolen from Benin City are on display. As Dan Hicks, at the Pitt Rivers Museum, Oxford, explains: "This throws a rather different light on the specter of empty galleries."[28]

Institutions opposed to restitution and repatriation have made the case for "universal museums," which ostensibly represent all humanity, across all cultures and times. One of the many arguments against returning cultural heritage to source communities dates back to 2002, when eighteen prominent institutions signed the "Declaration on the Importance and Value of Universal Museums."[29] Although the British Museum was not among the signatories, the declaration was widely seen as a response to Greek calls for the repatriation of the Parthenon Marbles. (Requests from Greece continue at the time of this writing.) The 2002 declaration argued that so-called "universal museums ... provide a valid and valuable context for objects that were long ago displaced from their original source,"[30] as if the context that the British Museum provides for the Parthenon Marbles were superior to that of the Acropolis Museum. (Note the word "displaced" instead of "dubiously acquired" or "looted.") This is not a sound argument, given the new museum in Athens is a few hundred meters from the Acropolis, which allows the marbles to be seen as intended in situ—in the context of the ancient citadel, a site covered with architecture, art, and artifacts venerating the gods.

"The universal admiration for ancient civilizations," the 2002 declaration continues, "would not be so deeply established today were it not for the influence exercised by the artifacts of these cultures, widely available to an international public in major museums." In other words, they argue that universal museums themselves should be credited with the broad knowledge today of an array of world cultures. I would call this a "means to an end" argument, whereby the museum justifies its holdings of looted objects by claiming that their ownership of the objects has aided in the promotion of important values, e.g., preservation, education and scholarship, and cultural pluralism.

As to the contested provenance of certain works within their museum collections, the declaration determined that "over time, objects so acquired—whether by purchase, gift or portage—have become part of the museums that have cared for them, and by extension part of the heritage of the nations which house them."[31] (Again, note that they do not use words like "looting" or "stolen" or "trafficked," opting instead to state that the objects were gifts, purchases, or simply "displaced.") They argue that the objects have become so integral to their collections and to their own national heritage that they now belong to the countries in which they are currently held. France's inalienability defense and the U.K.'s 1983 National Heritage Act certainly support this argument.

Ultimately, the 2002 declaration concludes, universal museums "serve not just the citizens of one nation but the people of every nation," presenting global art history for all humanity to appreciate. This, of course, reflects a perspective shaped by Western privilege.[32] As Tess Davis, a lawyer with the Antiquities Coalition, says: "The citizens of New York, London, and Paris may benefit, but those of Phnom Penh? Never."[33] Indeed, as Geoffrey Lewis, then Chairman, ICOM Ethics Committee, explained at the time, this declaration was not signed by the "international museum community," and in fact African and Asian countries were noticeably absent.[34] (Ten of the eighteen museums were in English-speaking countries, all led by white male directors.[35])

There were many outspoken critics of the declaration, including David Gill (professor, University of Kent), Kwame Opoku (formerly of the UN), and George Abungu (former director of the National Museums of Kenya), among others.[36] "The document is extremely important," Gill insists, "since we have no other modern document which spells out so well the selfishness and arrogance of the major museums, their desire to put themselves above morality and justice, their desire to take hold of the narratives concerning the cultural objects of others and to browbeat others into meek submission."[37] Opoku, for his part, calls the declaration a "singular failure of an arrogant imperialist project,"[38] and Abungu asks: "If the signatories of the Declaration are trying to create the idea that their collections are held in trust for all of humanity, then why do they still call themselves by their original names? Why not 'Universal Museum in Britain' rather than British Museum?"[39] As the critics make clear, the declaration was, in essence, "a statement of self-interest" that sought immunity from restitution claims.[40] Ultimately, however, it provided no defence for the eighteen institutions against claims from source communities seeking the return of their cultural heritage. Within a few years, for instance, Italy forced the leading American signatories of the declaration to return trafficked antiquities, including the Museum of Fine Arts (Boston), the Metropolitan Museum of Art (New York), and the Princeton University Art Museum (Princeton, NJ).[41] This was followed soon thereafter by a scandal surrounding 45,000 looted antiquities at the J. Paul Getty Museum (Los Angeles).[42]

INTERNATIONAL CONVENTIONS ON HERITAGE PROTECTION

Attempts to establish international guidelines for the repatriation and restitution, as well as the acquisition, of heritage have been made since the mid-20th century, by the United Nations, beginning with the Hague Convention in 1954. The convention, which was written in the wake of the widespread looting and destruction of heritage during World War II, sought precisely to protect cultural property during and after armed conflict.[43] (No international law prohibiting plunder of cultural objects during times of war existed before this. Imagine if such an international convention had existed in what is now Nigeria, or the United States, by colonial settlers.) But the pivotal moment in the safeguarding of heritage was UNESCO's "Convention on the Means of Prohibiting and Preventing the Illicit Import, Export and Transfer of Ownership of Cultural Property," adopted in 1970.[44] It stipulated that "it is essential for every state to become increasingly alive to the moral obligations to respect its own cultural heritage and that of all nations," and that "cultural institutions, museums, libraries and archives should ensure that their collections are built up in accordance with universally recognized moral principles."[45] Not all nations ratified the document, which has proven to be an ongoing issue—as has the fact that while the convention deals with the return of artifacts stolen and trafficked *since* 1970, there is no agreement on the rules that should govern the fate of objects illegally acquired prior to that date. The UNESCO convention, however, offered a legal framework within which governments could request repatriation of objects with undocumented, questionable provenance, and museums could respond. However, the convention is not itself enforceable by law; the expectation is that the governments and museums abide by it as the ethical standard.

Following the 1970 UNESCO convention there were many political steps taken to return artifacts back to source communities. In the early 1980s, Ekpo Okpo Eyo, a Nigerian archaeologist and director of his country's Federal Department of Antiquities, and Senegal-born Amadou Mahtar M'Bow, the first Black African director-general of UNESCO, elevated the repatriation and restitution of cultural heritage into a global political cause, culminating in the 1981 publication of a Restitution Form in three languages.[46] As Bénédicte Savoy explains: "This document shows how far this period went, and how close and how simple restitutions of cultural assets to the so-called Third World seemed to be."[47] French and German politicians were incredibly receptive to the idea of restitution of cultural heritage at the time. But, as Savoy explains, "museums across Europe were the 'major force' in opposing restitution 40 years ago."[48] Creating inventories of museum collections was "actively discouraged," and museums refused to engage in negotiations.[49]

The next significant international milestone in heritage protection emerged in 1995, with the UNIDROIT (International Institute for the Unification of Private Law) "Convention on Stolen or Illegally Exported Cultural Objects," which calls for the return of exported cultural property as well as objects illegally excavated from archaeological sites.[50] The convention established the principle of "due diligence," requiring dealers, collectors, and museums to ensure that cultural property is not acquired without a fully documented provenance.[51] Only thirty-five nations have ratified the convention to date; France, for instance, as of this writing, has signed but never ratified it.[52]

In 2007, the United Nations (UN) jump-started the conversation on restitution and repatriation again with Article 11 of its "Declaration on the Rights of Indigenous Peoples," which encourages states to restore "cultural, intellectual, religious and spiritual property" taken from Indigenous people without their "free, prior and informed consent or in violation of their laws, traditions and customs."[53] This declaration has proven difficult to enforce because many of the lands upon which Indigenous peoples live are not recognized as "states." For example, when Māori request the repatriation of ancestral remains, the application must be submitted by the government of New Zealand.[54] Or when Indigenous Australian artifacts and remains are requested, the Australian government must submit the request on behalf of the source community. In sum, the 2007 Declaration offers advice to "nations" but not specifically to museums or source communities. Again, while museums are encouraged to abide by the 2007 declaration, without an enforceable international legal framework, they are not obligated to return colonial-era objects.

PROFESSIONAL ARTS ORGANIZATIONS

Professional arts organizations have offered some guidance for museums on the subject of restitution, repatriation, and acquisition. In 2004, the international Association of Art Museum Directors (AAMD) issued "Guidelines on the Acquisition of Archaeological Material and Ancient Art."[55] In 2013, a revision of the guidelines advised museums to post all provenance information in the AAMD Object Registry, especially when seeking to acquire an archaeological object or ancient art.[56] Given the recent museum scandals surrounding ancient artifacts, one wonders to what degree museums like the Met abide by these guidelines. For their part, Arts Council England (ACE) published an extensive report in 2023, titled "Restitution and Repatriation: A Practical Guide for Museums in England," prepared in collaboration with the Institute of Art & Law (ILA).[57] The guide addresses every facet of museum operations impacted by these issues, urging institutions to act with collaboration, transparency, and fairness. The two-part guide recommends rigorous provenance research, which it suggests should be made readily available online. It recommends evaluating each claim through an ethical lens, considering the significance of the heritage to the claimant, the circumstances of its removal from its source community, and the museum's subsequent engagement with the object. Institutions should also perform a legal assessment to determine if the claimant has a "superior ownership right to that of the museum."[58] The guide offers a series of solutions in relation to claims, including transfer of legal ownership, rights of access or control, joint ownership, loan, or no change. All of these actions are subject to obtaining Charity Commission approval. While these guidelines will prove enormously useful to many museums throughout the U.K., they do not pertain to national museums and galleries, like Tate or the National Gallery, among others, since those collections are protected by the 1963 National Heritage Act (discussed below).

In 2021, the German Museums Association published "Guidelines for German Museums: Care of Collections from Colonial Contexts." Revised from its 2019 version, these recommendations broaden the original focus on transferring ancestral remains to embrace greater cultural sensitivity toward non-Euro-American perspectives.[59] The guidelines call for a complete digital inventory of museum collections that are readily accessible online. The Museums Association contends that the financial and human resources currently allocated to repatriation and restitution are grossly inadequate, urging individual museums to form dedicated teams to develop comprehensive inventories.[60] It recommends that Germany's sixteen states and local governments provide the money for these additional activities and personnel. It also suggests that all museum exhibition descriptions and object labels should clearly state how the items from colonial contexts came to be in their collections. Instead of recommending repatriation or restitution outright, the guidelines emphasize the importance of loans and partnerships with institutions in source communities.

The AAMD's, ACE's, and Germany's guidelines are simply recommendations. Museums have seldom been compelled to surrender artifacts; more often, they have voluntarily returned illicitly acquired objects from their collections.[61] Without these various declarations, conventions, and standards, there would be no ethical guidelines or, in some cases, legal obligations for the return of any tangible heritage. Few museums follow these directives, preferring instead to tackle repatriation and restitution claims on a case-by-case basis. Despite these declarations, there has been no uniformity of response. What is needed is a global convention to establish an agreed-upon set of ethical rules for all museums worldwide to follow. In lieu of that, many countries, museums, and arts organizations have developed their own policy frameworks for the protection and return of tangible heritage.

In the following pages, we will examine a series of case studies, highlighting practices that are more and less ethical.

THE U.S. AND NAGPRA

The U.S. was a frontrunner in attempting to address the need to restitute and repatriate artifacts to Indigenous communities. The Native American Graves Protection and Repatriation Act (NAGPRA), which has been part of U.S. federal law since 1990, mandates that every federally funded institution in possession of Native (Indigenous) American artifacts or ancestral bodies compile an inventory of its holdings, identify them by kin-group origin, notify existing communities of cultural heritage or remains that appear to come from that ethnic group's tradition or culture, and then facilitate their return to the respective communities.[62] According to a 2020 United Nations report, from 1990–2020, the law led to the repatriation of tens of thousands of ancestral remains, hundreds of thousands of funerary objects, and thousands of cultural artifacts from institutions in the U.S.[63] While this is progress, museums, universities, and federal agencies in the U.S. still house the remains of close to 120,000 Indigenous American ancestors and countless artifacts, most of which were looted by government, military officials, and archaeologists from burial grounds, massacre sites, and battlefields during western expansion.[64] Harvard University's Peabody Museum of Archaeology and Ethnology and the Hearst Museum of Anthropology (University of California, Berkeley), for instance, which have some of the largest collections, have been noncompliant for decades. (Peabody has the ancestral remains of more than 6,100 Indigenous Americans and 13,600 funerary objects in its collections and Berkeley has more than 9,000 Indigenous American remains.[65]) While Indigenous American artifacts have been continually stolen, since the colonizers' arrival, the unethical collection of ancestral remains reached a frenzied peak between the mid-1850s and the 1950s, when many scientists, museum curators, and archaeologists were embracing the U.S. eugenics movement, using plundered craniums to argue that Indigenous Americans were inferior to white people based on their skull sizes.

Critics have argued that federal funding for NAGPRA has fallen behind demand and that museums are not being held accountable. Enforcement of the act, for instance, has been inconsistent and carries penalties of only a few thousand dollars for institutions that flout the regulations. Museums, for their part, contend that the process is time-consuming and that determining the cultural affiliation of artifacts or ancestral remains can be exceedingly difficult—particularly, they argue, when the items are so old that they cannot be linked to any present-day, federally recognized kin-group. Museums have used this "affiliation" loophole in the act to justify their continued stewardship of the cultural objects and ancestral human remains. Another issue affecting NAGPRA compliance and cultural affiliation is that the act only applies to the 574 federally recognized Indigenous communities in the U.S., which leaves out the more than 200 kin-groups that do not have federal status. Adding to the difficulty, NAGPRA requires that cultural affiliation be demonstrated not only through geographic evidence but also through oral traditions, along with biological, archaeological and historical data. This mandate has created a substantial research burden, significantly slowing the process.[66] Critics of NAGPRA also argue that the act allows each museum to make its own decision on restitution and repatriation—in other words, the institutions act as both judge and jury, which perpetuates a dominant-subordinate structure that disempowers the Indigenous group. As Darrell Newell, a former vice chief of the Passamaquoddy Tribe, has said, "The wolves are in charge of how to deal with the sheep."[67] If museums were to collaborate with Indigenous communities in a fair and transparent way that honors their needs, including returning objects more promptly and removing insensitively displayed objects from view, then NAGPRA could function as restorative justice in which community healing is fundamentally integrated into the restitution and repatriation process.

Critics of institutions who have not made returns have complained they are exaggerating the complexity and are stalling the process. Indeed, very few institutions have completed inventories of their Indigenous American collections, despite the fact that the deadline to do so was 1995. So, while this act is excellent in theory, in practice many museums have failed to comply with the regulations. For instance, an April 2023 report by ProPublica found that 85% of 139 Native Art objects gifted and in some cases loaned to the Metropolitan Museum of Art by Charles and Valerie Diker lack complete provenance information.[68] ProPublica reported that the museum did not notify and consult with the Indigenous kin-groups about the acquisitions within six months, as is mandated by NAGPRA, especially for sacred and funerary objects, of which there are many in the collection. Unfortunately, NAGPRA does not mandate these requirements for loaned objects, which comprise many of the Diker collection objects at the Met.

To address institutional disregard towards NAGPRA, and the act's failure to expeditiously aid in the return of Indigenous ancestral bodies and culturally significant objects, Deb Haaland (Pueblo of Laguna), Secretary of the Interior in President Biden's administration and the first Native American to hold a cabinet post in the U.S., promised in 2021 to enact major changes to the NAGPRA regulations moving forward. The new guidelines, which went into effect in January 2024, require museums and federal agencies to assess and update inventories of ancestral remains and associated funerary objects within five years.[69] To overcome the loophole around cultural affiliation, the new NAGPRA regulations deem a kin-group's geographic connection or relations as grounds for "affiliation," and they remove the term "culturally unidentifiable" entirely from museums' inventory classification reports. Importantly, the new NAGPRA regulations prohibit institutions from studying or displaying Indigenous ancestral remains, funerary or sacred objects, or other cultural heritage without the "free, prior, and informed consent" of kin-groups or lineal descendants—or verifiable proof of a legally valid historic transfer of ownership, a standard that is often extremely difficult, if not impossible, to meet.[70] By insisting on sound provenance records and consent from a kin-group authority, Indigenous American communities are now empowered as both judge and jury under the new regulations, instead of the institution.

The effects of the alterations to the act were immediate and dramatic. Within days of the new regulations, the Field Museum in Chicago covered up several display cases of Indigenous objects in its Halls of the Ancient Americas and Hall of Northwest Coast and Arctic Peoples. In a statement, the museum explained that the "display cases will remain covered while Museum staff continue to review existing information about these items and contact affiliated Tribes and NHOs [Native Hawaiian Organizations] for their input."[71] Almost immediately, the American Museum of Natural History (AMNH) closed both the Eastern Woodlands and Great Plains Halls, which are expansive galleries dedicated to Native American history and culture. Cleveland Museum of Art, Denver Museum of Art and Harvard's Peabody Museum of Archaeology and Ethnology took similar steps soon thereafter. As of this writing the Met, which has an enormous collection of Native American objects and ancestors, has removed just twenty items from its musical instrument galleries, and has not taken steps to address works from the Charles and Valerie Diker Collection of Native American art currently on display.[72]

Besides the Met, other major institutions implicated in the ProPublica report included the AMNH, the Harvard University Art Museums, and the Hearst Museum of Anthropology, among others. In one of the many articles associated with the exposé, titled "America's Biggest Museums Fail to Return Native American Human Remains," the authors offer a history of U.S. institutions' collection of Indigenous bodies, especially during the height of western expansionism in the 19th century.[73] The Smithsonian reportedly holds the remains of approximately 10,000 people, more than any other U.S. museum. (The Smithsonian declared recently that they, in fact, have close to 30,000 remains—more than half of which are from Indigenous American communities.[74]) In March 2024, under Secretary Lonnie G. Bunch III, the Smithsonian adopted a new policy on human remains that centers on the principle of "informed consent," granting descendants the authority to determine the fate of their ancestors.[75] Bunch also announced that the museum will cease allowing scientific examinations of human remains that include racial profiling based on physical features, officially discontinuing a deeply entrenched practice dating back to the late 19th century.[76]

The implications of the new NAGPRA regulations are immense. Will all institutions across the U.S. be required to close wings or cover display cases dedicated to Indigenous American art, history, and culture? Yes, and they should. The question is: how quickly will they do this and how enforceable is it? NAGPRA is, after all, a federal law. What if museums were next required by federal law to shut galleries or cover display cases featuring all looted, trafficked, and stolen objects and ancestral bodies or simply those with dubious provenance, from any culture, especially those that might have been taken without consent? What would become of museums, especially the so-called encyclopedic ones like the Met, the British Museum, and the Louvre, who have already had to return large numbers of objects proven to be stolen, trafficked, or illegally acquired? Should all objects associated with smugglers be taken off view? And what of the large Egyptian, Greek, and Roman collections for which innumerable archaeologists no doubt plundered sites? The new NAGPRA regulations could have implications far beyond Indigenous American artifacts and their ancestral remains.

FRANCE AND THE HERITAGE CODE

In the wake of the Sarr-Savoy report in 2018, when President Emmanuel Macron permanently returned twenty-six objects from the Royal Palaces of Abomey to the modern-day Republic of Benin, those restitutions required approval from the Parliament, which made an exception to the restrictive French Heritage Code. However, since then there has been mounting pressure from the public to change the code to allow for more returns of cultural heritage to source communities and nations. In January 2023, three bills were proposed by French politicians that would make it possible to return objects in the national collections without individual approval from the French Parliament. The proposed bills aimed to address (1) ancestral bodily remains, (2) Nazi-looted art, and (3) colonial-era artifacts.[77] In July 2023, the first two bills were passed without much internal opposition. It was determined that the unethical collection of remains and artworks stolen from Jewish families during the Nazi occupation could be returned unconditionally to rightful owners, if requested. The new laws will be administered by special committees comprised of legal and scientific experts from France who are to collaborate with the respective countries or descendants requesting restitution. These special committees will determine whether an object meets the criteria to remove it from France's national collections and whether to return the object. A vote from Parliament will no longer be required.

The third bill proposed in 2023 has proven to be quite controversial, and there has been considerable pushback from many conservatives across the French cultural sector who are keen to maintain the French Heritage Code in order to avert repatriation claims from former colonies. Indeed, so heated has the debate been that, in April 2023, just four months after the new bill was proposed, Jean-Luc Martinez (the disgraced former president of the Louvre who was accused of purchasing objects of dubious origin for the Louvre Abu Dhabi but who, nonetheless, is overseeing the bill regarding the restitution of art) published a report, outlining several criteria as obstacles to restitution, including the legality of acquisitions and the geography of former colonies, which have changed over the years.[78] So strict are the criteria that Senator Pierre Ouzoulias of France's Communist Party declared that Martinez's report was "a way to bury the Sarr-Savoy report and to return the matter to museum curators' hands."[79] Throughout the report,

Martinez preferred to put emphasis on "cultural partnerships," instead of remorse for past "crimes against humanity," to use Macron's phrase. A key issue with the bill, according to the local press, is the parliamentary representatives' inability to acknowledge past wrongdoings: as one minister stated, the bill should not be "a text about repentance."[80] In April 2024, the bill was not passed, and the vote was postponed until autumn 2024. In July 2025, the bill was reintroduced and adopted by the Council of Ministers, with a debate and vote in the Senate scheduled for September 2025. That date was pushed back due to the current political climate, and a new date has not yet been announced as at the time of this writing.

Prior to the introduction of the new laws in France, the process of government approval had been onerous. For example, when the director of the Musée de Rouen sought to return a Māori head to New Zealand's Te Papa Tongarewa in 2007, the restitution took four years to work through the French legal system before approval. The question being debated was whether an ancestral human remain is or is not an artifact; if it is an artifact, then it can be considered French heritage. Amid the debate, there was concern on the part of the French government that they would be setting a precedent for the return of all remains in national collections. Eventually approved by the legislature in 2011, the Māori remains were returned to New Zealand with full tribal honors and a burial. In another instance, parliamentary approval took decades. Beginning in the early 1980s, the South African government requested the return of Saartjie Baartman's remains. Baartman was an African woman who was brought to Europe, and forced to perform seminude at carnivals, where she was promoted as an attraction: "the Venus Hottentot."[81] After her death, around 1816, her skeleton was preserved, and her brain and genitals bottled in jars, ostensibly for scientific study. Her bodily remains were publicly displayed at the Musée de l'Homme in Paris until 1985.

Following his 1994 election as president of South Africa, Nelson Mandela called for the repatriation of Baartman's remains. After years of political delays and legal hurdles, the request was finally granted in 2002, and she was reinterred in the Eastern Cape province. While the repatriation of Baartman's remains necessitated approval from the French government because, under France's Heritage Code, they were inalienable, with the new 2023 law, the transfer would have been streamlined, and would certainly not have taken decades to complete. The recent passage of the first two French laws—in favor of returning bodily remains and Nazi-looted art—is historic and will hopefully pave the way for other countries, like the U.K., who have equally restrictive rules regarding repatriation.

U.K. AND THE NATIONAL HERITAGE ACT

Of all the U.K. institutions, the British Museum has the most troubled history with looted objects. Indeed, as one headline in the *Guardian* in 2019 made clear: the "British Museum is world's largest receiver of stolen goods."[82] (In the 19th and early 20th centuries, the British Empire expanded into one of the largest empires in history, with colonies on every inhabited continent, including Australia, New Zealand, and Canada, as well as vast territories in Africa, like Nigeria, South Africa, and Egypt, among others.) There are countless plundered objects in the museum's collection, including, most famously, the Rosetta Stone, unearthed in Egypt by Napoleon's troops, then stolen from that country by the British;[83] sculptures from the Mausoleum at Halicarnassus, stolen in the 1850s from Turkey; the Ngadji, a sacred drum of the Pokomo people in Kenya that British colonial officials forcibly took in 1902; two large stone *moai* (ancestor figures), Hoa Hakananai'a and Moai Hava, taken from Orongo, Easter Island (Rapa Nui) in 1868; and countless others.

To highlight the loot in the museum, the activist group BP or Not BP regularly hosts "Stolen Goods" tours, during which they stop at over a dozen objects on permanent display that they argue should be returned to original source communities. One of the stops on the tour is at the display case for the Gweagal Shield, an artifact that Gweagal descendants claim was stolen 250 years ago when Captain James Cook and his soldiers, during their first landing in Australia at Botany Bay, shot a Gweagal warrior named Cooman. The bark shield bears a hole, clearly caused by a musket shot, which the Gweagal people say passed through Cooman's shield and wounded him in the leg. In 2015, the British Museum placed the shield and other Indigenous Australian artifacts in an exhibition sponsored by British Petroleum. This exhibition was followed by the shield's temporary loan, later that year, to the National Museum of Australia in Canberra for an exhibition called *Encounters: Revealing Stories of Aboriginal and Torres Strait Islander Objects from the British Museum*. Since that exhibition, Rodney Kelly, a sixth-generation descendant of the warrior Cooman, has been on a determined quest to restitute the Gweagal Shield to his people. During one of the "Stolen Goods" tours—punctuated by didgeridoo performances—Kelly told the crowd that the shield stood as a symbol of resistance to colonization. He added that returning it would acknowledge the "historic violence" inflicted on Indigenous Australians since their first contact with Europeans.[84] Kelly explained further that the restitution of the shield would be a way of acknowledging the historic violence enacted against Indigenous Australians from their very first contact with Europeans. As Kelly explains, "What I'm pushing for is not a loan, not just a permanent loan. The shield has got to stay in a museum in Sydney—that's the only place for it—then it's up to the elders of the Gweagal people what goes on with it, how the history relating to it is used for our people and other Australians."[85] In August 2016, the Australian Parliament adopted a resolution recognizing Indigenous Gweagal ownership of the shield and calling for its return.[86] However, as at the time of this writing, the British Museum, according to their website, is refusing to return the object to its rightful owners.[87]

In the U.K., the restitution and repatriation of artifacts and ancestral bodies from museums to source communities has been quite fraught. Many of the national institutions, such as the V&A, Tate, and the National Gallery of Art, are prohibited from permanently returning items by the National Heritage Act of 1983. The British Museum is also subject to the same act but is further prevented from doing so because of the British Museum Act of 1963, which bars the sale, exchange, or dispersal of museum objects except in very limited circumstances.[88] According to the National Heritage Act 1983, trustees of designated national museums are legally prohibited from disposing of objects in their collections except in strictly defined circumstances—for instance, if they are replicas or have been irreparably damaged. This statutory framework was explicitly designed to prevent trustees from selling or otherwise disposing of "unfashionable" or valuable works simply to raise funds—actions which might be regretted by future generations seeking broader access or ethical restitution.[89] It is these two acts that British institutions often turn to as a way out of not engaging in conversations about restitution and repatriation.

Given the inability of national museums in the U.K. to restitute and repatriate easily, there has been increasing public pressure on the government to determine how best to reconcile with their colonial-era collections. The result was a proposed amendment to the Charity Act of 2011, which would enable trustees to seek approval from the Charity Commission if they feel morally obligated to return property belonging to the charity—a non-obligatory payment made out of moral responsibility, termed an "ex gratia" payment.[90] Instead of the stringent restrictions of the National Heritage Act, the new act would allow decision-makers to be guided by ethical considerations. These new provisions would provide institutions and their trustees with a clear path to restitution and repatriation, thereby challenging the existing statutes that prohibit national museums in the U.K. from deaccessioning items except under limited circumstances.

Unfortunately, the new provisions were not approved when the legislature passed through Parliament in fall 2022, and the sections relevant to "ex gratia" transfers were suspended to offer the government additional time for review.[91] In January 2024, after careful review, the government's position on the bill was shared with the Charity Commission in a letter from the arts and heritage minister, Lord Parkinson of Whitley Bay, which explained that the "potential consequences of these provisions were not made clear by the Law Commission when the bill was introduced," and were not adequately scrutinized by Parliament in advance of the vote.[92] He noted that national museums would be categorically excluded from the scope of "ex gratia" transfer provisions, remaining legally bound by institutional statutes like the National Heritage Act of 1983.[93] He also said that any goodwill transfers to recipients outside of the U.K. would be denied outright. Some museum leaders, like Tristram Hunt, director of the V&A, described the new legislation as "infantilising," arguing that trustees should be afforded more latitude when making decisions related to the museum collections.[94]

Because the transfer process has become so onerous, many national museums in the U.K. are establishing renewable cultural partnerships with countries seeking repatriation of objects, including a collaboration announced in January 2024 between the British Museum, V&A, and Ghana, with the result being the long-term loan of Asante treasures, which were looted by British forces in the 1870s.[95] Partnerships and long-term loans appear to be the only way around the stipulations of the U.K. legislature at the moment.

RECOMMENDATIONS

To decolonize their collections, institutions can start by acknowledging that museums are still part of the colonial ideology of conquest and domination. As journalist and activist Ta-Nehisi Coates has explained, documenting the crime is an essential first step towards reparation.[96] In other words, museums must concede that theft of property occurred during the colonial era and must admit that the stolen and trafficked property in their collections does not belong to them. This will necessitate that museums reconceive of themselves as custodians or stewards, not owners, of the objects in their collections.

Philosopher Karen Warren has questioned the concept of ownership of heritage altogether, noting that among certain Indigenous American communities, for instance, cultural artifacts are not considered property.[97] Once museums have acknowledged their role in colonial possession and reconsidered themselves as custodians (not owners) of objects, they can choose to take a human rights-based approach to restitution and repatriation cases. Such an approach would focus on those who are most marginalized, excluded, and discriminated against—which is to say that the approach should focus on the needs of the source communities, not those of the museum. Such an approach would embody the tenets of common decency and respect: If one's property is stolen or illegally acquired, that property should be returned to the original owners, when possible. In a court of law, a thief cannot retain stolen property, regardless of how much time has passed since it was taken.

Further, as Isaac Kaplan argues, museums must reconceptualize artifacts and ancestral remains "not as static works of art" or specimens for study, but "as living pieces of significance" for many of the source communities from which they originate.[98] For example, artist Arianna Davis explained during a videotaped "Stolen Goods" tour at the British Museum, sponsored by BP or Not BP: "As an Indigenous person, it hurts to know that there are 2,300 taonga [treasures] locked away [in the British Museum], especially when you view these taonga as living objects containing the life force of your ancestors."[99] Or as artist Rosanna Raymond has explained, ancestral remains are spirits that linger among us: to keep remains locked away is to imprison a living being.

Even if it can be proven that an object was acquired legally, if a source community argues that the object has great symbolic value or national relevance for their peoples or nation, then the museum should open a dialogue with the community to determine how best to meet their needs. Such is the case with the Man-Eaters of Tsavo, two taxidermic lions from Kenya, purchased legally by the Field Museum, Chicago, in 1925. The lions—responsible for the deaths of over thirty laborers during the 1898 construction of a railway in Tsavo—are commemorated by many Kenyans as symbolic "first resistance fighters against British colonialism."[100] Therefore, the lions have significant symbolic value to the Kenyans for obvious reasons. Mzalendo Kibunja, then director of the National Museums of Kenya, said they are "extremely important" for the Mashujaa Museum (Heroes Museum) in Nairobi, which opened to the public in 2022.[101] During the Obama administration, there were attempts to persuade the Field Museum to return the lions, but the museum continues to refuse. Given their symbolic value to Kenyans, there is no question the museum should be in negotiations with the source country, so that the lions might be returned to their rightful owners.[102] The same could be argued for the stone Zimbabwe Bird in the Groote Schuur museum, Cape Town, and the Nefertiti bust in the collection of the Neues Museum, Berlin—these works have great symbolic value for the nations and peoples of Zimbabwe and Egypt, respectively.[103] The museums should confer with the countries' representatives to find a solution that the latter accept, whether it be unconditional return, long-term loan or something else altogether. Regardless, the solution should be driven not by the museum, but rather by the aggrieved, which is to say the respective source communities.

In other words, an ethical approach to restitution and repatriation will require that museums cede authority to source communities. Just as these communities should be given the space and opportunity in the museum to tell their unique stories on their own terms and in their own words, they should be granted a seat at the table, as equal players, when discussing the return of their heritage. This would entail rethinking the inherent power relations embedded in the restitution and repatriation process, in which museums tend to act as judge and jury in decision-making. Currently, the onus is typically on the source communities to construct a "case" for the return of cultural heritage to the museum. The source community must provide evidence and proof that they are entitled to the object. This process is overseen by the museums and universities they are petitioning. Requests are evaluated according to guidelines set by the institutions themselves, which ultimately decide whether the submitted evidence meets their criteria. In other words, the institutions, not the source communities, set the rules and make the final determination. This dynamic perpetuates a dominant-subordinate structure. It is a hierarchical and adversarial model that dictates a winner and a loser in the resolution of the conflict. In this unequal power dynamic, the museum maintains the position as the "authority" representing the "official" or "correct" point of view. It is assumed the museum's stance is a value-neutral, impartial point of view, which is often simply not true.

I would suggest that museums rethink the restitution and repatriation process so that it becomes positive, more inclusive, and reparative, rather than considering it a win-lose situation. In other words, museums could foreground an ethics of care. As Karen Warren explains, in contrast to a hierarchical model of engagement, in an ethics of care approach "the moral imperative is an injunction to care and avoid hurt, to discern and relieve the real and recognizable suffering of this world, to express compassion."[104] Applying a non-hierarchical approach to the restitution and repatriation debate would mean that museums would choose to "avoid hurt," acknowledge suffering, and replace the dominant-subordinate structure with a non-adversarial approach that is a "both/and" (which is respectful) versus an "either/or" win-lose situation. This would represent a consensus-based model of conflict resolution, in which all parties voluntarily participate in working toward mutually agreed goals. As returns of cultural heritage have become more common over the past several years, the processes appear to be less adversarial, principally because the museums are being analyzed by the watchful eyes of the public.

Utilizing a human rights-based approach, museums could choose to develop new commissioning policies, as well. Dan Hicks has suggested that museums can fill each gap left by returns with "new work made by artists, designers, writers and others from the dispossessed community paid for by the museum, to help museums remember and to bear witness to colonialism today."[105] Museums might alternatively opt to remit royalty payments to the legitimate custodians of looted objects held in their collections.[106] Where necessary, such payments could be sourced from revenue generated through admission charges or licensing fees for image reproduction. The activist Roxley Foley contends that although certain museums are willing to loan Indigenous Australian artifacts to their communities of origin, the dynamic should be reversed.[107] "How about you give the objects to us and we'll lend them back to you?" he said in October 2017 at a conference in Berlin.[108] It is certainly a valid suggestion. Indeed, in July 2022, after the Humboldt Forum in Berlin restituted 200 Benin Bronzes to Nigeria, 40 were loaned back to the museum for a ten-year period.[109] The strategies of long-term loans from source community to an outside institution, and financial reparation in the form of royalty fees, constitute a productive approach to the question of repatriation and restitution to nations or communities that may have the cultural but not the financial resources or latest technologies to care for the objects being returned.

A human rights-based approach to restitution might mean that museums pay loan fees to source communities in exchange for displaying looted objects. Illegally acquired objects could also be shared between museums and source communities. Or museums might consider transferring objects to their countries of origin through sales at a "symbolic market value," facilitated by a publicly administered trust established to ensure the object's preservation and stewardship.[110] Or perhaps the stolen objects could be copied using technologies like 3-D scanning so that the originals could be repatriated to rightful owners. Why can't museums display copies or replicas?[111] University of Chicago's Institute for the Study of Ancient Cultures (ISAC) Museum had no problem doing so. Before repatriating an ancient Sumerian artifact dated circa 3500 BCE to Baghdad in 2023, the museum produced a 3-D replica for display as well as a virtual reality video showing the artifact (which is in fragments) as a whole object, in the round.[112] Or perhaps, following the new NAGPRA regulations (discussed above), museums will simply remove from display objects with questionable provenance altogether, until such time as the source communities offer consent.

CONCLUSION

In August 2022, prosecutors from the Manhattan District Attorney's Office seized hundreds of objects from the Metropolitan Museum of Art that were allegedly connected to accused or convicted antiquities smugglers.[113] Since then, at least a dozen court-ordered seizures have taken place, citing statutes like "criminal possession of stolen property." Then, in March 2023, a month before the Diker collection scandal mentioned above, an exposé by the International Consortium of Investigative Journalists (ICIJ) determined that at least 1,109 objects within the Met's collection were found to have previously been in the possession of individuals who had faced indictment or conviction for crimes related to antiquities trafficking; of those objects, 309 were on display at the time the article was written.[114] Many of the items were acquired after 1970, in violation of the UNESCO treaty that sought to crack down on illicit trade in antiquities.

That same year, in August 2023, the British Museum disclosed the roughly 2,000 items had been stolen from its collections by senior curator Peter Higgs and sold off on eBay, in a scheme that may date back to 2014.[115] The irony, of course, is that an institution renowned for its resistance to the return of looted cultural artifacts had itself been robbed. As Dan Hicks explains, the British Museum "is the victim rather than the perpetrator of theft."[116] Immediately following the announcement of the thefts, Greece repeated its call to repatriate the Parthenon Marbles to the Acropolis, Athens; Nigeria renewed its formal request for the return of the Benin Bronzes; the Welsh, Scots, and Cornish demanded the return of national artifacts, as did the Chinese.[117]

These highly publicized recent crises at two of the world's most famous encyclopedic museums threw the sector into crisis. Max Hollein, the Met's director, promised to hire a new team of provenance investigators to examine its vast catalogue—a gesture that is a little too late to rectify decades of collection mismanagement. In response to its crisis, the British Museum fired its director (Hartwig Fischer) and deputy director (Jonathan Williams), and attempted to publicly defend itself, with the chair of the board of trustees, George Osborne, leading the charge, despite the fact the museum had known of the "potential thefts" as far back as 2021.[118] The museum promised to locate all missing items, as if that were possible, given that many had been sold off already, some to anonymous buyers.

While these gestures might have assuaged trustees, and some members of the public, the truth of the matter is that both collections, as noted above, include innumerable objects with dubious origins and incomplete record-keeping. As the news unfolded, the public was shocked to learn that the two museum collections had not been fully catalogued. Indeed, of the 1.5 million objects in the Met's collections, only 500,000 have been digitally itemized; while only 2 million of 8 million objects in the British Museum have been.[119] Without proper documentation of collection objects, it is no surprise that objects were stolen by an insider and/or that innumerable objects have suspicious provenances. This lack of documentation poses a challenge to restitution. Since the Sarr-Savoy report, calls have increased for museums to audit the provenance of their collections. Without accurate collection information, it is almost impossible for those seeking restitution to locate lost or plundered items.

The irony in both recent instances at the Metropolitan and British Museum, then, is that these are "universal" museums that have marketed themselves, indeed prided themselves, as the safest custodians for world culture. But can we really trust them with our cultural treasures?

CHAPTER 4
WHOSE MUSEUM IS IT? INCLUSION AND EXCLUSION IN MUSEUMS

INTRODUCTION

The ongoing and widespread discrimination in the art world is largely aimed at women, queer, disabled, and BIPOC (Black, Indigenous, and People of Color) artists. This discrimination permeates every aspect of the arts sector, from disparities in auction prices, gallery representation, and media coverage, to inequities in inclusion in permanent collections, group shows and solo exhibition programs. Despite various public commitments to support diversity, equity, access, and inclusion, many museums are woefully failing.

The authors of the 2019 Burns Halperin Report, published by Artnet, asked a large sample of U.S. museums to share information on the ratio of male to female artists in their annual exhibition programs. According to the data they collected, from 2008 to 2018, 86% of all museum exhibitions were either solo shows featuring male artists or group exhibitions in which males represented the majority.[1] An update to the report in 2022 revealed that from 2008 to 2020, only 11% of all works acquired by thirty-one top U.S. museums for their permanent collections were by women artists.[2] The disproportions in exhibitions and acquisitions are visible worldwide, not just in the U.S., as will become evident, and the figures are substantially worse for BIPOC women.

But these gender inequities are not restricted to exhibitions and acquisitions; museum directors are also overwhelmingly white and male. The last analysis completed by the Association of Art Museum Directors (AAMD, whose focus is the U.S., Canada, and Mexico) in 2017, entitled "The Ongoing Gender Gap in Art Museum Directorships," determined that women run just 23.6% of U.S. art museums with budgets over $15 million; and, in general, women museum directors are paid just 75 cents for every dollar earned by men in equivalent positions.[3] Boardrooms don't fare much better. A 2022 Black Trustee Alliance (BTA) Art Museum Trustee Survey, which polled close to 1,000 trustees throughout the U.S., Canada, and Mexico, confirmed that the majority of museum boards in North America are populated by white men.[4] Worst off are those with disabilities, who are almost entirely missing from the art world, whether as artists, curators, museum directors, or board members.

While these statistics are deeply discouraging, some mainstream museums (as distinct from activist museums like, for example, the Studio Museum in Harlem, New York) have made public commitments to support and acquire works by BIPOC and women artists. These kinds of pledges made by institutions across the globe, including the Museo Reina Sofía in Madrid, the Baltimore Museum of Art, the Museum of Contemporary Art Chicago, the Art Gallery of Ontario, Tate Modern in London, and the National Gallery of Australia, seem to be having an actual impact.

This is not to say that museums devoted to the work of specific groups of artists don't also play an important role in increasing representation in the art world. The new museum Femmes Artistes du Musée Mougins (Women Artists of the Mougins Museum, or FAMM), which opened in June 2024, will no doubt prove to be impactful as the first museum of its kind in continental Europe.[5] The FAMM, an all-women art museum representing art from the 19th to 21st centuries, was founded by British art collector Christian Levett, who has explained that he decided to collect women artists after learning that he could put together a "museum-quality collection of female artists for the price of one male artist," and soon realized that his collection could correct "a lot of wrongs of the past" by addressing long-standing art historical neglect that has functioned to devalue art by women.[6]

#METOO, BLACK LIVES MATTER, AND MUSEUMS

On November 3, 2018, Michelle Hartney staged an intervention at the Metropolitan Museum of Art (the Met), New York City.[7] Inspired by the #MeToo movement, she stealthily affixed her own wall labels throughout the museum to call out works by Pablo Picasso, Paul Gauguin, and Balthus—figures that Hartney deems to be among the worst sexual predators in the history of art. With her performance, titled *Correct Art History*, Hartney endeavored to highlight these misogynist artists—an intervention that was especially pertinent given museums' historical reluctance to take a stance on such issues. Her project was not without merit: Picasso was renowned for his womanizing, the seduction of underage girls, and for calling women "machines for suffering";[8] Gauguin was a pedophile who had three child brides while living in the South Pacific;[9] and Balthus hypersexualized (and allegedly raped) prepubescent girls.[10]

Hartney's label accompanying the Picasso painting *The Dreamer* (1932) quoted from the Netflix comedy special *Nanette* (2017) by comedian Hannah Gadsby. In the show, Gadsby condemns Picasso for his affair with a 17-year-old girl, Marie-Thérèse Walter, explaining, "Picasso suffered ... the mental illness of misogyny ... He said, 'Each time I leave a woman, I should burn her. Destroy the woman [and] you destroy the past she represents.'"[11] In 2023, the takedown of Picasso featured in *Nanette* played on a loop for visitors to *It's Pablo-matic*, the satirical, highly controversial exhibition Gadsby co-curated with the Brooklyn Museum on the occasion of the 50th anniversary of Picasso's death.

The new label by Hartney for Gauguin's painting *Two Tahitian Women* (1899) quoted from the words of author Roxane Gay: "We can no longer worship at the altar of creative genius while ignoring the price all too often paid for that genius. In truth, we should have learned this lesson long ago, but we have a cultural fascination with creative and powerful men who are also 'mercurial' or 'volatile', with men who behave badly."[12] In this article, "Can I Enjoy the Art but Denounce the Artists?" dated 2018, Gay cited a string of prominent actors, film directors and executive producers (like Bill Cosby, Woody Allen, Harvey Weinstein, Russell Simmons, among others)—who have been granted immunity, and, she argued, have built their success "on the backs of women." She concluded by suggesting that "there is no artistic work, no legacy so great that we choose to look the other way."[13] Hartney's intervention at the Met raised questions about the tendency of most museums to shy away from controversial subjects, which results not only in erasure of sexual harassment and gendered violence from art history but also in condoning the abhorrent behavior of some artists.[14]

Museum didactics typically comprise the artist, title, date, medium, and extended wall labels that describe the artwork in further detail, but in recent years, and as is evident in Hartney's work, labels have become a contentious arena. In the wake of the #MeToo movement, especially, museum wall labels have begun to include controversial information surrounding artists' questionable behavior. For example, in 2018, the Museum of Fine Arts (MFA) in Boston updated the label accompanying *Two Women* (1918), a work by the 20th-century Austrian artist Egon Schiele, who during his lifetime faced criminal charges for kidnapping and raping a 13-year-old girl. While those charges were eventually dropped, he was, however, charged and served time for exhibiting erotic drawings to a child. The revised label reads: "Recently, Schiele has been mentioned in the context of sexual misconduct by artists, of the present and the past. This stems in part from specific charges (ultimately dropped as unfounded) of kidnapping and molestation."[15] The MFA in Boston is opting for truth-telling over the erasure of ugly truths.

The issue of sexual predation came to a head in 2019 with a large-scale exhibition of Gauguin's portraits at the National Gallery in London. The portrait titled *Tehamana Has Many Parents* (1893), which depicts Gauguin's teenage wife holding a fan, was truthfully described by the museum as the "artist's 13-year-old wife."[16] The wall text accompanying the painting explained also that Gauguin "repeatedly entered into sexual relations with young girls, 'marrying' two of them and fathering children."[17] (In fact, as noted above, he had three teenage brides, between the ages of 13 and 14, during his time in the South Pacific.[18]) The label continues, "Gauguin undoubtedly exploited his position as a privileged Westerner to make the most of the sexual freedoms available to him."[19] Even the exhibition's audio guide made note of "the troubling issue of Gauguin's sexual exploitation of very young Polynesian women," and asked: "should we stop looking at Gauguin?" New Zealand art historian Caroline Vercoe answered that we should not expunge Gauguin from the canon as "an incredibly problematic figure" but rather use his "unconventional" lifestyle "to negotiate and understand how these kinds of hegemonies come into play today." (Note how Vercoe refers to Gauguin's behavior as simply "unconventional," which underplays the artist's inappropriate behavior.) Given that sexual exploitation and pedophilia are still very much with us, she implies, we can use the conversations around Gauguin's art as starting points to discuss their prevalence.[20] While many viewers expressed displeasure, if not anger, at being confronted with this information in the wall texts and audio guide, other museumgoers appreciated the honesty and transparency.[21] Still others have asked whether we should cancel Gauguin altogether.[22]

Sexism and objectionable behavior are not the only targets of art-world activists and museum professionals. In August 2020, after considerable public outcry in the wake of Black Lives Matter (BLM), the British Museum relocated and recontextualized a bust of Sir Hans Sloane (1660–1753), a wealthy physician, naturalist, and slave owner whose vast collection of artifacts, partly funded by his Jamaican sugar plantations, formed the basis of what became the British Museum. This relocation of Sloane's bust happened just months after the removal of a monument to U.S. Confederate General Thomas J. "Stonewall" Jackson, in Richmond, Virginia, and the toppling by protesters of another, dedicated to 17th-century trader of enslaved people Edward Colston in Bristol.[23] Sloane's bust now sits alongside artifacts that explain his legacy in "the exploitative context of the British Empire."[24] The wall label to his bust now reads, in part: "Together with his medical earnings and land investments, Sloane used income generated by enslaved people on plantations, inherited by his wife Elizabeth Langley Rose Sloane, to purchase 'curiosities' from around the expanding British empire and his wide network of contacts around the globe."[25] British Museum curator Neal Spencer explained that the BLM movement had provided "a certain level of urgency to the overhaul."[26] In an effort to face up to its colonial legacy, and no doubt in reaction to continued public criticism, the British Museum has recently begun offering self-guided tours called "Collecting and Empire," during which museumgoers visit fifteen objects in order to learn more about the "complex, varied—and sometimes controversial—ways" by which objects came to be in the museum collection.[27]

Like the British Museum, the Worcester Art Museum in Massachusetts has added historical context to some of the wall labels in their galleries that feature portraits of white male figures with links to slavery. One of the introductory texts now reads, in part, "Many of the people represented here derived wealth and social status from this system of violence and oppression, which was legal in Massachusetts until 1783 and in regions of the United States until 1865."[28] The museum has also amended the labels describing individual paintings: below a portrait of wealthy patron John Freake by a U.S. artist known as the Freake-Gibbs Painter, for example, the text indicates that Freake listed an enslaved person among his family's "personal assets."[29]

In an era of increased public awareness around the histories of slavery and colonialism, museums are re-examining the legacies not only of the artists themselves, but also of the individuals depicted in their works.[30] However, detestable biographies and behavior should not compel museums to throw out their Picassos and Gauguins—censoring artists is not the answer. Nonetheless, museums have a responsibility to present an uncensored, truthful account of an artist's life and work. Clear, unambiguous wall labels are essential in this respect—anything less is to construct a distorted narrative of art history and to disregard ethical standards and professional practices.

MOMA AND POMPIDOU: WHERE ARE THE WOMEN?

In 2019, the Museum of Modern Art (MoMA) reopened after a major building expansion, declaring that their intention henceforth was to tell a more inclusive, less definitive story. In their reinstallation of their permanent collection galleries—presenting art produced from 1880 to the mid-1960s—the organizers attempted a revisionist or integrative curatorial approach, inserting artists into the mainstream Modernist canon from which they had either been marginalized or made invisible. For example, in one room, a work by Ellsworth Kelly was placed next to a piece by Carmen Herrera. Both works date from 1951, yet Herrera has been omitted from the canon until relatively recently, only receiving critical acclaim in her nineties. In another revisionist example, *The Red Studio* (1911), by Henri Matisse, was placed beside *Fiery Sunset* (1973), by Alma Thomas. Despite both artists' exquisite command of color, Thomas, who was the first Black woman to have a solo exhibition at the Whitney Museum, in 1972, before her work fell back into obscurity until the mid-2010s, has not enjoyed nearly the same level of attention. Placing her next to Matisse was an innovative gesture. Nevertheless, the gallery was almost entirely devoted to Matisse, featuring just this one painting by Thomas.

During their 2019 reinstallation, MoMA received considerable attention for one dramatic juxtaposition of paintings, in particular. In a room functioning as a virtual shrine to Pablo Picasso, with thirteen early paintings and sculptures by the modern "master," MoMA's curators placed a monumental work by African American artist Faith Ringgold beside Picasso's *Les Desmoiselles d'Avignon* (1907). Ringgold's painting from 1967, titled *American People Series # 20: Die*, depicts a race riot in progress, with bloodied and contorted bodies strewn across the canvas. In the didactic, MoMA justified the placement of the painting in the Picasso room as follows: "Ringgold based her composition on Picasso's *Guernica* (1937)—the artist's response to the atrocities of the Spanish Civil War—which she regularly visited when the monumental canvas was on display at The Museum of Modern Art [in 1939]." Positioned as she was, Ringgold was, in my opinion, presented as a derivative of Picasso, or as a supporting character. At the time, I was thrilled that Ringgold was finally being given prominence in MoMA's permanent collection galleries. She certainly deserved it. However, I was disappointed in her placement. Why was she integrated into a room dedicated to a white male icon of art history?

Why didn't MoMA present an entire room dedicated to Ringgold, with multiple paintings and sculptures, and then place a single Picasso work therein? The museum certainly has enough money to purchase more Ringgolds to make this happen. Or, given that Ringgold's painting of the 1960s was not influenced by Picasso alone—she was also fueled by her admiration for the writings of U.S. writer and civil rights activist James Baldwin, the paintings of U.S. artist Jacob Lawrence, and the decorative work of the Kuba people in Zaire, to name just a few examples—it might have been interesting to include her work in relation to Lawrence's *Migration Series* (1940–41), also on view in the museum at the time.

MoMA's version of revisionism in 2019 was to sprinkle women, BIPOC, and non-Euro-U.S. artists throughout the galleries (another example was the placement of Lee Krasner and Grace Hartigan in the Abstract Expressionist room, where they belong). But while MoMA purported that the overall installation was non-chronological, the traditional narrative of Modernism as defined by the museum's founding director, Alfred Barr, was left intact, and the ghost of the mainstream Modernist timeline remained, again tracing Euro-U.S. art history from the 1880s to the 1970s.[31]

Despite the issues, MoMA's 2019 reinstallation of their permanent collections deserves some praise. Of the more than 1,400 works on display in the modern and contemporary sections, 25% were by women artists. In 1997, when I worked at MoMA, less than 1% of the works were by women—so this is a marked improvement. More recently, in 2024, my calculations demonstrated a slight improvement: 32% of the works on display were by women artists. At this rate, according to my statistics, it will take until about 2050 for MoMA to achieve parity: that is, if the curators keep up the good work.

Regardless of MoMA's inventive curatorial approach to the display of its permanent collection, there is an inherent problem with any revisionist approach to curating: it assumes the white, masculinist, Western canon as its center and accepts its hierarchy as a natural given. We should be wary of such revisionist curatorial strategies because they can become a sort of homage to the canon itself. Revising the canon to address the neglect of women and/or marginalized artists is also an impossible project because it does not grapple with the terms that created that neglect in the first place—it leaves unchallenged the concept of canonicity and the traditional definition of art history, both of which are sexist and racist paradigms. Despite these shortfalls, the benefits of the revisionist strategy are many, not least of which is that revisionism offers a more comprehensive view of art history, including artists such as Carmen Herrera or Faith Ringgold (or, in historical shows, Elisabeth Vigée Le Brun and Berthe Morisot). Even if their works are not shown on an equal footing with their white or male counterparts, they are afforded a place in the traditional (albeit problematic) canon.

Let's compare MoMA to the Pompidou Center in Paris. During a jaunt through the Pompidou's galleries in 2024, I determined that of the artists on display in the modern and contemporary sections combined, representing art from 1905 to 2024, 24% were women, which is almost comparable to MoMA. (This represents a 10% jump from the 14% women artists that were on display in 2022).[32] In 2024, the contemporary galleries, representing art from 1970 to the present, represented a huge improvement; of the artists on display, 39% were women. (In 2022, that statistic was 19%.) Incidentally, less than 1% of the artists on display in both 2022 and 2024 were gender nonconforming. As I walked through the modern art galleries at the Pompidou, however, I asked myself where the famous women artists of Modernism (1860s–1970s) were. There are many in their collection. But where, for example, was their Marie Laurencin (the Pompidou has 43 works in the collection, yet none was on view); or their Suzanne Valadon (the museum has over 100 works, yet there was not a single painting on view); or Tamara de Lempicka (there are 8 works in the collection, but none was displayed).

As I contemplated the Pompidou's modern art galleries, I thought of the brilliant exhibition *Pionnières: Artistes dans le Paris des Années folles* (*Pioneers: Artists in the Paris of the Roaring Twenties*), curated by Camille Morineau at the Musée du Luxembourg in 2022. *Pionnières* was an all-women exhibition showcasing the female geniuses of Modernism. I wondered why the Pompidou had not placed Danish painter Franciska Clausen next to French artist Fernand Léger, as they were contemporaries working between the two World Wars, each of whom painted in the Purism movement. "Marlow" Moss (Marjorie Jewel Moss) could easily have been presented near Piet Mondrian in the room dedicated to the De Stijl movement. Or Claude Cahun could have been installed next to Man Ray, both being famous Surrealist photographers. German textile artist Gunta Stölzl should have been included and presented near André Bloc in the Pompidou's installation.[33] It is particularly objectionable that Stölzl wasn't included, but Bloc was, especially given that it was the women of the Bauhaus that pioneered avant-garde tapestry, not the men. Yet the Pompidou chose to showcase the only man that was influential in avant-garde tapestry at the Bauhaus. In short, then, there are innumerable examples of brilliant women artists that the Pompidou could have installed—they have many works by such women in their storage units. They also, crucially, have the money for acquisitions.

THE 59TH VENICE BIENNALE, 2022

By contrast, the 2022 Venice Biennale, curated by Cecilia Alemani, demonstrated a broad commitment to women artists. In the op-ed that I wrote for *ARTnews* in April 2022, I noted that the statistics regarding women artists were historic: of the 213 artists in the Biennale, just

21 artists were men—which is less than 10%.[34] To put this into context: in the history of the Biennale's curated exhibition (since 1895), there has never been an edition that is majority-women. At the other extreme, the 1995 exhibition, curated by Jean Clair, was 90% male. Even some of the more recent editions curated by women have been majority-male, including Bice Curiger's in 2011 and Christine Macel's in 2017. When asked about the 90% women artists, Alemani explained: "I don't care about quotas ... but it's striking that people are obsessing about my exhibition and never found the dominance of men [in previous editions] shocking."[35] Indeed, when in the reverse, 10% women and 90% men, it's extremely rare for a mainstream (non-feminist) critic to note a dearth of women artists.

In her curator's essay and in interviews, Alemani spoke of wanting to challenge the "universal ideal of the white, male 'Man of Reason'—as fixed centre of the universe and measure of all things."[36] She spoke of an interest in historical narratives that are built around "forms of symbiosis, solidarity, and sisterhood,"[37] rather than "systems of direct inheritance and conflict," which are assumed male.[38] She titled her Biennale *The Milk of Dreams* after a book of the same name by Surrealist painter and novelist Leonora Carrington; and in her curator's essay, Alemani invoked feminist authors and activists such as Silvia Federici and Ursula Le Guin. She also embedded a feminist perspective into the installation plan of the show itself: the first artwork that viewers saw as they entered the central pavilion in the Giardini was a series of prints by printmaker Belkis Ayón describing an imaginary matriarchal society drawing from Afro-Cuban traditions—which was installed beside *Brick House* (2019), a sixteen-foot-high bronze sculpture by artist Simone Leigh, which combines the shape of the clay house seen in some parts of Benin, Togo, Chad, and Cameroon with a woman's form.[39]

For Alemani to curate a major international exhibition, arguably the most important one in the world, to be majority-women and some nonbinary artists is, despite her contentions, an overtly feminist and curatorial activist gesture and a much-needed turning of the tables—a powerful corrective to the erasure of women from art history and from the contemporary art scene. Major historical women artists (Sonia Delaunay, Sophie Taeuber-Arp, Dorothea Tanning, Meret Oppenheim, Claude Cahun, Hannah Höch, and others) were included, as Alemani put it, to trace "kinships and affinities ... across generations [of women]."[40] The avant-garde progression that she presented in the galleries at the Biennale is not of one male artist trumping another (as is the case at MoMA and the Pompidou), but rather a history of women artists inspiring others. In Alemani's mind, these are artists, past and present, who have offered up possible solutions during dark and confusing times—artists who have imagined "new modes of coexistence and infinite new possibilities of transformation."[41]

I'm hopeful that the 2022 Venice Biennale will set a precedent for other large-scale shows, much like Okwui Enwezor's 2002 edition of Documenta (a global exhibition held every five years in Germany).[42] This is not to say that I believe all exhibitions should be majority-women. What would be extraordinary, however, would be if other curators were courageous enough to follow Alemani's lead and use the platform of global biennales not only to give voice to those who have been historically silenced, but to show it in the numbers. This is the only way to truly offer new narratives of art history. In the future, much like the example set by the 2022 Venice Biennale, exhibitions should set the stage and provide inspiration for the next generation of curators interested in exposing systemic inequalities in the art world. Alemani's was, after all, intelligent curating, a practice rooted in ethics. The end goal of activist curating should be to normalize anti-sexist and anti-racist curatorial practice.

BIPOC ARTISTS, BLACK LIVES MATTER, AND U.S. MUSEUMS

In his now famous essay "Are Art Museums Racist?," first published in *ARTnews* in 1990, curator and critic Maurice Berger reported on the ways in which "white-identified, mainstream art venues" had historically excluded the voices of BIPOC artists.[43] "Who are the patrons of art, the museum board members, the collectors?" he asked. "Who is the audience for high culture? Who is allowed to interpret culture? Who is asked to make fundamental policy decisions? Who sets the priorities?"[44] Sound familiar? It should. While much has changed for the better since the 1990s, BIPOC artists and museum professionals continue to be discriminated against. Indeed, BIPOC artists and arts professionals have been systematically excluded from museums since their founding. As with society at large, structural racism is a widespread problem in museums. Statistics and reports on art institutions (by the Mellon Foundation, American Alliance of Museums, and the U.K.-based Art Fund) reveal that museums persist in supporting a majority-white, majority-male ideology.[45] Racial discrimination is visible in exhibition and public programs, staffing, boardrooms, and permanent collections. A 2019 Williams College survey of the works in the collections of eighteen major U.S. museums, for example, found that they are 87% male and 85% white.[46] These statistics become all the more shocking when understood in comparison with the U.S. population, which is 39.9% BIPOC and 50.5% women, according to the last census in 2022.

The statistics from the abovementioned 2022 Burns Halperin Report—that between 2008 and 2020, only 11% of works acquired by thirty-one major U.S. museums were by women artists—further substantiates claims of male-centrism in museums.[47] Even as some museums take action to counteract this disparity, the rates of acquisition, where reported, have historically been low for BIPOC women. According to the 2022 report, just 0.5% of those museum acquisitions were by Black American women.[48]

Racial discrimination is not only visible in museums' collections, but also on a staffing level: thirty years after Berger's essay was published, museum staff, on average, remain overwhelmingly white. In 2022, the Ithaka S+R group (who strive to expand access to knowledge and education globally) released their Art Museum Staff Demographic Survey, which reported that of the 328 museums surveyed, 64% of their employees identified as white.[49]

To begin to rectify racial inequities, museums—and curators, in particular—can build on the historiography of BIPOC art exhibitions, which for almost a century have either directly or indirectly addressed concerns of racism in the arts. Beginning with the first major museum exhibition of art by African Americans at the Art Institute of Chicago in 1927 to the exhibitions of today dedicated to BIPOC art, these shows have functioned as curatorial correctives to the exclusion of BIPOC artists from the dominant narratives of art history and the contemporary art scene. Some of these pathbreaking exhibitions have, however, proved problematic insofar as they have often excluded swathes of women artists. For example, the canonical *Two Centuries of Black American Art*, organized by U.S. curator David Driskell, and presented at the Los Angeles County Museum of Art (LACMA) in 1976, was the first "historically comprehensive exhibition of art by Black Americans ever to be presented by a major art museum" in the U.S.[50] Of the 205 works on display, only 25 were by women.[51]

Nevertheless, exhibitions that feature majority-BIPOC artists have had a profound impact on the art world, as was spectacularly evident in the U.S. by *The Decade Show* (1990) and the Whitney Biennial of 1993, both of which helped propel BIPOC artists to the fore of the contemporary art world and market.[52] One could argue that BIPOC artists have seen greater representation in the art world since the 1990s, as they have increasingly been included in group exhibitions and have had many more solo exhibitions at museums; and their auction prices and art press exposure have soared. Even the commercial galleries have improved. An example is the 2024 report card produced by the feminist art collective Pussy Galore, which analyzed a cross section of NYC contemporary art galleries (Fig. 9). The report revealed that 29% of the artists represented were BIPOC. A comparison with a 2016 report card by the same collective reveals a jump in representation of BIPOC artists from 14% to 29% in just eight years. The gallery representation has doubled. Incidentally, the NYC gallery with the best representation of BIPOC artists as of 2024 is Jack Shainman (64% BIPOC).

The activism associated with Black Lives Matter (BLM) has clearly had a profound effect on the industry. Founded in 2013 in response to the rampant white-on-Black police brutality in the U.S., the BLM movement took on renewed urgency following the murder of George Floyd, an unarmed Black man, by a white police officer in 2020. Since then, cultural institutions are being held accountable for what critics characterize as their complicity in sustaining toxic and racist environments. In the museum world, in particular, BLM protests have prompted a more serious look at issues of equity in their hiring practices and governance structures, as well as with exhibitions and acquisitions.[53] In the summer of 2020, for example, museum staff across the U.S. wrote a number of forceful public letters denouncing racist practices within their institutions.[54] The letters demanded a range of actions, including leadership resignations, partnerships with external racial equity consultants, and the implementation of more equitable hiring practices.[55] In addition to these open letters, the exposure of institutions has been made public in a myriad of ways—including Instagram posts (especially those shared to the Instagram account Change the Museum), social media campaigns, and leaked internal documents—all of which speak to the widespread discriminatory practices plaguing cultural institutions.

Museums in the U.S. have reacted to these allegations very differently. Some are reinstalling exhibitions and permanent collection displays to reflect their audience's cultural diversity more adequately; some are diversifying their governing boards; while others are committing to acquiring more art from BIPOC communities. Several museums, including the Baltimore Museum of Art, have sought to deaccession expensive, canonical works by white male artists to fund the acquisition of multiple works by BIPOC artists. These deaccessions have proved to be controversial, and a recent, significant attempt by the Baltimore Museum of Art did not go ahead, but the impulse to improve collection holdings is laudable.[56]

However, to truly begin to rectify racial inequities more effectively, museums must write and implement racial equity plans (and/or anti-racism plans) written by DEAI (diversity, equity, access, and inclusion) working groups, who would also advise on a regular basis as issues arise. Becoming a more equitable, anti-racist institution is an ongoing journey, and museums need to commit long term to the effort. Most U.S. museums now feature DEAI plans on their websites, which are individualized accordingly, but, in general, these plans all share common denominators. Each starts with a call for racial equity training of staff, focus groups, and forums to discuss and identify priorities, the establishment of specific working groups to oversee museum-wide DEAI planning and activities, followed by the writing of strategic action plans with benchmarks and timelines. Typically, these plans aim to address equitable hiring practices and staff retention, to ensure exhibition and public programs continue to feature majority-BIPOC voices and intersectional viewpoints, and to assess organizational culture and policies with respect to DEAI principles. Ongoing actions can include governance analyses to implement board slates that are at least 40% BIPOC, and newly conceptualized resource allocation to ensure DEAI initiatives are integrated into department budgets. These are just some of the many initiatives that museums are taking to address systemic racism.

NATIVE AMERICAN ART AT THE METROPOLITAN MUSEUM OF ART

The representation of living Indigenous artists is abysmal in U.S. museums.[57] Contemporary Indigenous artists have been excluded from the canonical narratives of Euro-American art history since their founding. The first time a contemporary Indigenous artist was included in a widely used art history textbook, for instance, was in 1995 in the form of a single painting by Kay WalkingStick, which appeared in H. W. Janson's *History of Art* (more than thirty years after the first edition was published). Incidentally, these white-male-dominated texts included women and Black artists for the first time in 1986 and 1995, respectively.

There are, of course, museums and art galleries dedicated exclusively to Indigenous art in the U.S. But few of them feature contemporary art, preferring instead to showcase historical objects as if they were ethnographic artifacts from another era. Some museums, such as the Met, are making broad efforts to dismantle such stereotypically derogatory exhibition displays.

It should be noted that there is no universally agreed-upon term to refer to Indigenous communities, as different kin-groups have different preferences. Some communities prefer "First Nations," others

"Indigenous," and still others by their specific kin-group name. Because the Met Museum uses the term "Native American," that term is used in this chapter in connection with their collection.

In 2023, the Met reinstalled *Art of Native America: The Charles and Valerie Diker Collection*, in the American Art wing, which is a retake on a permanent collection exhibition of the same name that opened in 2018. Unlike the earlier iteration, there was a concerted effort to present contemporary art alongside objects of spiritual or ritualistic value. For example, one gallery features a striking maskette, *circa* 1780–1830, created by a Tsimshian or Tlingit artist from British Columbia or Alaska, which represents a principal spirit helper that would have been worn during healing practices. Nearby, a 2016 video by Cannupa Hanska Luger features performers carrying mirrored shields embodying the values of a Water Protector. These shields are modeled on those used at the Oceti Sakowin Camp at Standing Rock in November 2016, which was established to block the Dakota Access Pipeline from crossing the Missouri River. While the maskette represents spiritual practices of the distant past, the video is a political statement about the illegal usurpation of Indian land by oil companies.

Another gallery features a 19th-century guardian-figure staff produced by a Lower Chehalis or Quinault artist. Adorned with a necklace of deer hooves, this standing figure would have provided protection for its owner. Displayed nearby is a 2015 photograph by Cara Romero, titled *Water Memory*, depicting two Pueblo corn dancers engulfed by a sweeping flood. The image reflects on the history of human interventions in Indigenous American landscapes—most notably the 1940 construction of the Parker Dam on the Colorado River, which submerged thousands of acres of Chemehuevi homelands in Southern California. In placing historic objects in juxtaposition to contemporary artworks, the curator is emphasizing the concept of "survivance," which underscores that Indigenous Americans are "still here" through an emphasis on their contemporary survival.[58]

These decolonial curatorial innovations are thanks to curator Patricia Marroquin Norby, who was the institution's first full-time curator of Native American art in its 150-year history.[59] Her appointment came two years after the first iteration of *Art of Native America: The Charles and Valerie Diker Collection*, which had been simultaneously lauded and quite controversial. One the one hand, the exhibition was celebrated as the first instance in which the Met featured Native American art in its American Art wing. Critics also noted the art historical importance of displaying Native American art alongside canonical works by white male artists like Gilbert Stewart and

John Singer Sargent. However, the advocacy group Association on American Indian Affairs (AAIA) criticized the exhibition principally because, it argued, the museum had not satisfactorily consulted with tribal representatives during the curatorial process. In a statement, moreover, the AAIA claimed that most of the objects in the exhibition were not art, but rather "sacred ceremonial objects, cultural patrimony and burial objects."[60] They also objected to these objects being displayed alongside the "greats" of North American art. Interestingly, Norby's 2023 installation makes clear that she viewed the sacred ceremonial objects as art, referring to the makers in each label as "artists."

During her appointment, Norby transformed the institution. In addition to her new installation of the Diker collection, the series *Native Perspectives*, in the American Wing, invites Indigenous American artists, authors, community members, curators, and historians to engage with 18th- and 19th-century American artworks, bringing forward myriad voices and narratives that expand and complicate our understanding of American art and history. During her time at the Met, Norby made substantive changes. One can only hope that other encyclopedic institutions will make similar strategic hires, which will have a transformative impact.

Modern and contemporary art museums, on the other hand, have made less progress. Until recently, Indigenous art in general has been almost entirely overlooked. It was not until 2023 that the Whitney Museum of American Art, for example, presented its first-ever retrospective of an Indigenous American artist, Jaune Quick-to-See Smith. MoMA and the New Museum of Contemporary Art have never done so. In 2025, Tate Modern presented its first major solo exhibition dedicated to one of Australia's greatest Indigenous artists, Emily Kam Kngwarray. Also in 2025, the Zimmerli Art Museum presented the largest museum exhibition of contemporary Indigenous art from the U.S., titled *Indigenous Identities: Here, Now & Always*, curated by Jaune Quick-to-See Smith. While museum exhibitions of Indigenous art are becoming more frequent, mainstream, non-Indigenous commercial galleries in the U.S. have only just begun to represent Indigenous artists. Art-market representation is critical to an artist's success: without a gallery, artists have little chance of being identified and seen. The art world has a long way to go with respect to contemporary Indigenous art. While great strides have been made in the past several years, it often appears that the "I" in BIPOC is overlooked. This must change.

MANCHESTER MUSEUM: A CASE STUDY IN EMPATHY

The South Asian community, too, is often ignored in mainstream museums in Europe and America. However, Manchester Museum (an encyclopedic collection with 4.5 million objects from around the world), in partnership with the British Museum, has received considerable positive press since opening its South Asia Gallery in February 2023.[61] Acknowledging the city of Manchester's links to the British Empire and the tremendous wealth generated by enslaved labor, the museum is reassessing its colonial past and contemplating its present. This includes the fact that Asians comprise 21% of the city's population, the majority being of South Asian descent—a presence shaped in part by historic ties to textile production in the Indian subcontinent. As museum director Esme Ward explains, "We are an institution born of empire. How are we grappling with the complexity of that? What does an ethics of care look like for an institution like ours?"[62] She insists that the institution's mission be extended beyond caring for objects and collections to caring for people and their untold stories.

The multilingual South Asian Gallery, which draws on some of the best of the British Museum's national collections, formed the centerpiece of a huge building expansion and renovation in 2023, which included a new entrance, larger temporary exhibition space, and increased public facilities. Unlike most museum spaces that are curated by in-house curators, the South Asian Gallery was co-curated by thirty-one people from Manchester's South Asian diaspora communities, including artists, historians, journalists, scientists, musicians, educators, and students, among others. For the installation, they chose to include a cycle rickshaw from Dhaka decorated with flowers and ribbons by communities in Manchester; woven Muslin cloth; an opium pipe; a World War I uniform worn by one of the organizer's great-grandfathers; a panoramic mural by artists The Singh Twins, which presents a visual archive of the diasporic experience, from images of Queen Victoria (who holds an emblem for the East India Company) to Queen Mary's Crown, set with one of the largest cut diamonds in the world, known as the Koh-i-Noor, mined from India; and a large self-portrait titled *I Beg You to Define Me* (2018), by Azraa Motala, portraying a young woman dressed in richly embroidered South Asian attire layered over a tracksuit.[63] This combination of objects in the gallery reveals the multitude of identities within Manchester's present-day South Asian community. The gallery is also significant as it is the first exhibition space in a U.K. museum to celebrate the experiences and contributions of the South Asian diaspora.

ACCESSIBILITY AND MUSEUMS

If you look in most museums, you'd think disabled people didn't exist, but they're the world's biggest minority."
Richard Sandell, *New York Times* (2019)[64]

According to the World Health Organization, 1.3 billion people living in 2023, or 16% of the world's population, experienced some form of disability.[65] In 2022, the U.S. Centers for Disease Control and Prevention, or CDC, indicated a higher percentage for the U.S. population, reporting that 26% of adults have some type of disability; in its most recent analysis, Arts Council England has reported that 20% of adults in the U.K. identify as having a disability.[66] In 2023, the British Council reported that 48% of the respondents from European museums surveyed present work by disabled artists only occasionally (that is, less than once a year) and 23% never do it.[67]

People with different access preferences or people with disabilities (which are the terms the community prefers) can include those with a chronic illness, impairment, or condition that reduces their ability to carry out daily activities, such as ADHD or multiple sclerosis. They can be people with vision and hearing impairments, as well as those with sensory needs, including autism-spectrum conditions and learning difficulties. Those with mobility concerns, such as people who use wheelchairs and canes or those from senior citizen centers are also considered part of the disability community. For museums not to tackle accessibility barriers for this huge constituency of people is irresponsible and ableist. Yet most people with disabilities describe museums as unwelcoming spaces. Buildings are difficult to navigate by wheelchair users or those with white canes or walkers, spaces are often too loud or populated for those who are neurodiverse or autistic, and public programs make few concessions to those who may require closed captioning or sign language, for instance. So unwelcoming are U.S. museums to people with disabilities, for example, that a 2015 study by the National Endowment for the Arts found that fewer than 7% of people in the U.S. who visited art museums or attended performing arts events identified as disabled.[68] Given that there has been no study in the U.S. on this since 2015, one hopes that the situation has improved over the intervening decade.

The major failings of museum accessibility famously made international headlines in August 2019, when Ciara O'Connor, a wheelchair user, shared her experience on Twitter after a gallery attendant at Olafur Eliasson's exhibition titled *In Real Life* at London's

Tate Modern instructed her to "go around the side" of a mirrored tunnel installation that was accessible only by two steps.[69] Tate and Eliasson later apologized, explaining that "even if a ramp were added, the mirrored walkway that is an integral part of the sculpture is structurally too narrow to be made safe for wheelchair use."[70] The museum continued, "We recognise that this has caused an access issue for wheelchair users for which we are sorry and the comments we have received will be taken on board in future decision-making."[71] To their credit, a few weeks after the tweet storm, Tate Modern installed a video of the Eliasson work as a way for people to see and experience it if they weren't able to physically access it.

The physical barriers for people with disabilities are daunting. As Ciara O'Connor explained at the time of the Tate Modern incident: "I never get to lose myself in a picture, or wander in a reverie. I am always, ALWAYS aware of my body, how it's blocking people, how it's taking up space, how it's inconvenient and cumbersome."[72] It is not just physical barriers that are at issue. Museums are failing on the programmatic side, as well. Only in recent years have a handful of institutions begun to stage exhibitions centered on the experiences, perspectives, and contributions of people with disabilities—such as *Smoke & Mirrors* (Zimmerli Art Museum, 2024) and *Being Human* (Wellcome Collection, 2019), both discussed below. In most museums, however, representations of artists with disabilities remain "either absent, skewed, or stereotypical," as Richard Sandell (a U.K.-based disability advocate and professor of museum studies) and others have explained.[73] It is no surprise visitors with disabilities feel unwelcome and alienated. But what if museums were to make access for all a grounding principle central to exhibition and educational development processes? Instead of merely focusing on compliance with the law, how could museums begin to serve people with disabilities in meaningful ways? The pages that follow indicate some possible ways forward.

BEING HUMAN: A CASE STUDY IN INCLUSIVE CURATION

In 2019, the *New York Times* labeled the Wellcome Collection in London the "world's most accessible museum."[74] The compliment centered on the institution's reinstalled permanent collection, titled *Being Human*, curated by Clare Barlow and Kate Forde (Fig. 10). The curatorial mandate from the institution in organizing the exhibition had been "to challenge the ways we all think and feel about health by connecting science, medicine, life and art."[75] As an activist curator dedicated to marginalized populations, for her part, Barlow aimed to challenge the limitations of the art world by avoiding what is considered "normal," or, in her words, "works that privilege a white, non-disabled, straight, male and/or cis gaze."[76] Instead, *Being Human* articulated "a vision of humanity as frail, leaky, and flawed, yet also infinitely various, creative and, for better and worse, inevitably connected."[77] During the exhibition's planning stage, to ensure a broad representation of artists and perspectives, Barlow consulted broadly with people with different access preferences, including those with autism, mental health conditions, HIV+ people, and other marginalized communities.[78] The consultants provided guidance on matters such as the height at which artworks were installed, the wording of display labels, video-screen access, the number of exit signs (so people with anxiety know they can leave), and audio and visual guides, including one in British Sign Language (BSL).[79] The museum also created a "social story"—a narrative tool designed to help visitors anticipate and navigate the experiences they will encounter during their visit—that they worked on with the British charity Ambitious About Autism.[80] They also invited visitors to select an object to touch or smell from a curated list of multisensory artworks and offered in-person deaf-led BSL tours.[81]

The exhibition's accessible design and programming were laudatory. Its curatorial approach was equally impressive and important—rather than presenting disabled people as patients in need of a cure, it foregrounded their stories and centered their humanity (hence the exhibition's title).[82] Barlow and Forde included two films by British artist Katherine Araniello that challenge representations of disability with both humor and rage. The curators also featured a large sculpture by disabled artist Yinka Shonibare and in a display nearby the curators presented a 'reserved parking' placard that had been spray-painted orange to turn a passive wheelchair user into an active one. Elsewhere, the curators presented a case filled with prosthetics that had been donated by some of the consultants, which included a didactic that raised questions about the future of body modifications and robotics, connecting what is traditionally viewed as an object for a person with a disability with innovations of the future.

Being Human was created *with* and *for* disabled people—it is principally for this reason that the exhibition has emerged as a benchmark for inclusive exhibition design. Sandell, who consulted on the show, claimed the new Wellcome Collection installation was "a real game changer."[83] More museums need to present exhibitions and offer programs that either feature and/or cater to individuals with different access preferences.

SMOKE & MIRRORS: A CASE STUDY IN INCLUSIVE CURATION

In 2024, the Zimmerli Art Museum at Rutgers University presented the exhibition *Smoke & Mirrors*, which featured an international group of fourteen contemporary disabled artists and two disability art collaboratives. The decision to organize the exhibition was the result of a Disability Roundtable, hosted by the museum in 2022, to which the institution invited thirty-five people with disabilities to an in-person seminar in order to listen and learn from them directly about how best to meet the community's myriad access needs. One of the key outcomes of the roundtable was that, while the community appreciated all the accommodations the museum agreed to implement (large-print materials, Braille, audio descriptions, sign-language interpretation, and so on), what they really wanted to see was themselves *represented* on the museum's walls.

As a result of this astute advice, the museum invited prominent disability arts activist and curator Amanda Cachia to organize an exhibition of artists with different access preferences. Cachia's curatorial concept for *Smoke & Mirrors* foregrounded a new genre of art called "access aesthetics," which highlights the inequities within museum spaces for people with disabilities.[84] As Cachia explained, "For the non-disabled visitor, wayfinding through a museum can be a straightforward experience with few obstructions. For disabled visitors, however, wayfinding and experiencing exhibitions is challenging owing to barriers within the museum environment that are designed without disabled embodiment in mind."[85] These barriers within museums are typically invisible, that is, unless the visitor is disabled.

The featured artists showcased artworks that investigated innovative approaches and conceptual frameworks that disrupted conventional modes of spectatorship within art museums.[86] Drawing on the artists' diverse backgrounds, the exhibition adopted an intersectional approach to disability, fostering dialogue around its connections to race, gender, and sexuality. In doing so, it cultivated a more inclusive understanding of the disabled experience.[87] For instance, a film by JJJJJerome Ellis, *Impediment Is Information* (2021, Fig. 11), examined, as the curator explained, "how histories of Black resistance intersect with his experience of having a speech impediment and its impact on how he navigates the world." Fayen d'Evie's multimedia installation *With Cane in Hand, I Dance a Duet for One, for Two, for Three, for Four…* (2021) included a two-channel video work that documents her performing a duet dance with her mobility cane, as well as two touchable, 3-D printed sculptures that traced the motions of the mobility cane, with which audiences were invited to interact through touch and movement. Emanuel Almborg's *Talking Heads* (2016) was a film about a pioneering school for deaf-blind children, which was established in 1963 in Zagorsk, north of Moscow.

Given that it was an exhibition *about* and *for* the museum's disabled community, it was incumbent upon the institution to ensure the exhibition itself, and the correlating programming, were fully accessible to visitors with diverse access preferences. As such, within the galleries, the museum offered audio description of artworks, closed captioning, Braille labels, and, importantly, the artworks were hung lower than usual to account for persons of small stature. Sign-language interpreters and real-time captioning were provided at all public events, the in-person events were live-streamed, and both in-person and virtual sessions were recorded and made available on the museum's website—all to ensure that any participants with limitations, physical, audio, visual, or otherwise, would feel welcome.

In contrast to the Wellcome Collection and the Zimmerli Art Museum, and according to museumgoers with different access preferences whom I surveyed, most museums make minimal accommodations and offer few opportunities for artists with disabilities to exhibit. Even fewer seem to be making the effort to hire people with disabilities, which could vastly improve how a museum analyzes and enacts inclusive practices.[88] Without staffing that is truly inclusive of people with different access preferences, or their representation in galleries and on boards, museums will continue to fall behind in their efforts toward inclusivity for all.

DISABILITY INCLUSION ACTION PLANS

Engaging with organizations and communities that are experts in the field of access (such as Adapt Community Network in the U.S. or Accentuate in the U.K.), institutions can write Disability Inclusion Action Plans (DIAP) in which they outline a series of prioritized action items that concentrate on the needs of a broad spectrum of people with different access preferences. These should focus on all types of disabilities: mobility, vision, hearing, cognitive/learning, psychological, and invisible (disabilities that may not be observable). The goals would be, of course, to address building and equipment needs, but they should also focus on what will be done in terms of programming to create safe spaces—that is, how best to represent people with disabilities in museums, public programming, and in exhibitions. Of equal importance is the need to overcome the negative attitudes and perceptions as well as the physical and communication barriers that people with disabilities regularly face.

Several U.K. and European museums are making great efforts to address accessibility barriers, many of them associated with a European Union–funded research project called ARCHES (Accessible Resources for Cultural Heritage Ecosystems),[89] which, in 2020, engaged 200 people with disabilities to co-design and test digital technologies that support visitors with diverse access preferences in navigating collections. Outcomes of the initiative include tactile maps now available at the Kunsthistorisches Museum in Vienna, orientation videos at the Thyssen-Bornemisza and Lázaro Galdiano museums in Madrid, and life-drawing classes for visitors with visual impairments at London's Wallace Collection.[90] These are just a few of the pioneering museum initiatives that are attempting to ensure access for all.

Action items may also include virtual reality simulation or access video of artworks for wheelchair users who are unable to enter spaces with narrow platforms, as was the case with Ciara O'Connor, discussed above. (In 2017, the Hirshhorn Museum, Washington, D.C., created one of these for their monumental exhibition of the Infinity Mirror Rooms of Japanese artist Yayoi Kusama.) Additional physical upgrades—such as accessible restrooms and compliant doorways—require the expertise of building-access specialists. For visitors who are hearing-impaired, museums can provide induction hearing loops, compatible with hearing aids and cochlear implants, that amplify sound while reducing background noise. Access is also greatly enhanced through closed captioning and sign language. For blind or visually impaired visitors, resources such as audio guides with visual descriptions, tactile tours, large-print text, high-contrast labels, and Braille offer vital support. The Victoria and Albert Museum (V&A) in Dundee, Scotland, offers Sensory Friendly Days and a Quiet Room, which prioritizes the needs of visitors with autism-spectrum conditions. Other museums are adapting their opening times to accommodate flexible visiting options for museumgoers with different access preferences.

One way in which museums might address lack of access for visitors with disabilities is by expanding digital access to their collections and activities. All museums' websites should be reviewed to ensure they're employing best practices in access and inclusion. These measures might include accessibility pages outlining how to visit the museum or join digital events, along with downloadable accessible documents and a dedicated "contact us" page featuring an accessibility-specific phone number and email address. Social media posts should consistently include image descriptions, while events can be promoted through access and disability organizations as well as specialized listings. Where budgets allow, in-person programs should also provide sign language interpreters.

For in-person visitors, entrance signage and communications could be enhanced and CCTV footage of entry points could be utilized to help reception staff anticipate and accommodate visitors with access needs.[91] Some museums have, and all could, create advisory committees composed of people with disabilities who could offer guidance on all access concerns and who could help identify additional services, as needed. These committees could also advise on how best to *prioritize* the many accommodations associated with making buildings, exhibitions, and programs accessible, undertakings that often require fundraising, and could prove to be prohibitively expensive for some museums.

Finally, and crucially, in addition to hiring full-time staff members with disabilities, museums could expand their networks of disabled arts workers by actively including them in public programs and marketing initiatives.[92] In writing DIAPs it is important to understand that the disability community is not monolithic—what's needed for someone with a visual impairment or cognitive difference is not always what is needed for someone with a physical disability.

CONCLUSION

In 2005–6, artist Carrie Mae Weems offered up a powerful museological intervention. In a series of black-and-white photographs from the *Museum Series*, she stands, often with her back to the camera and wearing a floor-length black dress—gazing upon some of the world's leading museums and cultural institutions: the Louvre Museum in Paris, the British Museum in London, the Philadelphia Museum of Art, the Guggenheim Bilbao, Tate Modern in London, Galleria Nazionale d'Arte Moderna in Rome, Project Row Houses in Houston, and the Pergamon Museum in Berlin (frontispiece, Fig. 12). Close to, yet still outside these institutions that have historically excluded her as both a woman and an African American.

Weems's series serves as a reminder to those in the art world who believe that equality has been achieved for women and artists of color. Discrimination in the art world is widespread. People with disabilities, BIPOC, and women remain significantly marginalized. Hence the urgent need for Racial Equity Plans, Disability Inclusion Action Plans—and I'd argue for Anti-Sexism plans too, which are of equal importance. These plans must include action items that are achievable with strict benchmarks and timelines for completion. Crucially, it will take financial resources to implement the ideas put forth in future action plans. Hence the need for prioritization. Institutions cannot transform overnight, but they should be held publicly accountable and make a serious and sustained effort towards doing so.

CHAPTER 5
PRIZING OPEN THE MUSEUM'S CLOSETS: QUEERING THE MUSEUM

INTRODUCTION

Museums are storehouses—and, like most storehouses,
they are full of closets."
James Saslow[1]

Museums have always struggled with how to deal with and acknowledge non-heteronormative sexualities. By relegating lesbian, gay, bisexual, transgender, and queer (LGBTQ+)[2] materials to museum "closets," hidden along with other objects considered "obscene" or "abominable,"[3] LGBTQ+ experiences have largely been ignored or marginalized. This kind of lesbo-homo-trans-phobia and curatorial bias perpetuates the belief that heterosexuality is the default, preferred, and "normal" mode of sexual orientation and, within the museum context, privileges such histories and perspectives. For example, in 2013 the Museum of Modern Art (MoMA) presented *Johns and Rauschenberg*, an exhibition of the work of Jasper Johns and Robert Rauschenberg from the mid- to late 1950s that made no mention of the fact that the two artists were lovers during a six-year period of artistic triumph, when they were moving away from Abstract Expressionism toward Pop art. Instead, the introductory placard described them as "friends" who were "in dialogue with one another" during this period.

As museologists Renaud Chantraine and Bruno Brulon Soares have argued, the concept of heritage—so central to cultural institutions—is itself heteropatriarchal, adhering to the "patriarchal logic of transmission of goods and legal rights from fathers to sons."[4] The dominant culture's vertical transmission of history differs radically from what artist Michael Petry calls "horizontal history," a term that, in this context, describes how stories, memories, or information have passed from one same-sex lover to another.[5] Given that LGBTQ+ people are among the only minorities whose culture is not transmitted through familial relations, they have had to devise "alternative means of keeping their excluded history viable."[6] As such, the documentation of LGBTQ+ lives has been all the more difficult logistically. LGBTQ+ people have historically self-censored for fear of exposure, surviving friends and relatives have destroyed evidence posthumously—covering up what they perceived to be embarrassing information—and historians, curators, and archivists have suppressed material or inaccurately catalogued and interpreted it. (One need only think of the U.S. poet Emily Dickinson for an example of suppressed queer material.) The obvious result is that there is a dearth of available collection items in museums about the LGBTQ+ community and an overabundance of material about heterosexuals. Moreover, institutional reluctance to display objects that may make museum visitors feel uneasy, or that may impact funding, has also greatly affected the representation of LGBTQ+ people. Given this, how can museums foreground minority communities that historically have been rendered insignificant? How can they excavate material hidden within their storage units that reflects this history? And, if they conceal any queer material, can museums reinterpret and re-present their collections with a "queer eye," that is, from a queer perspective? What does "queer" mean anyway?

The word "queer" is an umbrella term used to encompass the full diversity of non-heterosexual individuals, those who may—in different times, locations, and cultures—have been referred to and identified variously as lesbian, gay, bisexual, transgender/trans, intersex, and homosexual. "Queer" also holds room for a range of other, often insulting and derogatory, terms associated with sexual dissidence: sodomite, sapphist, fairy, fag, invert, dyke, drag king, pansy, bumboy, polyamorous, hermaphrodite, drag queen, cupcake, tranny, M2F, poofter, *maricón*. It embodies and accounts for all of these beings and identities. As pioneering cultural theorist Nikki Sullivan has pointed out, the word "queer" can also function as a verb, as in "to make strange, to frustrate, to counteract, to delegitimize."[7] To queer a museum, then, is to challenge, query, and critique the institution itself as an always already heteropatriarchal institution. Queering contests heteronormativity.[8] Or, as scholar Elizabeth Freeman has argued, queering is a form of "talking back" to history.[9] It is a form of misbehaving.

Curators can intervene in existing collections in ways that challenge heteronormativity by highlighting LGBTQ+ stories and themes, presenting queer readings of works of art, exploring hidden histories and truth-telling in didactics, and targeting and promoting LGBTQ+ themes in educational and public programming, which can be marketed to queers and non-queers alike. Curators can also organize museum exhibitions exclusively dedicated to LGBTQ+ histories and visual culture, from solo exhibitions of LGBTQ+ artists to blockbuster group shows. There have been numerous examples of the latter since the 1970s across the globe, including, but not limited to, the following canonical museum exhibitions: *Extended Sensibilities: Homosexual Presence in Contemporary Art* (New Museum, New York City, 1982); *Becoming Visible: Lesbian & Male Homosexuals—From Oppression to Liberation* (Constitutional Museum, Adelaide, 1982); *Love and Democracy* (Poznań Art Fair in the Kulczyk Foundation Galleries and Center of Contemporary Art "Laznia" in Gdańsk, 2005–6); *Prejudice and Pride* (Museum of Brisbane, 2010); *Hide/Seek: Difference and Desire in American Portraiture* (National Portrait Gallery, Smithsonian Institution, Washington, D.C., 2010–11); *Queer British Art* (Tate Britain, London, 2017); *Hors de la nuit des normes, hors de l'énorme ennui* (Palais de Tokyo, Paris, 2023–24); and *Queering the Crip, Cripping the Queer* (Schwules Museum, Berlin, 2023).[10]

THE GAY MUSEUM

To queer a permanent collection is a different curatorial project from the examples given above insofar as it entails a systemic examination of a museum's relationship to histories of non-heteronormative sexualities as manifest in its own collection holdings. *The Gay Museum* (2003), curated by artist-curator Jo Darbyshire for the scientific and ethnographic Western Australian Museum, Perth, was one of the first exhibitions to queer an institution (Fig. 14). For this show, Darbyshire appropriated and recontextualized seemingly unrelated LGBTQ+ and non-queer objects from the museum collection and queered them through carefully conceptualized juxtapositions and snippets of written text (dictionary definitions, quotations drawn from newspapers, oral history interviews, scholarly articles, and so on). "Unlikely objects, thrown together casually or juxtaposed with text, may evoke new meanings," Darbyshire wrote.[11]

One display case, for example, featured a mannequin in a fancy dinner suit; the jacket was open at the front to reveal bound breasts, accompanied by a text on lesbian butch-femme practice. Another case presented a powder puff next to a text about the etymology of the word "poofters." In one particularly witty display, a multicolored packet of cupcake wrappers was accompanied by the text, "Cupcake: an effeminate male, possibly a homosexual (U.S. slang 1900s)"; while elsewhere the words "Lickety Split" were linked to a display of open mussel shells, mink muffs, and late 19th-century purses—which Darbyshire described as "a perfect metaphor for cunnilingus—that never mentioned activity of 'lesbians.'"[12] The exhibition also featured extensive listings of formerly active gay hotels and clubs, curated excerpts of widely reported romantic scandals sourced from historical newspapers, and narratives exploring drag culture and queer identities within Indigenous Australian communities.[13] Darbyshire shared tales of a 1940s murder-suicide of two motorcycle-riding lesbians from Perth, alongside an enlarged photograph of Dykes on Bikes, a staple at every Gay Pride march.[14] One display case, titled *Sodomy*, included two disco balls, an antique spirit level, a squid and an arca suspended in formaldehyde, a 19th-century police baton, pyrite specimens, and a letter from Peter Foss (then Shadow Attorney General) to a community member, dated 2001, which partially read, "We do not consider it appropriate that law should permit sodomizing of our young people."[15] In another display case, small fragments of used hand soap and other artifacts were displayed alongside an electric shock machine accompanied by a didactic about changing homosexual orientation through treatment. In this instance, as one reviewer noted, "the associations of dirt, guilt, the body, and technology collide and linger."[16] To Darbyshire, the accompanying texts and didactic labels were critical, as they allowed her to move away from the guiding voice of the museum's authoritative narrator towards a more experiential, personal and subjective voice—one that allowed for visitors to participate actively in the process of interpreting the objects queerly.

Since *The Gay Museum*, the queering of museums has become a widely adopted approach to addressing the exclusion of LGBTQ+ lives from the historical record, including other important permanent collection interventions at the National Museum of Poland (2010), the Birmingham Museum & Art Gallery, U.K. (2010–11), and the National Gallery of Victoria, Australia (2021).

ARS HOMO EROTICA AT THE NATIONAL MUSEUM IN WARSAW, POLAND

Ars Homo Erotica, curated by Paweł Leszkowicz and presented in 2010 at the National Museum in Warsaw (NMW), Poland, culled over two hundred artworks from the museum's permanent collection to trace the theme of homo-lesbo-erotic desire from antiquity to the 21st century (Fig. 13). It should be noted that most of these works dealt with gay male subjects, with very little focus on lesbian imagery. This was not an exhibition of LGBTQ+ art, but rather a survey of works by heterosexual and LGBTQ+ artists that demonstrated the presence of homo-lesbo-erotic motifs throughout the history of art.

The exhibition served as a "curatorial outing" of artworks in the museum's permanent collection, most of which had been forgotten or relegated to storage rooms, or whose homoerotic content had been overlooked by museum labels.[17] Contemporary homo-lesbo-erotic works, mostly by artists from Central and Eastern Europe (with a few contributions from U.S. artists), were scattered throughout the galleries and juxtaposed with historical works. By setting the recent work into historical context, Leszkowicz sought to validate and legitimize contemporary LGBTQ+ art practice. The exhibition espoused personal and political aims: to "challenge the heteronormative visual canon" by highlighting alternative erotic narratives and different canons of art and love,[18] and to "reinvent the National Museum and turn it into an active agent of cultural and political debate and change in the region."[19] As Leszkowicz explained, "An exhibition about homoeroticism radically subverted any kind of nationalist concept, because the notion of nation and nationality is always connected with the heteronormative, patriarchal ideology." He continued, "This was a chance to rethink the authoritarian concept of the museum and the collection. What is in, what is out, bringing outside what is hidden, suppressed, breaking the heteronormative filter imposed on the cultural institution, but also on the concepts of personal and national identity."[20] He also leveraged the museum's stature as a respected cultural institution to champion equality for Poland's LGBTQ+ community; he hoped the exhibition would function as a protest against the persistent inequalities faced by those who are LGBTQ+ in the country, and that it would help to promote widespread tolerance of sexual difference.[21]

Ars Homo Erotica evolved over nine sections. The exhibition opened with "A Time of Struggle"—a section devoted to the current political conflicts around LGBTQ+ rights in Central and Eastern Europe—in the museum's main hall. The 1911 bronze sculpture *Struggle* by Edward Wittig, depicting three nude men wrestling, laid the groundwork for early 21st-century works by artists such as the Polish art collective Blue Noses Group, whose photograph *Kissing Policemen* (2005) showed two policemen kissing in a Siberian forest; and Karolina Breguła's series of photographs *Let Them See Us* (2003), which offered straightforward portrayals of same-sex couples holding hands, and which had first appeared on billboards in Poland several years earlier, and were censored.

Visitors moved on to "Homoerotic Classicism," focused on heroic and sensual male nudes from the classical and contemporary periods, ranging from ancient sculptures of Greek gods and satyrs (male nature spirits, half-man, half-goat) to Egyptian pottery with homoerotic scenes and a plaster cast of a male nude by Krzysztof Malec from 1994. In the third section, the "Male Nude" was presented as a foundational homoerotic subject, in contrast to the way the female nude forms the foundation of heterosexual art, and in recognition that the male nude was frequently censored as pornographic in Communist Poland only to return triumphantly, uncensored, in the 1990s. This section included a plethora of academic nude sketches and paintings from the mid- to late 19th century, as well as late 19th-century photographs of nude boys by German photographer Wilhelm van Gloeden, and recent works by artists Adám Dallos and Katarzyna Kozyra.

"Iconography of Male Couples in Mythology" presented works depicting male-to-male physical contact—both platonic and romantic—including representations of gods and heroes from ancient mythology, such as Zeus and Ganymede, Apollo and Hyacinth, Achilles and Patrocles, Hercules and Antheus, David and Goliath; these appeared alongside contemporary art depicting amorous pairings of male bodies by Łukasz Stokłosa and Krzysztof Jung, among others. A subsection "Ganymede" was explained by the curator: "In medieval court and monastic culture, the word 'Ganymede' had the same meaning as 'gay' today and explicitly referred to homosexual circles."[22] This section juxtaposed recent images of the mythological figure (including one by Barbara Falender, *Ganymede II*, 1987, in marble), 18th- and 19th-century watercolors and etchings, as well as examples from the 1st century BCE in white marble.

A section of the exhibition was devoted to St. Sebastian, the early Christian saint and martyr most frequently associated with homoerotic iconography—usually represented as an ecstatic and penetrated (by arrows) male body—including 16th- and 17th-century paintings, as well as a recent photograph by Stasys Eidrigevičius and a video by Karol Radziszewski. The seventh section, "Lesbian Imaginarium," featured historical and mythical subjects with lesbian themes (such as the ancient Greek poet Sappho, the Roman goddess Diana, and nymphs), 19th-century portraits of "romantic friendships," juxtaposed with contemporary lesbian photography and video by various artists, including Tanja Ostojić and Marina Gržinić, Catherine Opie, and Hanna Jarzabek; the *Da Boyz* series of photos (2009–10) by Jarzabek about the everyday life of lesbians in Poland was particularly strong. The "Transgender" section presented works related to the act of moving beyond and between genders, as well as images of androgynous figures, such as the *Genderqueer* series (2008) by the art collective KKJR, and George Grosz's watercolor *Carnival* (1930–32). The final section was devoted to the "Archive," and included film and theater materials related to postmodern LGBTQ+ culture.

Ars Homo Erotica provoked significant controversy within a sociopolitical context in which the Catholic Church maintains substantial influence over public discourse and cultural norms.[23] Far-right politicians and intellectuals reacted vehemently when, in the autumn of 2009, the museum announced plans to mount an exhibition on art and homosexuality. In a formal letter to the Minister of Culture, politicians demanded the project's cancellation, while members of the ultra-conservative Law and Justice Party denounced the exhibition both in Parliament and across media.[24] An MP for the Law and Justice Party asserted that, like pedophilic and zoophilic art, homosexual art does not exist, while another MP declared, "The Polish culture minister should ban this obscene exhibition, which is a waste of taxpayers' money. The National Museum should focus on wholesome, patriotic topics."[25] However, when the show opened as planned on June 11, 2010, it was received peacefully, and there were no protests or attacks throughout its three-month run. Indeed, it attracted not only 44,000 visitors, but also tremendous international attention, with hundreds of articles and mentions in global media—more than any previous exhibition at the NMW.

QUEERING THE MUSEUM AT THE BIRMINGHAM MUSEUM & ART GALLERY

Queering the Museum (2010–11), by artist-curator Matt Smith, was another major exhibition that sought to queer a museum collection. It took place at the Birmingham Museum & Art Gallery, one of the largest regional museums in England, renowned for its wide-ranging collections encompassing archaeology, fine and decorative arts, and natural and social history.[26] Rather than presenting the "queered" objects in just one gallery, Smith distributed them in nineteen separate locations in the building, creating what he called "a queer seam" throughout the museum.[27] Each queered display was identified by a green carnation graphic—again signifying LGBTQ+ identity. A green carnation was famously worn on the lapel of the Irish poet and playwright Oscar Wilde (1854–1900) and several of his associates; it became a symbol of gay identity in the 19th and 20th centuries. According to Smith, the signal of the green carnations throughout the exhibition mirrored the performance of "cruising," as visitors, in an ostensibly heterosexual setting, searched "for queer signifiers that they can then choose to either engage or ignore with."[28]

In *Queering the Museum* and another exhibition he curated, titled *Other Stories: Queering the University Art Collection* (Stanley and Audrey Burton Gallery, University of Leeds, 2012), Smith sought "to unpick the interrelationships between Queer Theory (and LGBT experiences) and museum and gallery exhibitions, exploring how queer could be brought into and interpreted within museums and art galleries that hold collections of material culture." He also aimed "to investigate why LGBT experiences are so seldom included in museum and gallery displays."[29] In looking at the museum's collection through a queer lens, he explored the heterosexual assumptions that underpinned the institution and how they impacted the development and interpretation of the collection. By adopting a "queering" curatorial strategy, he unearthed the heteronormative bias inherent in standard curatorial practice.

The exhibition opened with a dramatic installation that functioned to queer a famous bronze statue titled *Lucifer* (1945) by U.S.-British sculptor Jacob Epstein (1880–1959). The sculpture takes the form of a woman's head on a man's body, resulting in a cross-gendered figure. Although a permanent fixture of the museum, the artwork was, for the duration of the exhibition, draped in a green cape created by Smith and embellished with green silk carnations.[30]

Many of the works in the exhibition were new ceramic pieces produced by Smith specifically for the exhibition that blended in seamlessly with the historic objects he had chosen. Smith was keen to tell his "queer stories" via the use of craft—it is a familiar medium to him as he was trained as a ceramicist. But he was also drawn to the gendered connotations associated with craft as "women's work," such as embroidery and sewing, which have a traditional connection to domesticity. He liked using a medium with "homely connotations" to convey potentially "unsettling messages."[31] Using clay as a medium was important for him, as it "has an ability to take on form—casting allows for similar, but slightly different, copies to be made—and coupled with its permanence after firing, clay is able to fill the invisible gaps in the collection with permanent reminders of missing histories."[32]

Smith's insertion of his own work into the displays, alongside objects from the permanent collection that he'd chosen, made for a radical intervention into the museum itself. This curatorial strategy follows on from Fred Wilson's landmark exhibition *Mining the Museum* (1992–93), which—through unprecedented combinations of objects in the permanent collection of the Maryland Historical Society, Baltimore—drew attention to racial blind spots and inherent biases within the institution.[33] Like Wilson's strategy, which exposed "a legacy of violence, exclusion, and selective looking,"[34] Smith's intervention was a form of institutional critique that presented his new ceramic works and museum artifacts—some of which had little to do with LGBTQ+ lives—as stand-ins for the unrecorded and multidimensional experiences of LGBTQ+ communities, past and present.

In one display, amid an existing collection of works depicting heterosexual couplings, Smith placed a new ceramic sculptural portrait of the "Ladies of Llangollen," Eleanor Butler and Sarah Ponsonby (Fig. 15). The "ladies" were two upper-class Irish women who had lived together as a couple for fifty-one years in Plas Newydd, rural Wales, during the 18th century. Their contemporaries were both scandalized and captivated by the unconventional relationship, which sparked great interest in society. During their time together, the women were visited by several eminent figures, many of whom were writers, including Sir Walter Scott and Lord Byron; William Wordsworth wrote a sonnet about the couple after meeting them in 1824. Smith's new depiction of the women, placed amid earlier collection works, functioned to solidify their historic importance.

One display, *Tribute to Simeon*, featured collection works by the Pre-Raphaelite artists Simeon Solomon (1840–1905) and Frederic Leighton (1830–1896). These were presented together in a display case, accompanied by a new ceramic artwork by Smith of "a bear playing the part of the tortured St. Sebastian."[35] The wall label examined how Solomon's sexuality detrimentally shaped his artistic practice and career, in contrast to Leighton's experience. Solomon's homosexual relationships led to his arrest in both London and Paris, effectively ending his career. Leighton, however, was far more discreet about his sexual relations with men, which meant that his career continued to flourish; he was knighted in 1878 and given a peerage in 1896.[36]

Other displays addressed themes such as the representation of gay slang and the perpetuation of stereotypes, including Smith's combination of permanent collection objects—of bears and otters—which, in gay slang, refer to large, hairy gay men with beards and slimmer, hairy gay men, respectively. In another work exploring gay slang, titled *Looking for a Chicken Hawk*, the label explained that "chicken" is gay slang for younger men and "hawks" are older men who are attracted to them; the label accompanying a double-spouted teapot explained that "tea-rooming" is U.S. gay slang for anonymous male-male sexual encounters in public toilets. While slang was a common theme in the exhibition, so was "polari," a coded language once used by gay men, popular in the 1950s and '60s, that enabled discreet conversation about same-sex relationships at a time when homosexuality was punishable by imprisonment.[37] One polari work, a new piece by Smith titled *Bona Arm*, translating as "nice penis," showed a dapper male figure with an enormous penis protruding from his zipper.

Another display featured four historic medicinal jars beside another by Smith with a willow-pattern motif and a bathhouse depicting the tale of two lovers who, upon execution, were transformed into a pair of doves.[38] The label explains that despite advances in drug technology, the gay male community has been hit particularly hard by HIV. While some displays were darkly serious, others were whimsical. In one witty pairing, a young boy in a hat from the museum collection is shown "cruising" a handsome figurine created by Smith. To emphasize one of the definitions of "queer" as odd or unusual, Smith also employed "jarring, confusing, or provocative juxtapositions," such as false eyelashes "borrowed from Lady James," placed beside well-worn high heels, topped by a decorative shoehorn with a butterfly pattern, an object produced by Smith.[39] Another "odd" object included *Donkey Man*, a ceramic piece by Smith, representing an upright donkey in a business suit, standing before two green lobster claws.

Smith's interventions queered the Birmingham's permanent collection by reintroducing biographical references to same-sex relationships that previously had been omitted from the museum's interpretation—heterosexual references, by contrast, were commonplace.[40] In one particularly striking display, Smith juxtaposed an 18th-century figurine of a heterosexual couple with a Baroque-style *Civil Partnership Figure Group* depicting two men arm in arm atop an ornate base. With displays like this, he countered the cultural silencing of LGBTQ+ communities—a practice that renders lives and histories as insignificant and thereby invisible. Instead, *Queering the Museum* negated the heterosexual filter so commonplace in museums and made absence visible, by reappropriating objects that told new or revised stories, by recontextualizing collection objects and placing them center stage, and by placing new objects within the collection to fill historic LGBTQ+ gaps.

QUEER AT THE NATIONAL GALLERY OF VICTORIA

A historiography of collection interventions curated from a queer perspective is not complete without the inclusion of *Queer*, the 2022 exhibition at the National Gallery of Victoria (NGV) in Melbourne. In queering their permanent collection, the NGV opened new ways of looking at and interpreting its vast encyclopedic holdings, isolating approximately four hundred objects for presentation. It was not an exhibition of visual art by exclusively queer artists, nor were the subjects depicted necessarily queer in content. Instead, we encountered heterosexual artists representing LGBTQ+ figures and subjects; LGBTQ+ artists representing heterosexual figures and subjects; LGBTQ+ artists representing LGBTQ+ figures and subjects; heterosexual artists representing LGBTQ+ figures and subjects with queer references; and other variations. Queerness functioned as an illusory category, one with no single definition or aesthetic. Museumgoers were invited to explore the myriad ways in which both people and works might be interpreted as queer. The thrust of the exhibition was less about who was/what is queer but rather, as Robert Mills has argued: "why and how one finds queerness historically or culturally."[41]

Here the didactic label, like the notes in the margins, became the salient entry point. Take, for example, two objects that demonstrate the slipperiness of the term "queer:" one was a photograph by the heterosexual portrait photographer Athol Shmith of heterosexual gay icon Elizabeth Taylor; the other was a portrait by heterosexual photographer André Kertész of bisexual author Colette. Similarly, an image of the heterosexual Napoleon Bonaparte was accompanied by a label that informed us that during his reign the decriminalization of homosexuality, which began during the French Revolution, was legally ratified. And a simple photograph of Hyde Park in London, by William Thomas Owen dated 1926, was accompanied by advice that at the turn of the 19th century, Hyde Park and St. James's Park were locked at night to prevent "scandalous practices." Similarly, a label accompanying an etching dated 1821 depicting a large gathering of men at the Royal Exchange in London noted that its arcades were known as a "buggery haunt."

The majority of the objects in the exhibition were overtly queer. Some involved "household" (LGBTQ+) names, such as Andy Warhol, Duncan Grant, Edward Burra, Noël Coward, David Hockney, Nan Goldin, Robert Mapplethorpe, William Yang, Agnes Goodsir, David McDiarmid, and Margaret Preston. Gay icons abounded (for example, Judy Garland, Elizabeth Taylor, Divine, Madonna, Kylie Minogue, Colette, Jean Cocteau, Greta Garbo, Isadora Duncan, and Leigh Bowery). Other objects presented undeniably queer subject matter, as in kabuki theater, costumes from gay fashion houses, portraits of the notoriously bisexual Bloomsbury Group, and images of St. Sebastian. But the "smoking gun" was not always evident. Often there were historical references that led curators to believe the individuals may have been LGBTQ+. The "Royally Queer" and "Classical Queer" sections of the exhibition were particularly provocative in this regard, claiming a variety of historical characters as members of the queer tribe: from King Richard I of England, Henry III of

France, and Louis XIII of France to Christina of Sweden, King Gustav III, and Sardanapalus. In other sections of the exhibition, ostensibly un-queerable figures, such as Julius Caesar, Nero, and Petronius, were queered. We also encountered images of and by artists, or of subjects, whose sexual identities were uncertain or debatable—for example, Sandro Botticelli, Leonardo da Vinci, William Shakespeare, Joan of Arc, Michelangelo—to challenge the historical heterosexual filter.

Exhibition texts revealed certain long-concealed information on some well-known figures. For example, that Alastair Cary-Elwes's 1887 portrait of Rupert Bunny is indeed a depiction of his lover, and that the actor Charles Laughton, husband of the actor Elsa Lanchester, featured in a 1958 portrait by Bryan Kneale, was bisexual. Sharing these public figures' queerness openly was invaluable in affirming LGBTQ+ lives that were once hidden in the museum's archives—literal and figurative closets—but have now been retrieved. As curator and historian Anna Conlan has explained, "Omission from the museum does not simply mean marginalization; it formally classifies certain lives, histories and practices as insignificant."[42] Hence the importance of archival research that offers new insights. All information about LGBTQ+ lives lived is proof of existence and *significance*.

The manner of exhibition of many extraordinary objects sourced from the NGV's holdings demonstrated the extensive curatorial research undertaken in order to collect queer references, annotations, and observations that might otherwise have remained hidden and undetectable to the non-LGBTQ+ viewer. Photographer André Kertész's *On the Boulevards, Paris* (1934), for example, is a seemingly quotidian photograph of a street scene in Paris showing a woman resting on a bench, while, behind her, a man walks by wall posters advertising a then-popular aperitif, Dubonnet (Fig. 16). But upon closer inspection, at the center of the composition is a cutout silhouette of a gender-non-conforming individual in a suit and top hat. The figure is literally attached to the bench, part of an advertisement for a film called *Georges et Georgette*, which the seated woman is ignoring. The film is the French-language version of the 1933 German film *Viktor und Viktoria*, precursor to the 1982 film *Victor/Victoria*, wherein a woman pretends to be a male female impersonator and, after enjoying great success on the stage, struggles to conceal her secret when she falls in love with a man. It takes queer vision on the part of curators to notice and re-present these details, allowing for a queer reading of a now-canonical image. In contrast, to demonstrate how LGBTQ+ content like this is generally overlooked in museums or how queer interpretations are thwarted, the Metropolitan Museum's wall label for the same photograph describes the top-hatted silhouetted figure as a "fellow," a male, whose "inviting smile" the seated woman is oblivious to.[43] The Met has presented this as a heteronormative image.

Strong curatorial research and accompanying didactic materials highlighted the queer content of another unlikely image in the exhibition. In his 1810 etching of *Chaucer's Canterbury Pilgrims*, the artist William Blake has chosen to depict, among the other pilgrims, a portrait of The Pardoner, who is shown on horseback just center right of the composition. The figure is described in Chaucer's text as a man of slight build, beardless, with wispy blond locks, and a high-pitched voice. The accompanying label text quotes novelist and critic Peter Ackroyd, writing about the character of The Pardoner in *Queer City*, his 2017 history of gay London: "The narrator of *The Canterbury Tales* eventually declares that 'I believe he was a gelding or a mare'—that, literally, he was either a eunuch or a woman. But 'mare' was also used as a term for effeminate men."[44] Ackroyd proclaims Chaucer's literary character as "one of the first portraits, or caricatures, of a London queer."[45] A heteronormative label would not have focused on the queer character—and might indeed have left his description, because it was ambiguous, out of any corresponding didactic. It requires a LGBTQ+ lens to focus on this specific pilgrim, amid all of the other characters. In both the Kertész photograph and the Blake etching, it is clear that it takes a "queer eye" to uncover, seek out, reinterpret, and re-present LGBTQ+ content.

Some of the most profound works encountered in *Queer*, all presented under the umbrella "Anxiety/Shame/Discrimination/Loss," reminded us that LGBTQ+ people have been persecuted across time and place and that lesbo-homo-trans phobia has always run deep. Via a careful selection of works and smartly written didactics, we learned of the arrests for homosexuality of artists Angus McBean and Simeon Solomon, of Thomas Hart Benton's disdain for homosexual men, and of James Stuart MacDonald's outright condemnation of "degenerates and perverts" who he insisted had invaded the fine art realm (MacDonald served as the NGV director 1936–40). We learn also of many other historical figures who were vicious homophobes, including Justinian, the Emperor of Constantinople, who believed that homosexually inclined men were responsible for earthquakes and should, for this reason, be "burned alive."[46] A label alongside a portrait of King Henry VIII explained that he was the first to criminalize sexual activity between men when he codified the Buggery Act of 1533; a mirror etched with a portrait of Queen Victoria was accompanied by a label explaining that she signed the Criminal Law Amendment Act in 1885 that outlawed oral sex between men—the act under which Oscar Wilde was prosecuted.

A beautiful etching of Newgate Prison was accompanied by a didactic that explained that queers were hanged at this prison for the crime of sodomy.

What the exhibition made clear is that the condemnations and executions for nonconformist sexuality were specific to men. Lesbianism appears not to have been a threat—except in passing, for instance, with Marie Antoinette's unsubstantiated relationship with Princess de Lamballe, her confidante. Indeed, lesbianism has never (to my knowledge) been outlawed, because, as philosopher Judith Butler has explained, a lesbian is an "unviable (un)subject,"[47] a cipher with no meaning outside of the heterosexual matrix—hence the 19th-century French synonym for lesbians *faut de mieux* ("for lack of something better"). A phallogocentric understanding of lesbianism precludes its existence, as in the notion of a Boston Marriage. Indeed, when an image is lesbo-erotic—as in the case of Diana and her nymphs, who are typically shown naked with bodies tipped towards the (presumably male) viewer—it is clear it is composed so as to maximize heterosexual male visual consumption. Only a few images in the exhibition were unambiguously lesbian in content—for example, two photographs by Ponch Hawkes. And, except for several images of drag queens, the only reference to gender nonconformity was the famous 1932 Brassaï photograph of *Le Monocle*, which depicts a grouping of butch-femme lesbians in a bar in the Montmartre neighborhood of Paris, a few of whom don "masculine" attire.

CONCLUSION

While the exhibitions described above are signs of progress toward increased queer representation in the art world, no exhibition can be all things to all people. It must be said that most LGBTQ+ exhibitions are themselves homonormative, which means they normalize white middle-class cis men in gay communities and their histories. Differences of race, ethnicity, class, and gender are often overlooked. This criticism has been leveled at blockbuster queer exhibitions like *Hide/Seek* and *Ars Homo Erotica*—and rightly so. The marginalization of certain identities within the queer art world mirrors the marginalization of the queer community in the art world as a whole. Clare Barlow, curator of the 2017 exhibition *Queer British Art* at Tate Britain, has written of the curatorial challenges presented by the limitations of mounting a queer, historical exhibition. She states: "This lack of surviving material reflects power dynamics within society that were replicated in the queer community and the art markets."[48] "Long histories of racism, misogyny, transphobia, and class prejudice," she continued, "have not only caused works to be lost but also stifled careers before they could flourish."[49] Indeed, one of the most difficult aspects of curating an exhibition with queer content from the past is that history itself is homo-lesbo-trans-phobic. The task of a curator is to make those absences visible. Not to do so runs the risk of essentializing dissident sexualities—as if all LGBTQ+ experience is the same regardless of the myriad differences among and between individuals. As scholar Carolyn Dinshaw has expressed, we are not "a feel-good collectivity of happy homos."[50] What differentiates collection interventions like those explored in the case studies above from group shows of LGBTQ+ art is that they do not purport to speak for all members of the LGBTQ+ community. Rather, they adopt the queer lens to focus on the collection itself. It is a useful model, as the curators are not presenting the LGBTQ+ community in a monolithic form.[51] Here, the strength of "queer" as a concept is its flexibility.

In his seminal essay, "Theorizing the Queer Museum," Robert Mills argues that "the objective, narratorial voice of museum authority is not the only voice to be heard."[52] In their drive towards democratization and inclusivity, museums must continue to challenge their exclusionary practices by reconciling with colonization, sexism, racism, classism, ableism, Western-centrism, and, yes, heteronormativity. As museums enact LGBTQ+ initiatives, one must ask if systemic change is even possible without a complete reconfiguration of the inner workings of the museum. The queer turn, after all, is not just a change in content; it must also simultaneously decenter institutional authority and intensify accountability. To truly queer a museum also necessitates avoiding tokenistic gestures, which only serve to reinforce power hierarchies without confronting complicities and silences. Challenging heteronormativity must be an ongoing and sustained project.

What these queer museum interventions revealed is that museums are capable of acting productively upon contemporary social issues and concerns; that they are capable of challenging their own heteronormative biases. Museums have the unique potential to act differently, to tackle prejudice and foster more respectful ways of seeing difference; to build support for progressive values and equality for all. Cultural organizations of all kinds have both an ethical responsibility and rich untapped opportunities to stimulate and support progressive social change. The museums highlighted above have proven that they are indeed capable of doing the hard work of confronting institutional biases. We can return to Jasper Johns and Robert Rauschenberg for one hopeful example. In 2022, nine years after the MoMA show that failed to acknowledge the true nature of their connection, Johns's major career retrospective *Mind/Mirror* at the Whitney Museum of American Art explicitly described their "romantic and creative relationship."[53]

CHAPTER 6
HOW BLOODY IS TOO BLOODY? TOXIC PHILANTHROPY AND THE CORPORATIZATION OF MUSEUMS

INTRODUCTION

Since the 2010s, a spate of scandals and protests in the U.S. and U.K. has plunged some of the world's most prominent public museums into crisis. Most of these incidents, which are linked to board members, art patrons, and corporate sponsors, have been sparked by so-called "toxic philanthropy"—that is, when funds donated to institutions are derived from questionable sources. As a museum director and a senior curator at various institutions, I have accumulated considerable inside knowledge not only of art patrons, but also of the make-up, function, and inherent problems with some museum boards. In this chapter I give an overview of some of the most significant challenges facing museums vis-à-vis philanthropy. My primary focus is on U.S. museums—particularly those that receive minimal government subsidy and are therefore often dependent on donations from private philanthropists and corporate sponsors. What follows, then, is an analysis of public art museums and boards of *governors* (those who are responsibility for overseeing the management of assets and resources). This is distinct from boards of *advisors*, who (like the advisory board of the Zimmerli Art Museum, with which I am currently associated) offer guidance without the expectation of financial oversight or control of operations. The analysis that follows is specific to nonprofit museums and the 1% patrons (who represent the highest echelon of wealth in the U.S.) on governing boards.

While most art museums genuinely work quite productively with philanthropists who have the best of intentions, others—especially those with larger endowments like the Museum of Modern Art, the Whitney Museum of American Art, and the British Museum—appear to be entertaining a gallery of disreputable funders that include fossil fuel oligarchs, opioid and war profiteers, private-prison racketeers, climate-change deniers, real estate tycoons, sexual predators, and individuals pushing right-wing agendas. In such cases, museums are, to use art critic Rhonda Lieberman's phrase, "art-washing"—trading "filthy lucre for cultural capital, civic glory, and good PR."[1] They are, quite simply, laundering the reputations of patrons whose business practices are far from ethical.

Many wealthy patrons who join fiduciary museum boards do so primarily for tax benefits, taking advantage of deductions on contributions to nonprofits and charities. Donations are also frequently tied to naming rights, allowing patrons to affix their names to a museum's wing, building, gallery, entrance—or, in some cases, the entire institution. At the New Museum of Contemporary Art in New York City, for example, even the public bathrooms have been named (after the former venture capitalist Jerome L. and Ellen Stern).[2] Naming serves as a means of securing one's legacy through a conspicuous display of wealth, now and sometimes into the future, since some named gifts come with perpetuity clauses ensuring that they can never be changed; that is, unless there are reputational controversies, as shall be outlined below. Buying the right to name a building, or part of it, after oneself is a symbol of ego, and principally male ego, since it is only in recent years that women have begun donating to nonprofits for naming purposes.

A trustee's role in a museum is slightly different from a donor's. Unlike a donor, a trustee has a fiduciary responsibility to the museum. (While a trustee is by definition a donor, a donor is not always a trustee.) Donors are third parties who have a contractual arrangement, which amounts to a simple exchange: *I give you money, I get something in return, and our agreement must include certain terms*. These are restricted, rather than unrestricted, gifts. Under these conditions, the museum receiving the gift is entering into a legally binding relationship with the donor, as it would be with any third party with whom it signs a contract. Typically, terms include time frames: for example, that a donated art collection or artwork must remain on display in perpetuity, or for a certain number of years. Sometimes, museums sign a contract with a donor to build a new museum, or part of one, that will bear the donor's name forever. For a museum to accept such gifts is unwise—a donor's name may, for example, become embroiled in controversy. Once the museum has entered into a contract with the named entity, it can be extremely difficult to back out of it. Un-naming is a complex process.

Aside from tax advantages, ego boosts, and art-washing, the benefits of donor status or board trusteeship can include admission to an exclusive club where collector-trustees can network and interact with other rich and (sometimes) famous people. By gaining access to top curators, collector-trustees can quickly discover the "hottest" emerging artists before they become market commodities. Is this insider trading or just an unfair advantage? While many CEO board members are undoubtedly altruistic and have a genuine desire to share their wealth, some are invariably eager to be known and recognized for their philanthropy. Otherwise, why not give anonymously?

During their tenure as trustees, members of boards of governors can vote on policy, bylaws, strategic planning, acquisitions, financial investments, deaccessioning, and general management of the museum. A trustee's power on the board often mirrors the size of their financial contributions—as exemplified by billionaire cosmetics executive and collector Leonard A. Lauder at the Whitney Museum of American Art. Over his tenure from 1977 to 2011, Lauder donated major works, poured in vast sums—including $131 million toward the new Renzo Piano building—and wielded disproportionate influence over the museum and its directors.[3] In my experience, the members of boards of governors who give the most tend to meddle the most in the day-to-day operations of the organization.

I would argue that the current issues surrounding philanthropy are directly tied to the corporatization of museums, which began in the 1980s and continues today. The for-profit ethos driving corporations in an era of global expansion has seeped into nearly every corner of the museum sector, evident in everything from boards dominated by the economic elite and blockbuster exhibitions to the race for flashy architectural trophies—"starchitecture"—designed by celebrity architects to project power and prestige. Finally, I argue that de-corporatization is essential if museums are to become ethical, democratic institutions.

THE SACKLERS AND PURDUE PHARMA

In Europe, the U.K., and the U.S., the Sackler family name has become synonymous with dirty money. The Sacklers are the owners of Purdue Pharma, the pharmaceutical company responsible for creating the highly addictive painkiller OxyContin. Since the late 1990s, this drug has resulted in approximately half a million overdose deaths in the U.S. alone (as at the time of this writing).[4] Purdue Pharma's role in these deaths traces to its decade-long, aggressive marketing schemes of the drug after its 1995 launch—falsely assuring that it carried little to no risk of addiction while pushing prescriptions for chronic pain in dangerously excessive quantities. The company further incentivized doctors to adopt and perpetuate these practices.[5] Subpoenaed emails in 2019 from Richard Sackler have substantiated that the company was fully aware of the potential for Oxy abuse and about its impact on the company's profits: "If OxyContin is uncontrolled, it is highly likely that it will eventually be abused ... How substantially would it improve our sales?"[6]

Purdue Pharma has faced a barrage of mass-action lawsuits for nearly two decades. In 2007, the company pleaded guilty to federal criminal charges, and was fined $600 million "for misleading regulators, doctors, and patients about the drug's potential for abuse," according to the *New York Times*.[7] Then, a decade later in 2019, as opioid deaths mounted, Purdue Pharma filed for bankruptcy—no doubt in an effort to avoid paying out large sums of money to plaintiffs, and only after they withdrew billions from the company.[8] (Incidentally, the members of the Sackler family who owned a majority share of Purdue Pharma since 1952 are collectively worth a total of $11 billion, as of 2024.[9]) The company reached a bankruptcy settlement in 2021, requiring the owners, members of the Sackler family, to dole out $6 billion to thousands of plaintiffs in exchange for complete immunity from future lawsuits.[10] In 2023, the US Department of Justice challenged the provision, arguing that the non-bankrupt party cannot obtain such protections, a decision upheld by the US Supreme Court in 2024.[11] In November 2025, a revised bankruptcy plan dissolved Purdue and reconstituted it as a public benefit company, Knoa Pharma, while requiring the Sacklers to relinquish ownership and pay up to $7 billion over fifteen years.[12] The plan provides resources for states, municipalities, tribes, school districts, hospitals, and roughly 150,000 personal-injury claimants, with initial distributions expected to begin as early as spring 2026.[13] Importantly, the Sacklers no longer receive immunity from future opioid-related lawsuits, though the plan establishes a legal-defense reserve (funded by withholding $200 million, with potential replenishment of up to $800 million) to support litigation should claimants pursue future cases against the family.[14]

Since the market introduction of OxyContin in the mid-1990s, as their own fortunes have continued to rise, the Sacklers have donated significantly to U.S., U.K., and European arts institutions, theaters, and universities. In return for these gifts, their name has been prominently displayed in and on institutions worldwide—including at the Metropolitan Museum of Art (Met), New York; the Guggenheim, New York; Tate, London; Harvard Art Museums, Cambridge, Massachusetts; the American Museum of Natural History, New York; the National Portrait Gallery, London; the Serpentine Galleries, London; the Victoria and Albert Museum (V&A), London; the British Museum, London; and the Louvre, Paris, among many others.[15] Even the Elizabeth A. Sackler Center of Feminist Art at the Brooklyn Museum, of which I am founding curator, bears their name.

The Sacklers's actions represent the clearest and by far the most powerful example of using nonprofit institutions to art-wash blood money. However, following a series of protests, the family's attempts to hide behind the skirts of these museums have failed miserably. In 2018, the artist Nan Goldin—a former OxyContin addict (and her activist group, Prescription Addiction Intervention Now, or PAIN) launched a full-scale campaign against the Sacklers, urging museums to sever ties with them. She compared the family to notorious drug barons such as El Chapo and Pablo Escobar and demanded that Sackler money be diverted from museums to fund addiction and treatment centers for the drug they push. Goldin's first action took place in 2018 in the Met's Sackler Wing, home of the ancient Roman Egyptian Temple of Dendur, where she and her allies staged a "die-in"—lying down en masse to symbolize Oxy-related deaths—and threw Oxy prescription bottles into the moat surrounding the temple. Subsequent Goldin-led protests have taken place at the Louvre, the Guggenheim, Harvard's Arthur M. Sackler Museum, the National Portrait Gallery in London, Smithsonian's Freer-Sackler Galleries, and the V&A, among others.

The highly publicized Goldin-led protests, and the media circus that ensued, have had a major impact, particularly in forcing museums to reconsider sponsorship policies, gift acceptance, and naming opportunities. Several museums have now renamed spaces that bear the Sackler name (from galleries and libraries to courtyards and education centers), including the Louvre (2019), the Metropolitan Museum of Art (2021), the Guggenheim (2022), the Serpentine Galleries (2022), Tate (2022), the V&A (2022), the British Museum (2022), the Ashmolean Museum (2023), and the Smithsonian's Freer-Sackler Galleries, which in 2024 were rebranded as the National Museum of Asian Art.

The PAIN protests have rendered the Sacklers cultural pariahs whose "Oxycash" is now too tainted to art-wash through patronage.[16] The damage to the family name has been so severe that in 2019 the German artist Hito Steyerl likened exhibiting at the Sackler-funded Serpentine Galleries in London to "being married to a serial killer."[17] In 2019, the State of New York stated that in taking Sackler money, "arts institutions had allowed themselves to be used as lubricant in a death machine."[18]

Goldin's anti-Sackler actions have thrown into high relief the fact that some of our most beloved museums are directly involved with drug pushers and other disreputable patrons. How can they justify doing so? Yet the museum world has been more than willing to take millions from the Sacklers, and in some instances have remained resolute in their continued support for their problematic benefactors, refusing to un-name properties (despite protests).[19]

Some museums are willing to accept money from loathsome people even when they know the patron's financial activities and personal politics contradict the very *mission* of the museum. The U.S. heiress and Republican Party sponsor, Rebekah Mercer, for example, has given millions to right-wing organizations that deny climate change and engage in disinformation campaigns.[20] For several years, she sat on the board of the American Museum of Natural History, a museum that has organized exhibitions about the damaging effects of climate change. It took years of protests and outside pressure before the museum convinced her to resign from the board in 2020.

WHY MUSEUMS CONDONE TOXIC PHILANTHROPY

When pushed on the issue of toxic philanthropy, cultural institutions—large and small—claim that they accept money from and turn a blind eye to dubious patrons in response to mounting budgetary woes. However, while the U.S. and U.K. arts sectors have suffered financially from government funding cuts since the 1980s and, more recently, from the impact of Covid-19, many institutions are embarking on exorbitant building projects with prestigious or celebrity "starchitects." Growth for growth's sake is valued over living within economic means; the symbolic power and prestige of dazzling public architecture are prioritized over operating expenses. The claim that blood money is essential to alleviate financial woes applies only to a few. Mega-museums such as the Met, the Museum of Modern Art (MoMA), the Whitney, and the Guggenheim possess vast endowments and should face no financial hardship. It is the smaller to mid-sized arts institutions that are struggling to stay solvent. Very few of the smaller museums are embarking on major building projects. For these institutions, the issue is not about capital campaigns or new buildings—it is about keeping the lights on.

With the growth-for-growth's-sake ideology now in place, many rely on board dues and donations for up to one-third of their annual budgets. In their most recent report looking at U.S. museums' revenue streams, the Association of Art Museum Directors (AAMD) revealed that, on average, 33% of total revenue from 2003 to 2017 derived from "private support," defined as individual and family gifts, foundation gifts, and corporate support.[21] When looking at individual board contributions, a few examples will suffice: as the *New York Times* reported in 2019, "At the Whitney, some 10 to 12% of the $60 million annual operating budget comes from board contributions. Museum of Modern Art estimates that its trustees contribute as much as 20 percent of its $175 million budget.

At the Los Angeles County Museum of Art [LACMA], officials pegged that support at about 30 percent."[22] On average, then, some 20 to 30% of a museum's revenue can come just from board contributions. As culture reporter Robin Pogrebin has argued, "Thanks to trustees' support, the public gets to enjoy Picassos, Rembrandts, Shakespeare in the Park."[23]

When challenged about toxic philanthropy, some museums shrug it off with the cynical refrain that "all money is dirty," so why bother objecting? In other words, this is just business as usual, and since their inception, most museums have relied on 1% patrons, many of whom made their money in dubious ways. They offer examples such as the Met, where the Italian-U.S. diplomat Luigi Palma di Cesnola persuaded a group of prominent New Yorkers to buy his plundered trove of Cypriot antiquities—they then appointed him director of their new public art gallery. Or they point out that J. Paul Getty of J. Paul Getty Trust was a ruthless oil tycoon; or that Sir Hans Sloane, an early patron of the British Museum, was a doctor whose vast wealth was fueled by slave labor in Jamaica. These museums argue it is an inescapable fact that many vast fortunes in the U.S.—including the business tycoons who established institutions such as the Frick Collection, Carnegie Mellon, and the Morgan Library—were built on exploitation. As Maxwell Anderson (who from 1987 to 2015 directed art museums in five cities in North America) explained in 2019, "wealth creation is rarely from someone who manufactures unicorns and rainbows."[24] So, if museums were to forensically examine the investments of every donor, would they find any suitable candidates beyond reproach? Sometimes it is difficult to determine whether a donor's money is dirty. Undoubtedly, there are complexities, and there is a long history of toxic philanthropy, but this does not make its continuation acceptable.

Another persistent argument voiced by institutions accused of whitewashing their patrons' money is that it is irrelevant where the money comes from if it is serving the public good. As one critic put it, "Would you rather visit a new Sackler-funded wing at a museum or see the Sacklers buy another private home? ... Let's not put the goal of shaming wrongdoers above the goal of furthering the common good."[25] Or, as journalist Anand Giridharadas asks, "Can it still be called bribing when millions are the recipients?"[26] Well, yes, it can. Museums are tax-exempt, charitable institutions and, as such, belong to the public, not to the trustees or donors. They have a responsibility to the public whose tax and/or membership dollars support them. If the public is demanding change and asking for accountability, then it is a museum's ethical responsibility to address their concerns. In sum, they are not serving the public good by accepting donations from 1%ers with questionable ethics.

THE MUSEUM OF MODERN ART

In August 2019, *Vulture* magazine published a list of New York City's most toxic museum boards.[27] The Met topped the ranking, principally because of its then-trustee emeritus David Koch, a businessman and aggressive backer of right-wing political efforts, including climate-change denying organizations. MoMA ranked second for its trustees Larry Fink and Leon Black—both of whom have come under fire during protests over the past several years. Fink serves as the CEO of BlackRock, a global investment and technology firm that has faced criticism from activists who accuse the company of war profiteering due to its financial holdings in major weapons manufacturers, including Boeing, Raytheon, and General Dynamics.[28] Equally contentious is BlackRock's role as a major investor in the nation's two largest private prison corporations—GEO Group and CoreCivic—whose profit-driven operations disproportionately exploit incarcerated people of color.[29] Fink's fortune also depends on investments in companies (including CoreCivic) that contract with U.S. Immigration and Customs Enforcement (ICE), the U.S. government agency widely denounced for its mass detentions of undocumented immigrants at the U.S.-Mexico border, under harrowing conditions.[30] BlackRock also holds investments in Lockheed Martin, a company that has provided arms to the Israeli army, including F-35 fighter jets, since 1971—an association that many people consider unacceptable.[31] As of 2026, Fink remains a MoMA board member.[32]

The other MoMA board member on the *Vulture* magazine list is billionaire investor and former chair of the museum's board, Leon Black. He was the co-founder of the private equity firm Apollo Global Management, which has investments in General Electric—a company that supplies the Israeli army with military equipment. Pro-Palestine campaigners, who have agitated at the museum since 2021, have found this particularly egregious.[33] Black was directly affiliated with disgraced sex offender Jeffrey Epstein, and has been the subject of a series of campaigns spearheaded by the International Imagination of Anti-National Anti-Imperialist Feelings, the coalition of activists that have been leading "Strike MoMA" demonstrations since 2021. Of particular interest has been Black's payment to Epstein of $158 million for tax and estate planning services between 2012 and 2017, that is, *after* Epstein's first conviction in 2008 for sexual misconduct.[34] Black has also been accused of war profiteering because of his investments in Blackwater (now Constellis Holdings), a security contractor with a gruesome track record in Iraq.[35] In 2021, Black was accused of sexual abuse in a widely publicized lawsuit; the following year, he was accused of raping a woman at Epstein's Manhattan townhouse.[36]

As the scrutiny of Black's finances and sexual misconduct intensified in 2021, Chinese artist Ai Weiwei said he would not exhibit at MoMA if Black remained as board chair, and an open letter calling for his removal was signed by more than 150 artists, including Nan Goldin, Nicole Eisenman, William Powhida (Fig. 17), Andrea Fraser, and Michael Rakowitz.[37] After two years of protests, Black announced in March 2021 that he would not stand for reelection as MoMA's board chairman; in April 2021 he stepped down as chairman and CEO of Apollo Global Management. As of 2026, Black remains on the MoMA board.

In April 2021, MoMA announced that Marie-Josée Kravis, former executive director of the conservative think tank Hudson Institute and ally of Donald Trump, would be Black's successor, thereby reconfirming MoMA's lack of concern about the business practices of its board members. Kravis and her husband have direct ties to the fossil fuel industry—a point highlighted in June 2023 in a protest outside MoMA's annual Party in the Garden. Activists erected a 20-foot-tall handmade oil rig topped with a reproduction of a painting of a gas station engulfed in flames by Ed Ruscha, who was one of the gala's honorees.[38] Text overlaid on the painting read, "MOMA DROP KRAVIS." As gala attendees arrived, the protesters chanted slogans like "We need clean air, not another billionaire" and "Henry Kravis you can't hide, we charge you with ecocide."[39] As of 2026, Kravis remains as board chair.

So, given the extensive negative publicity, why did it take Leon Black over two years to resign as chair of the board? Why did the MoMA board and its then-director Glenn Lowry not encourage him to resign far earlier? There are several reasons. It is well known that Black contributes massive sums of money to MoMA, including $40 million towards the museum's 2019 expansion project (for which he was thanked by having the film center named after him), and that is in addition to his board dues of $10 million, annually. Black also loans major works of art to MoMA, including an 1895 version of Edvard Munch's famous painting *The Scream*, which he purchased for $120 million at auction. Black's financial contributions are staggering and given MoMA's continual quest for grandeur (in scale and with its collection), it is understood that his money is indispensable.

Ultimately, the question remains: how can an educational, tax-exempt institution such as MoMA tolerate individuals like Fink,

Kravis, and Black on their boards? Do they not comprehend, as the activists CodePink explained, that their museum practices are "complicit with oligarchical structures"?[40] In an open letter to MoMA from April 2021, the "Strike MoMA" organizers challenged the institution's continued support of billionaires "whose names have become synonymous with patriarchal violence, the carceral state, climate destruction, neo-feudal landlordism, and direct support for the NYPD Foundation."[41] They ask that the future institution, which they refer to as "Post-MoMA," should consider being "controlled by workers, communities, and artists rather than oligarchs."[42]

THE WHITNEY MUSEUM OF AMERICAN ART

While trustees of the American Museum of Natural History (AMNH) and MoMA received sustained negative press, the most widely publicized of these museum-board protests in the U.S. to date was leveled against Warren Kanders, former vice-chairman of the board of the Whitney Museum of American Art. Since 2012, Kanders has been chairman and CEO of Safariland, a U.S. manufacturer of tear gas, which they supply to the U.S. government. In November 2018, U.S. border patrol agents fired Safariland tear gas at asylum seekers along the U.S.-Mexico border, launching it into crowds that included children.[43] Then, after an article published in *Hyperallergic* revealed the incident's connection to the Whitney board member, around a hundred Whitney staff members signed an open letter demanding that leadership remove him. It read, in part, "We work to bring in artists who are immigrants and artists of color to the collection .... Upon learning of Kanders's business dealings, many of us working on these initiatives feel uncomfortable in our positions," and declared, "To remain silent is to be complicit."[44]

Kanders fired back at the signees in his own letter. "I am not the problem," he wrote. "While my company and the museum have distinct missions, both are important contributors to our society."[45] No one disputes that museums "contribute to society." But can Kanders seriously claim that his company, Safariland, does the same when it manufactures an arsenal of weapons used to suppress and kill civilians? Amid the fiasco, Whitney director Adam Weinberg sent a memo to staff and trustees that evaded the controversy—indeed, the letter did not even mention Kanders. He described the museum as "a place of great promise, hopes and dreams, often against great odds."[46] Without directly addressing the employees' letter, Weinberg also stated that "staff does not appoint or remove board members," and explained that he understood if some staff members opted to resign from their positions at the museum.[47] He also asked his staff to simply accept that our culture is full of "profound contradictions."[48]

Safariland weapons were also used against protesters at Standing Rock in the U.S. and, in 2019, against pro-Palestinian protesters in the Gaza Strip.[49] In sum, Kanders has openly profited from activities that directly contradict the museum's stated commitment to diversity and inclusion.

Over a six-month period in 2019, activist groups, artists, and the public demanded Kanders step down from the Whitney board, accusing the museum of whitewashing his reputation. The protests, demands, and resulting publicity storm converged with the museum's biennial, where the London-based collective Forensic Architecture presented *Triple-Chaser*, a video exposing Kanders's unethical business dealings. As the *New York Times* explained, "The video suggested that by selling bullets to the Israeli government, one of Mr. Kanders's companies may have abetted what United Nations investigators have called possible war crimes."[50] The activist collective Decolonize This Place (DTP), the most vocal opponents of Kanders, staged highly visible actions—unfurling banners across the museum's façade and galleries (Fig. 18), maintaining months-long pickets outside the institution, and protesting directly in front of Kanders's townhouse, chanting: "Warren Kanders, you can't hide. We charge you with genocide." A month later, the DTP activists delivered an open letter to the Whitney, accusing the institution of being complicit in Kanders's injustices. "We know this goes beyond Kanders," the signatories wrote. "He is a stand-in for an entire system." The letter argued that museums, "as structured today, are undemocratic, ignoring broad public interests to favor the rich."[51] Despite weekly demonstrations, Kanders refused to step down.

In July 2019, pressure on Kanders escalated when artists and writers Hannah Black, Tobi Haslett, and Ciarán Finlayson published "The Tear Gas Biennial" in *Artforum*, calling on all seventy-five participating artists to pull out of the exhibition in protest.[52] Eventually, eight artists, including the high-profile Nicole Eisenman, requested that their work be removed from the museum on the grounds that they refused "further complicity with Kanders and his technologies of violence."[53]

The Kanders debacle ended in July 2019, with Kanders resigning from his position on the Whitney's board. In his resignation letter, he presented himself as the victim, citing "the targeted campaign of attacks against me and my company."[54] He wrote: "The politicized and oftentimes toxic environment in which we find ourselves, across all spheres of public discourse, including the art community, puts the work of this board in great jeopardy." He added, "I hope you assume the responsibility that your position bestows upon you and find the leadership to maintain the integrity of this museum."[55] This, after months of protests.[56]

Kanders's resignation and the MoMA board controversies, along with the surrounding media frenzy, sent shockwaves throughout the museum sector. As *New York Times* critic Robin Pogrebin explains, "If board members can be forced out because of what they do for a living, what does that mean for cultural institutions that depend on their generosity to survive?"[57] The fear in the museum sector at that time was that if an institution becomes too precious about who can serve on boards, then it will become increasingly difficult to attract and retain board members. Major donors may back away from donations to museums for fear of facing controversy. Or worse for the museum, donors may direct their giving toward other worthy causes, such as health or educational initiatives. In other words, there was a fear of effective altruism, which, some argued, if it gained traction, could put the arts out of business.

In the end, the protests over the Sacklers, Fink, Kravis, Black, Kanders, and other board members have activated a public reckoning. It is clear that by not asking these patrons to step down earlier, the museums in question demonstrated their collusion with dirty money.

CORPORATE SPONSORS

It is not just art patrons such as the Sacklers, Mercer, Black, and Kanders who are being accused of using museums to whitewash their reputations. Art-washing is also practiced by corporations with dubious business activities or nefarious aims. In the case of corporate sponsors such as Purdue Pharma, the company's charitable contributions are often being used to mitigate their unpopularity. While the pharmaceutical industry is among the most criticized in the U.S., it is also one of the most active in charitable giving.[58] Many corporations, including the big oil companies, boast that they have departments and programs dedicated to "corporate social responsibility" (CSR), which make charitable donations. Economist John List has argued that CSR leads to "moral licensing"—or that doing good cancels out any negative acts.[59] Corporations frequently deploy philanthropy as a form of "tax-exempt lobbying," boosting donations in congressional districts whenever those districts' representatives gain seats on committees tied to the company's business interests.[60]

BRITISH PETROLEUM

Corporate sponsors of cultural institutions have been taken to task for decades by climate change activists. Since the 2010s, there has been increased scrutiny of corporate donors such as oil giants British Petroleum (BP) and Shell. In her book *Artwash: Big Oil and the Arts*, artist and campaigner Mel Evans contends that fossil fuel companies are bankrolling arts sponsorships worldwide on an "epidemic" scale as a "cynical PR strategy" to launder their reputations.[61]

In the U.K., BP is considered a particularly heinous offender by climate change activists. BP is the third largest contributor to climate change of any oil company in history, preceded only by Shell and Exxon.[62] Its drilling and extractive activities have been linked to countless human and environmental abuses directly threatening the lives, lands, and cultures of all people who share our planet. The most notorious of these abuses was the 2010 BP Deepwater Horizon Oil Spill, which is the single largest environmental disaster in the world to date. In 2017, the company successfully lobbied the Trump administration to open up all U.S. coastal waters to offshore drilling and to expand the company's drilling in the Arctic—to the horror of many citizens across the globe who care deeply about the environment. In 2017, protests by the Sioux and their allies began against the Dakota Access Pipeline, a 1,200-mile pipeline, built by BP, that extends directly through the Sioux's Standing Rock reservation. (Safariland tear gas was used against these Standing Rock protesters.) Moreover, BP has turned its back on the green energy revolution. According to a 2022 report commissioned by Greenpeace, BP was 97% invested in fossil fuels and allocated less than 2% of their annual profits to solar and wind power.[63] In 2019, BP committed to a 40% reduction of carbon emissions by 2030. But, in 2022, the company backtracked on that commitment, offering instead a less ambitious reduction of 25%.[64] Yet, contradictorily, in 2024 there was a statement on their website which read: "Our purpose is reimagining energy for people and our planet. We want to help the world reach net zero and improve people's lives." In February 2025, they announced a strategic shift (no doubt emboldened by today's conservative politicians who deny climate change), further reducing its planned annual spending on low-carbon energy projects, while increasing investments in oil and gas production.[65] Meanwhile, BP reports billions in profit annually, while receiving exorbitant tax credits.[66]

Since the early 2010s, fossil fuel-free activist groups in the U.K. —such as Liberate Tate, Art Not Oil Coalition, Extinction Rebellion, BP or Not BP, Platform London, Culture Unstained, and many others—

have been staging interventions at major U.K. museums that accept BP funding. Since these anti-oil protests began, several institutions in London have disassociated from BP, including Tate, which ended their sponsorship deal with the corporation in 2017. Since then, the National Galleries of Scotland, the Royal Shakespeare Company (London), the National Portrait Gallery (London), and the Royal Opera House (London) have also ended their fossil fuel partnerships.[67]

The British Museum, however, has refused to sever ties. While there had been much speculation recently that the historic partnership between the two organizations had ended, in December 2023, the museum announced a $63 million partnership with the oil giant.[68] In its statement, the museum announced that it will allocate BP's funding toward advancing its environmental initiatives, as part of its "Rosetta Project," a $1.2 billion master plan designed to address numerous infrastructural inefficiencies in the museum's 170-year-old building.[69] The ten-year master plan—funded, in part, by BP—includes a large-scale renovation of the museum's aging electrical, plumbing, and mechanical systems, the redevelopment of a third of its galleries, a new government-funded Energy Center, and a new Architectural Research Collection.[70] These goals are intended to phase out the museum's reliance on fossil fuels, the museum reported, and to chart a path toward achieving "net zero" operations.[71] The British Museum has defended its decision to maintain the partnership with BP, stating that corporate funding is essential to the master plan. In 2019, when queried about the museum's continued relationship with BP, the British Museum's then-director, Hartwig Fischer, explained that BP's funding has helped "create learning opportunities," and that "this sort of support is vital to [the British Museum's] mission."[72] Fischer made no attempt to explain how he reconciled the museum's cultural mission with BP's record of environmental plunder.

News of the December 2023 deal came as a shock to environmental campaigners in the U.K. Despite the decade-long protests by fossil fuel-free activist groups at the museum, their highly publicized objections to the partnership had been ignored. The director of Greenpeace UK described the partnership as "one of the biggest, most brazen greenwashing sponsorship deals the sector has ever seen."[73]

The issue of unethical sponsorship from fossil fuel companies is not just specific to BP. Shell, Statoil, Equinor, and DONG Energy also sponsor arts and culture at U.K. institutions such as the National Gallery, the Science Museum, and the Natural History Museum in order to "greenwash" their reputations.

Another controversy over fossil fuel sponsorship took place in April 2021, when London's Science Museum Group (SMG) faced backlash over an exhibition on climate change titled *Our Future Planet*, sponsored by oil company Shell. Activists from Culture Unstained argued that the museum's emphasis on climate change was fundamentally undercut by its sponsorship from Shell—a corporation whose continued exploitation of fossil fuels directly accelerates the climate crisis. What struck many as especially disquieting was the exhibition press release's assertion that Shell "aims to become a net-zero emissions energy business by 2050," even as the company actively perpetuates fossil fuel production and marketing.[74] To imply that Shell is (or will ever be) an environmentally friendly company is beyond disingenuous. The partnership with the SMG was clearly Shell's attempt to greenwash its reputation, and, as one commentator noted, the Science Museum is "supping with the devil."[75]

When London's Science Museum announced plans in October 2021 for a new green energy gallery sponsored by Adani Green Energy—a subsidiary of the Adani Group—critics reacted sharply, citing the company's substantial investments in coal mining and power as incongruous with the exhibition's climate focus.[76] The new exhibition space, Energy Revolution: The Adani Green Energy Gallery, which opened in March 2023, is intended to examine pathways toward a more sustainable future in response to the climate crisis.[77] (The Energy Revolution gallery replaced the Atmosphere Gallery, the museum's first permanent exhibition dedicated to climate change, which opened in 2010. That gallery was sponsored by Shell oil.[78]) The museum's partnership with Adani ignored the company's ongoing destruction of Indigenous Australian lands, where its coal mining activities continue to expand despite widespread protests.[79]

Two years after the sponsorship deal, in March 2023, Fossil Free Science Museum, a coalition of climate activist groups, published a book called *Science Museum Group: An Unravelling Tragedy*, which features extracts from an internal report, produced by the SMG in December 2020, which showed that it was fully aware of the damaging impact of Adani's coal mining activities on the environment, as well as allegations of human rights violations and poor conditions for workers.[80] Despite the damning evidence in the report, the SMG moved ahead with the deal. In July 2024, the SMG announced an end to their sponsorship deal with oil giant Equinor. As of this writing, activists are still calling for the board to divest from its sponsorship ties with Adani and BP.[81]

AIRBNB

A 2019 sponsorship deal between the rental property conglomerate Airbnb and the Louvre, Paris, similarly met with public outcry. The museum endorsed a marketing campaign with Airbnb whereby winners of a competition could spend a night in the Louvre and enjoy a "cozy Renaissance-inspired aperitif, while relaxing," the organizers explained, "on a sumptuous Parisian lounge sofa, listening to the atmospheric sounds of French music on vinyl records."[82] In addition, guests enjoyed a private visit to iconic works like the *Mona Lisa* and *Venus de Milo*, a dinner and acoustic concert in Napoleon's apartments, and an overnight stay under the Louvre's iconic glass pyramid.[83]

The French public was outraged that their beloved institution was being privatized by an international real estate predator. Ian Brossat, Paris's then-city deputy mayor in charge of housing, criticized the Louvre over the sponsorship, calling it a "political gesture that is both disastrous and shocking."[84] The Louvre's decision was particularly unwelcome in a city where, as Brossat explained, "an increasing number of its inhabitants are more aware of the adverse consequences of Airbnb on the Parisian real estate market."[85] Airbnb was also called out for not complying with French law and for its practice of tax optimization. Brossat had been mounting a long-running campaign against Airbnb, explaining to *Le Parisien* in September 2018 that he wanted to ban Airbnb rental apartments in the center of Paris. "When we see that in the first, second, third and fourth arrondissements, 26% of the properties are no longer occupied by Parisians, we have to ask—do we accept that Airbnb is taking control of entire neighborhoods in Paris?" he queried.[86]

Museums seem to have become increasingly "married to the mob," as Rhonda Lieberman puts it.[87] By allowing real estate predators, tear gas magnates, and opioid profiteers on boards, accepting gifts from climate change deniers and earth destroyers, some museums have become enablers of dirty money. To change this will take a widespread collective revolution. These problems are structural, embedded into museums' foundational identities, so what is needed, I believe, is the de-corporatization of museums themselves.

THE CORPORATIZATION OF MUSEUMS

The corporatization of museums emerged in the 1980s, when art institutions began cultivating partnerships with corporate sponsors and major businesses, signaling their increasing alignment with—and subordination to—the interests of capitalism.The business values that

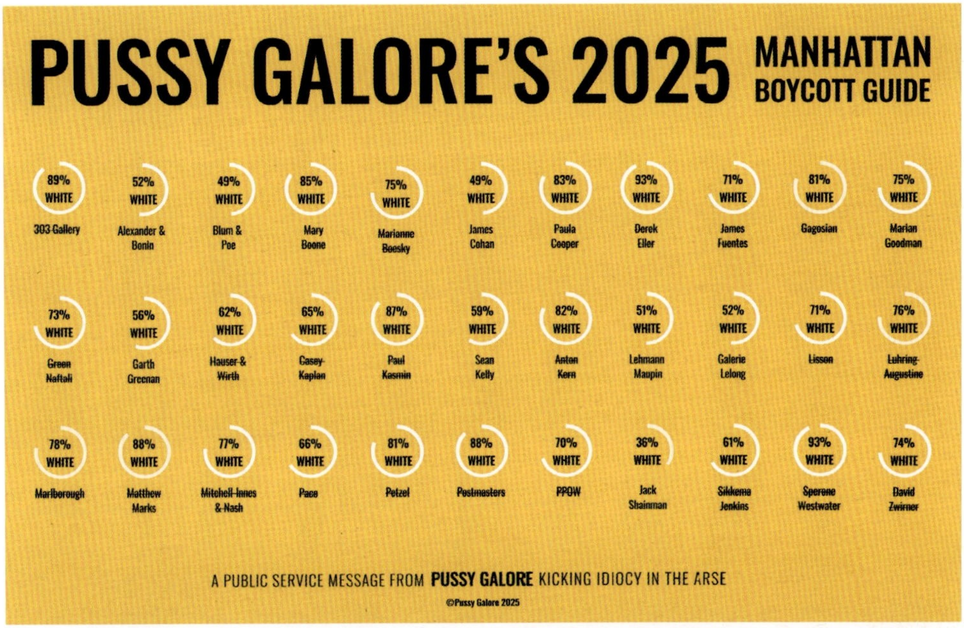

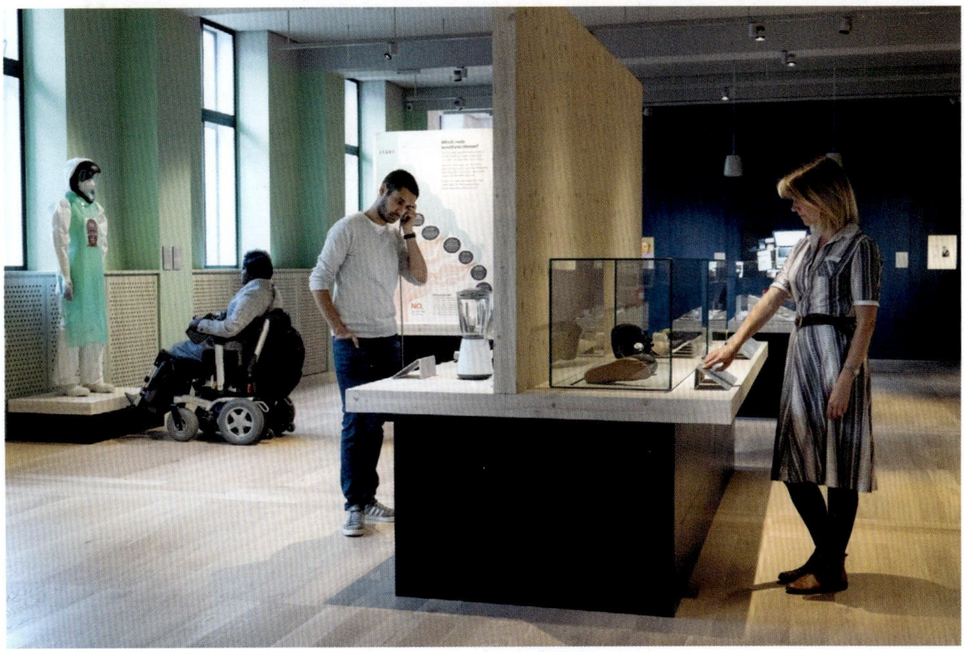

9 Pussy Galore, *Manhattan Boycott Guide*, 2025.

10 *Being Human*, exhibition installation, Wellcome Collection, London, 2019–present.

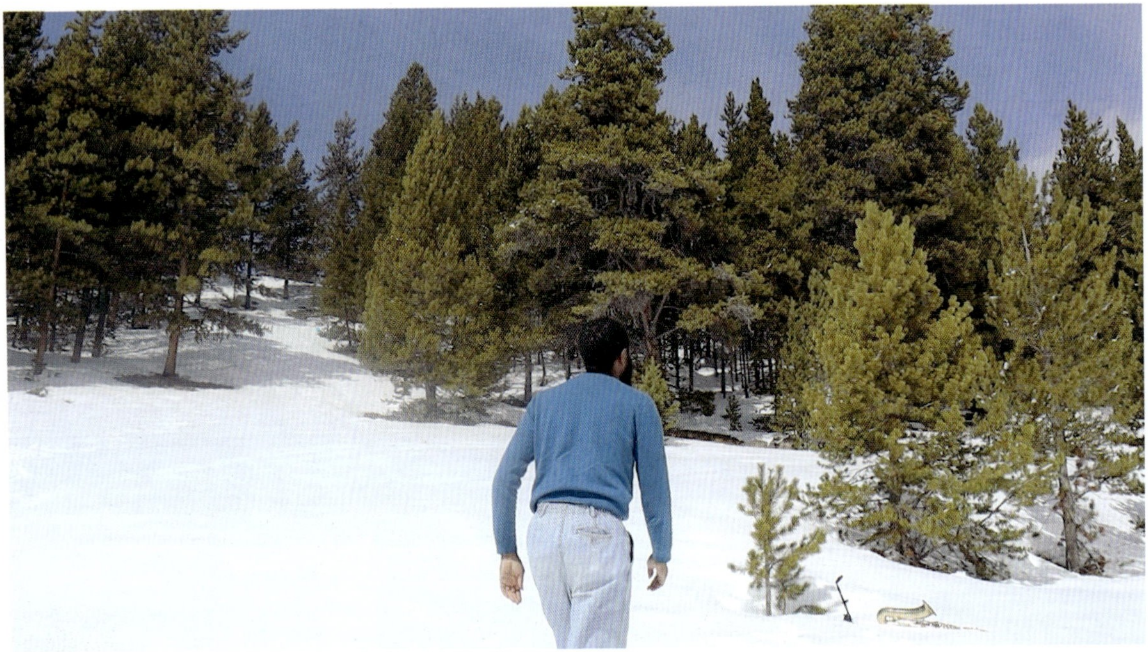

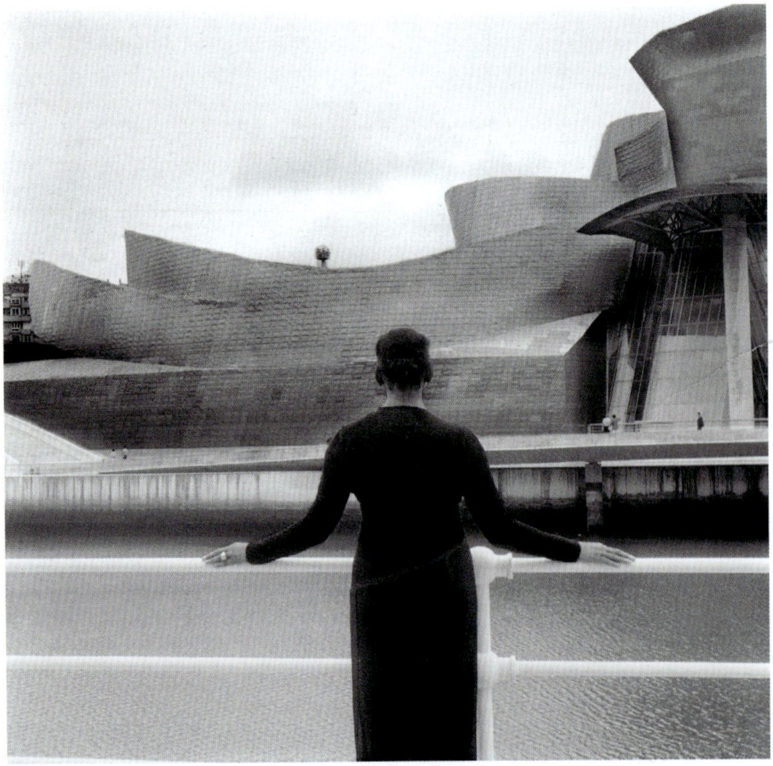

11 JJJJJerome Ellis, *Impediment Is Information*, single-channel video, 2021.

12 Carrie Mae Weems, *Guggenheim Bilbao*, 2008, from the *Museum Series*, 2006–present.

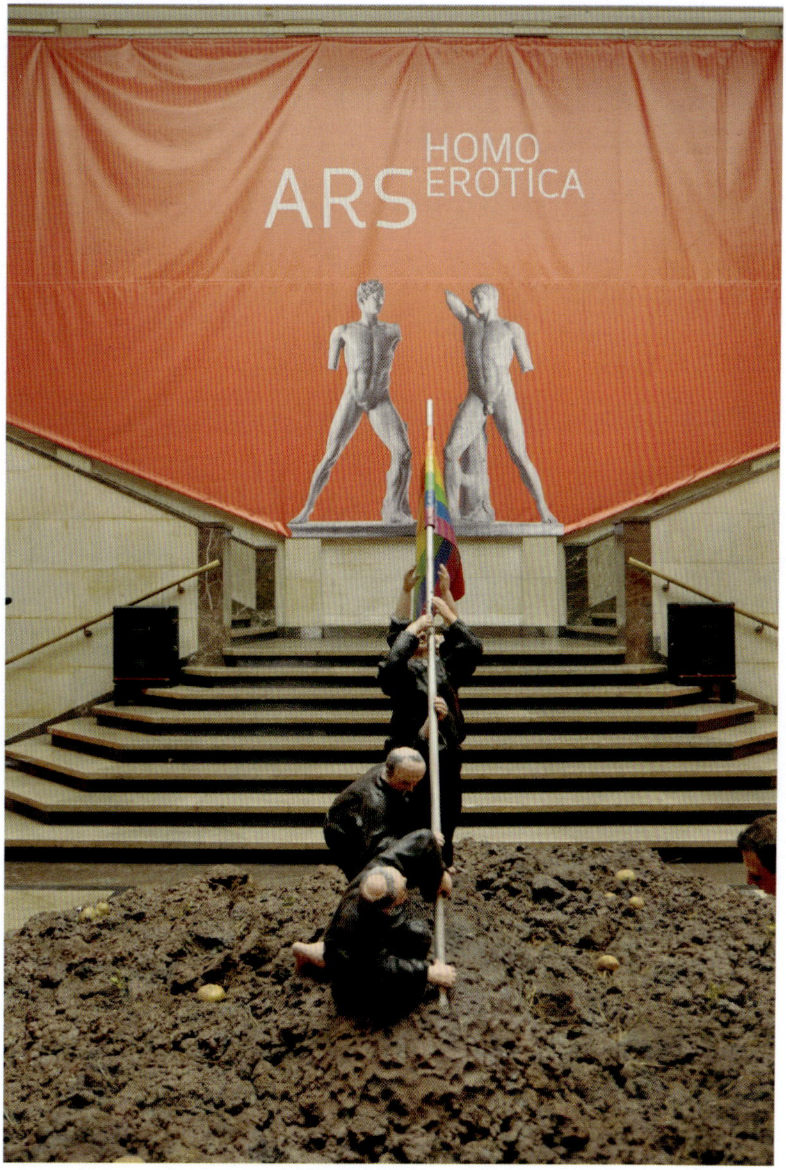

13 *Ars Homo Erotica*, exhibition installation, National Museum in Warsaw, 2010.

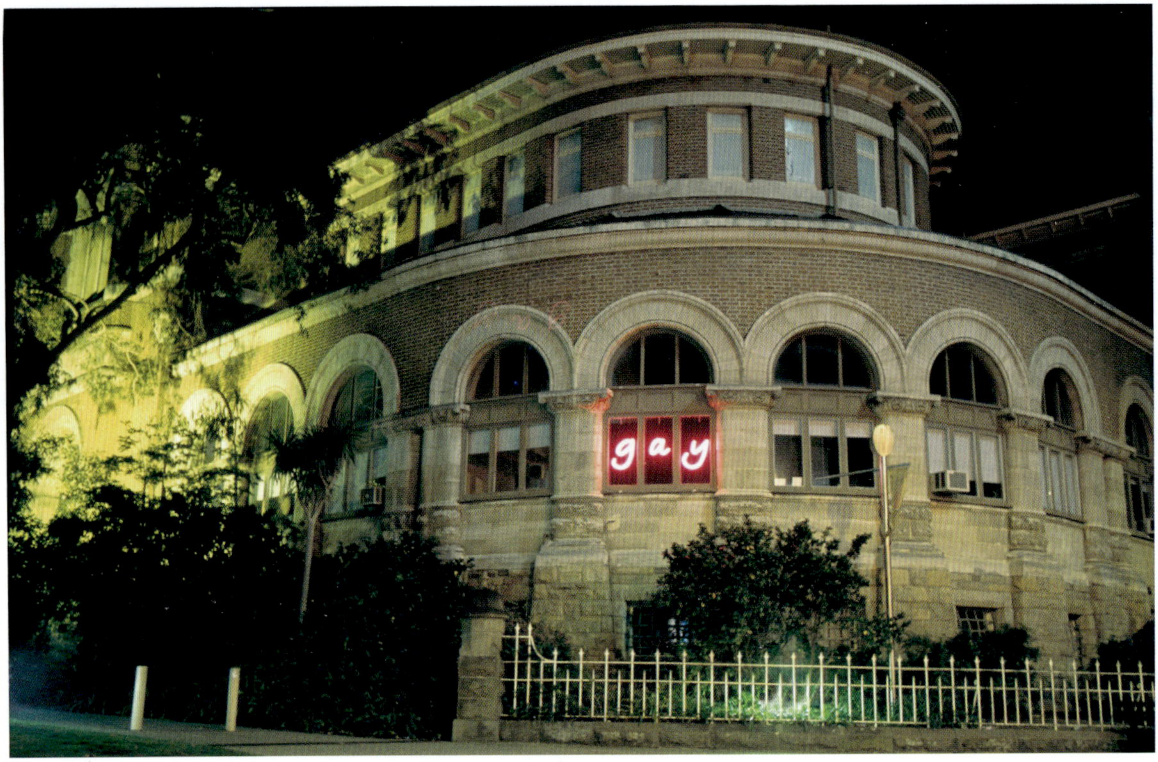

14 Jo Darbyshire, "GAY" neon artwork, from the exhibition *The Gay Museum*, Western Australian Museum, Perth, 2003.

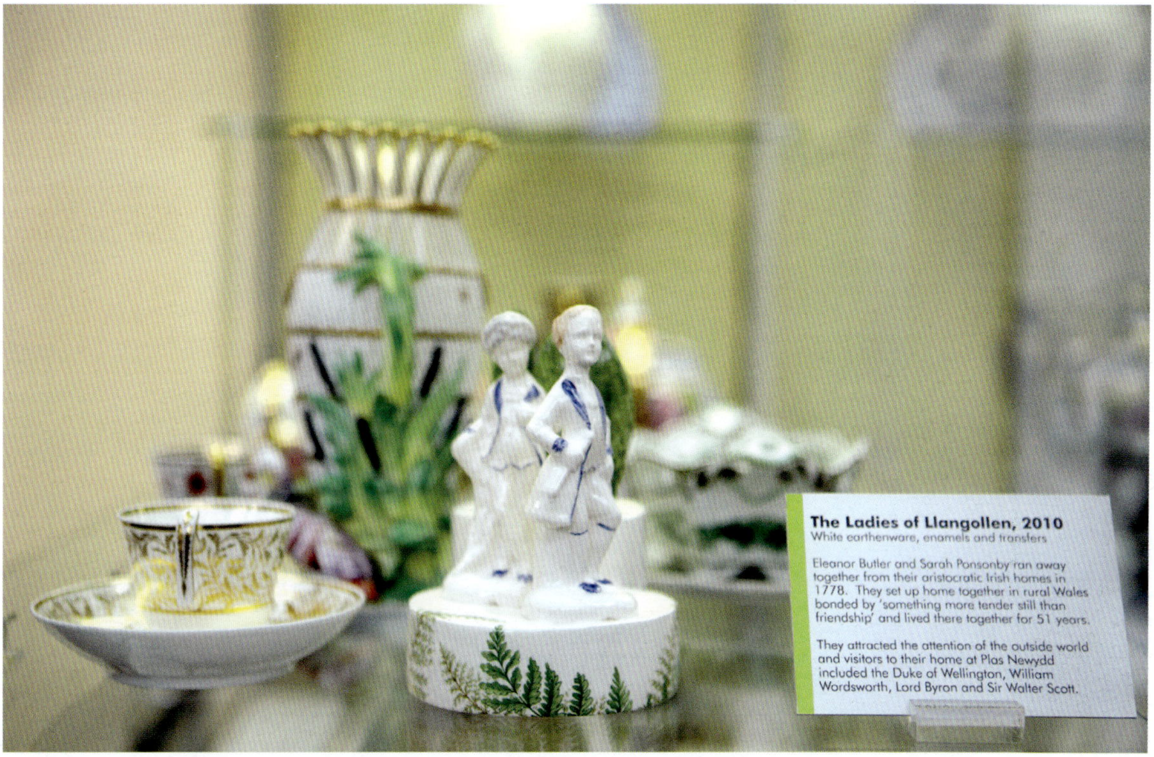

15 Matt Smith, *The Ladies of Llangollen*, from the exhibition *Queering the Museum*, Birmingham Museum & Art Gallery, 2010–11.

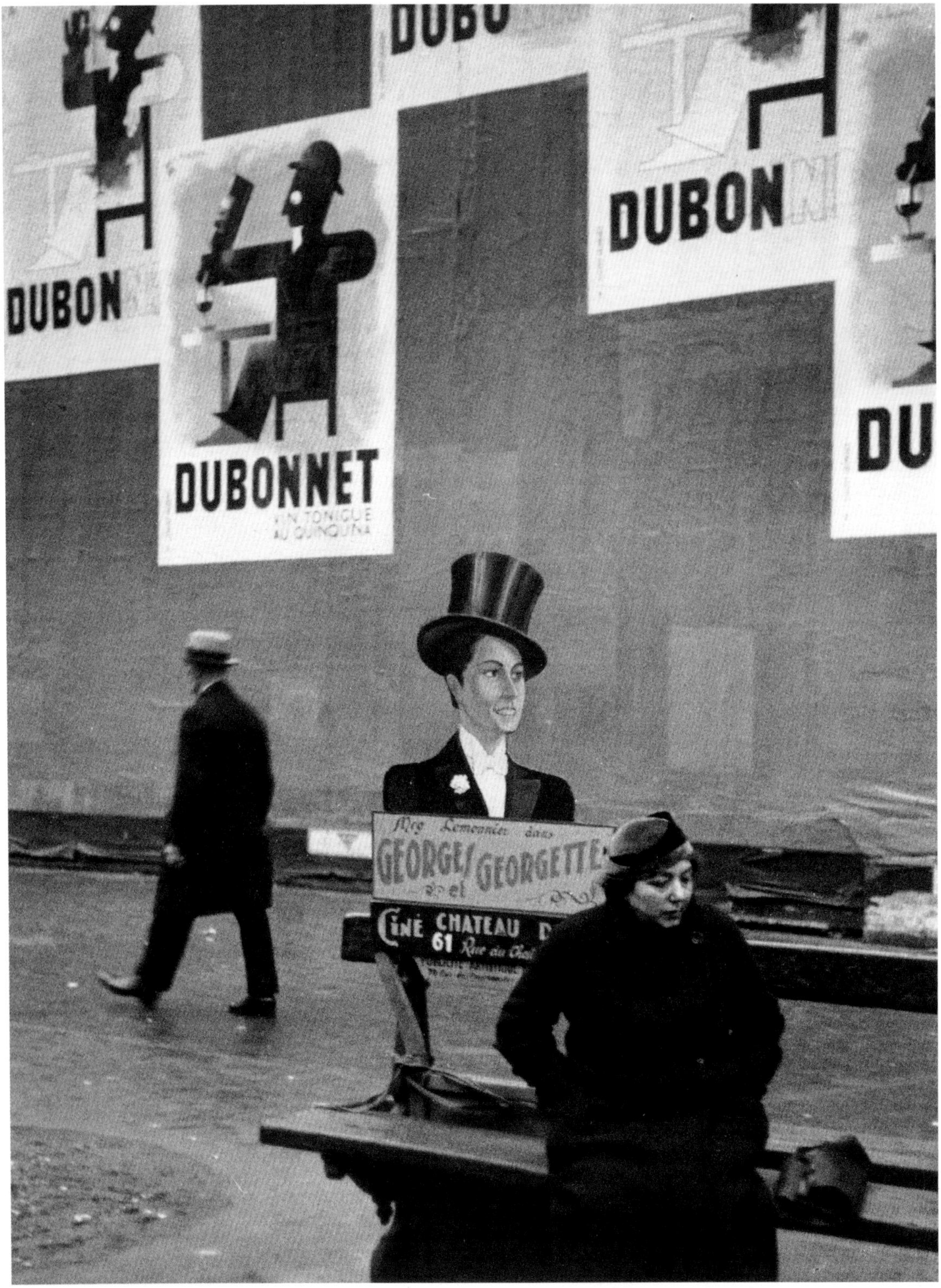
DUBO
DUBON
DUBON
DUBONNET
VIN TONIQUE
AU QUINQUINA
DU
GEORGES
et
GEORGETTE
CINÉ CHATEAU
61

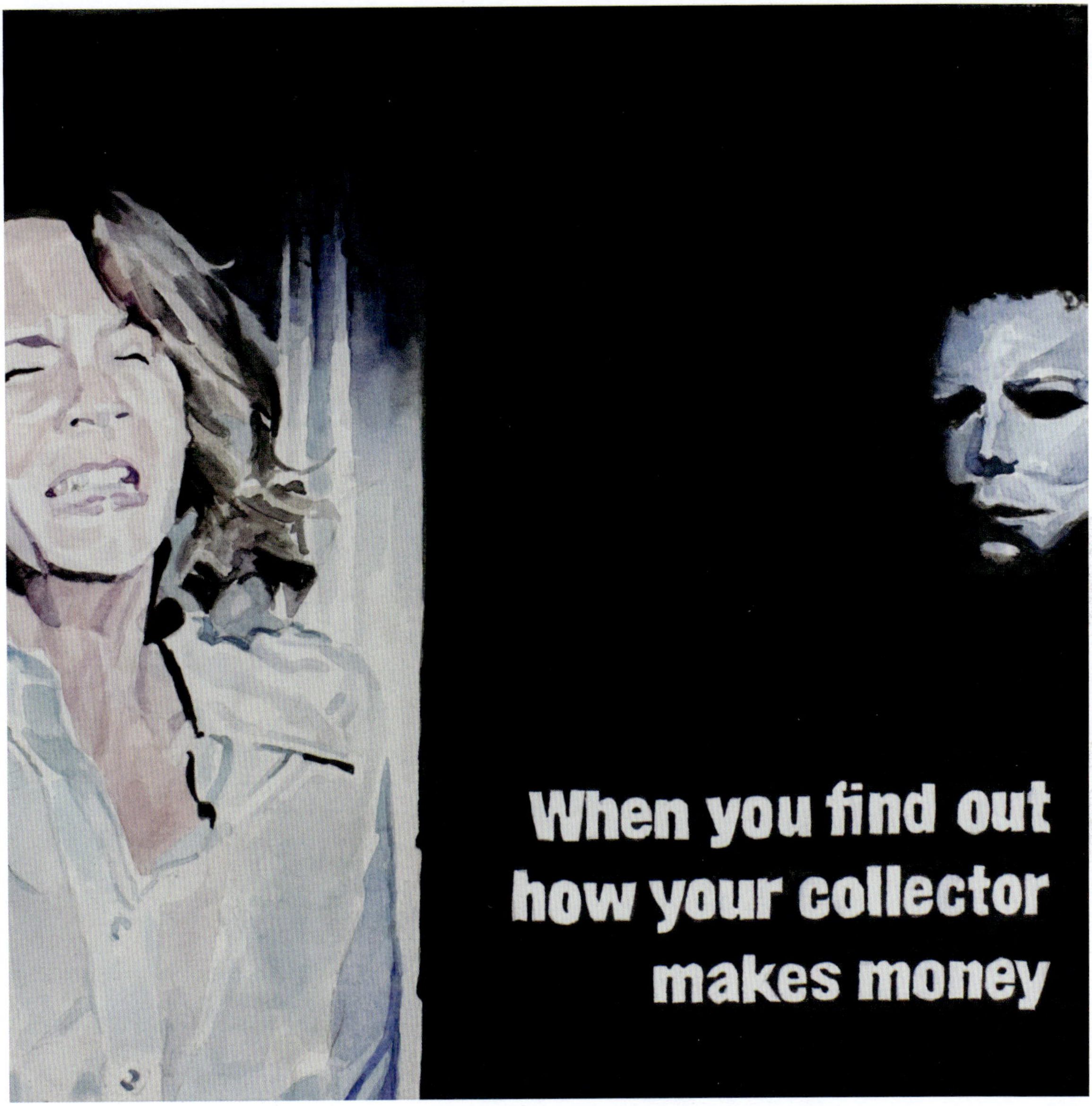

16 André Kertész, *On the Boulevards, Paris (Dubonnet)*, 1934.

17 William Powhida, *Collectors (Halloween)*, 2019.

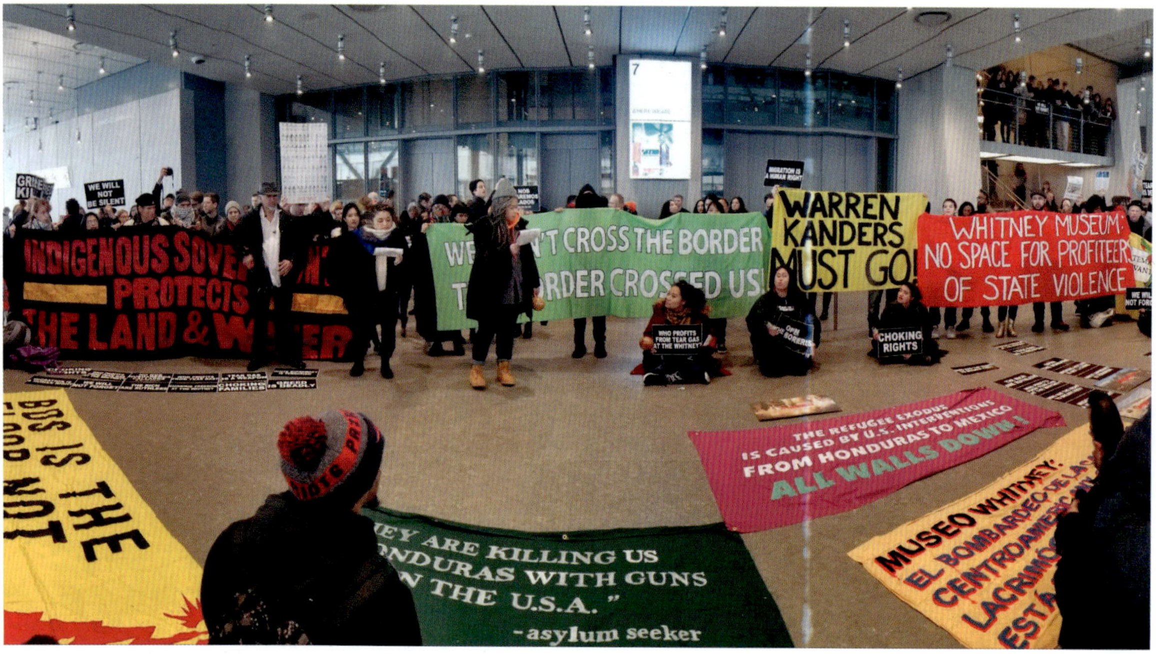

18 Decolonize This Place,
Crisis of the Whitney,
December 2018.

emerged then permeate every level of the museum world today, from curatorial integrity and capital projects to hiring strategies and labor relations. The marketplace model is manifest in, among other things, grossly unequal salaries, hierarchical and for-profit management style, board make-up of 1%ers, massively expensive capital projects, populist and blockbuster exhibitions designed to drive earned revenue, and global expansionist models.

Today's museums operate increasingly like corporate enterprises, embracing a business model that measures value primarily in terms of revenue and relentless expansion. The corporatist focus has overshadowed qualitative analysis. The institution's earned income (from shops; cafés; traveling exhibitions; admission fees, when charged; membership dues; space rentals; and blockbuster exhibitions) has become more important than the quality of curated exhibitions, especially those with academic integrity, which might draw smaller crowds and less revenue. The previously referenced 2018 AAMD report, which looked at museums' average revenue streams, demonstrated that on average an American museum derived 30% of its annual income from earned revenue from 2003 to 2017.[88] However, earnings should be watched carefully. In the U.S., because museums are categorized by the Internal Revenue Service as nonprofit and tax-exempt, they must pay unrelated business income tax on their profits. If they start operating more like businesses than nonprofits, these financial advantages could be at risk. The corporatist growth model and art-washing are not just morally wrong, they can also have negative tax implications in the U.S.

Why did museums become corporatized in the 1980s? Why did the private sector move in and assume control? The simple answer is that many (but not all) museums were struggling financially. In the U.S., at least, this coincided with massive cuts in arts funding from the National Endowment for the Arts (NEA). Museums turned to private patrons and corporate sponsors for a bailout. Tax breaks allowing private and corporate donors to write off the appreciated value of their donated possessions made philanthropy attractive to the wealthiest 1%. The situation worsened in the 1980s when right-wing fanatics such as former Republican Senator Jesse Helms censored a number of artists, including Robert Mapplethorpe, Andres Serrano, and Karen Finley, which itself resulted in funding cuts to the NEA. These additional government cuts deepened dependence on the wealthiest 1%.[89]

During the 1980s, a financial innovation emerged whereby art collectors could borrow money using their artworks as collateral—effectively rendering fine art into liquid capital.[90] The art-credit system, then, enabled artworks to serve as assets—alongside stocks, boats, and jewelry—that could be pledged for credit, thereby blurring the line between aesthetic and financial value.[91] The system also allowed for some questionable practices, including "flipping" artworks—that is, reselling artworks quickly and for profit. The art market is famously one of the largest unregulated markets worldwide, which allows for some unsavory business dealings and tax havens. During the Great Recession of 2008, the art and luxury goods markets initially experienced sharp contractions before rapidly rebounding, reflecting both speculative investment behavior and sustained consumer enthusiasm for high-value assets.[92] As German historian and art critic Isabelle Graw noted in her book *High Price: Art Between the Market and Celebrity Culture*, "Practices that in other fields would be denounced as criminal or insider-trading are commonplace in the art market."[93]

The corporatization of art museums is reflected in the rise of museum directors who often have neither expertise in the museum sector nor (in the case of art museums) extensive knowledge of art history; increasingly, some directors are hired for their business prowess and MBA degrees. Or, pressured by the governing board in the endless quest for growth, directors are now frequently hired for their expertise in fundraising and populist marketing strategies. Boards of governors shaped by corporate logic implement business-style incentive structures, offering directors bonuses for achieving or exceeding performance targets. Thus, labor relations in corporatized museums mirror those of for-profit corporations, where directors are often grossly overpaid and (sometimes) receive valuable assets as part of their contracts (Glenn Lowry, then-director of the Museum of Modern Art, for example, made $2 million in 2023 and was also the recipient of a $6 million rent-free apartment).[94] The disparity has become so severe that museum staff across the U.S. are unionizing for "living wages," with protests at the New Museum of Contemporary Art, Philadelphia Museum of Art, Art Institute of Chicago, Museum of Contemporary Art in Los Angeles, and MoMA, among others. In fact, in 2018, MoMA's annual Party in the Garden, a fancy fundraiser, was picketed by underpaid MoMA workers, who protested, "Modern art, ancient wages."[95] Meanwhile, Lowry, who had raised $450 million for a building expansion, was given a substantial bonus. Disgruntlement over salary differentials resulted in a publicly leaked spreadsheet in 2019, in which U.S. museum professionals listed their salaries, throwing into high relief extreme pay inequities.[96] The assumption in the museum sector is that employees are there for the love of art, not for salary. It is understood that people will make sacrifices to work in the arts sector, which is why it appeals more to individuals who are either independently wealthy or have other means of subsidizing their measly earnings. And a museum's nonprofit status is often used to justify the allocation of barely livable wages, despite the high salaries of upper management.

Another indicator of the corporatization of museums is the high price of museum admission. For-profit boards cannot tolerate free admission (with the exception, offered by some institutions, of a limited number of free entry dates per month). As of 2026, MoMA, the Guggenheim, the Met, and the Whitney charge $30 for adult admission, the Louvre raised its standard admission price in 2024 from €17 to €22 (and will be implementing a surcharge for non-EU visitors in 2026), and the Alte Nationalgalerie in Berlin increased its admission price by 10% in 2024.[97] Meanwhile, the federally subsidized U.K. national museums are free. These high prices at mega-museums in the U.S. are shockingly elitist and classist. And that's just the price for general admission; it often doubles when there is a blockbuster exhibition. Governing boards appear to care less about the content of the exhibition than its ability to drive revenue. Hence the endless exhibitions of Impressionism and Picasso with large gift shops placed strategically at the exits.

Many of those who now govern museums have minimal knowledge of museum practices and are often uninformed about the challenges of nonprofit management. The for-profit mindset views a nonprofit as a business in need of their expert assistance, especially given nonprofits' often precarious financial situations. This means CEO-board members are keen to run the museums as businesses and often try to assume control of day-to-day operations. (I have experienced this first hand.) This museum-as-business model often assumes a hierarchical management style—senior management make the decisions, with little or no input from those lower down the chain of command. The (now ubiquitous) practice among museums of hiring headhunting companies to source candidates for senior leadership positions (a common practice in the corporate world) is a further sign of their corporatization. Consider the qualified candidates who may have been dismissed outright simply because museums rely on the same recruiters used by large corporations. After more than three decades working in the industry and having had conversations with dozens of headhunters, I have only known of one recruiter who had worked in a museum.

Another sign of the corporatization of museums is the high cost of securing a position on the board. Much like a golf club, the more expensive the annual dues, the more prestigious the position is perceived to be. And the more prestigious, the more unattainable, the more coveted. On top of which, the limited number of board seats makes them even more valuable. According to the *New York Times* (2019), the most recent figures available show that securing a place on the Metropolitan Museum of Art's board requires an upfront donation of $15 million plus annual contributions; at MoMA, the entry cost is $10 million; and at the Whitney, a new trustee is expected to give $5 million to join and $200,000 each year to remain on the board.[98] (I am referring here to the mega-museums. A board seat at mid-sized museums, such as the Kalamazoo Institute of Arts or Columbus Museum of Art, for example, generally runs between $25,000 and $100,000 annually.[99]) The substantive board fees do not include fees associated with galas, tax-deductible gifts of art, or donations to capital campaigns. Trustees unable to contribute from their own funds are expected to raise an equivalent sum from outside sources or secure coveted artworks for the museum—a practice in the cultural sector summed up by the adage, "give, get, or get off."

Because of the steep cost of entry, museum boards in the U.S. and Europe are overwhelmingly dominated by donors from finance, real estate, and the energy sector—including oil and gas. Unsurprisingly, most boards are white and most often male, just like CEO Wall Street suites in general.[100] It is a vicious cycle as board members invite those from their majority-white social circles into their museum "club." Like attracts like. How likely are trustees to make choices with an awareness of systemic racism, sexism, income inequality, or any social justice issues that don't directly affect them?

Over the past few years, however, this homogeneity in the boardroom suites has begun to be challenged as diversity, equity, access, and inclusion (DEAI) has become a priority. This is the result of decades-long political and social activism, with an increased awareness that to entice new audiences, museums must diversify their staff and boards. Some progress has been made, but not enough. For example, the 2022 Black Trustee Alliance (BTA) Art Museum Trustee Survey, which polled close to 1,000 trustees throughout the U.S., Canada, and Mexico, revealed shocking disparities. The survey concluded that just 3.2% of 926 trustees in North America are Hispanic/Latino/Latina/Latinx and 18.1% are Black, while 68.5% are white.[101]

Corporatization is evident in the sponsorship of museum exhibitions by private collectors and luxury brands. The Met set the precedent in 1997 with a Gianni Versace fashion exhibition bankrolled by Condé Nast—the media conglomerate behind *Vogue* and *Vanity Fair*, magazines that are dependent on Versace's advertising dollars. Since then, the museum has hosted lavish exhibitions dedicated to Chanel, Tiffany, the House of Fabergé, and Cartier, each effectively paying for prime cultural real estate to market their products under the guise of art.[102] The Met Gala, the museum's annual fundraiser, is subsidized by non-art companies, including the 2024 edition, which was sponsored by TikTok and the LVMH-owned fashion label Loewe.

The Brooklyn Museum is also notorious for its populist marketing methods, beginning with the 1999 exhibition *Sensation: Young British Artists from the Saatchi Collection*, which showcased the private collection of advertising executive Charles Saatchi, and was sponsored by Saatchi himself. The British auction house Christie's and the dealers representing the artists on view also contributed money towards the exhibition. The blockbuster show—which attracted immense press interest due to the display of controversial works and drove earned revenue for the museum via massive ticket sales—greatly enhanced the value of the collection, which meant that the donor stood to gain financially with future sales of artworks.

In 1997, the National Air and Space Museum of the Smithsonian Institution in Washington, D.C., premiered the blockbuster exhibition *Star Wars: The Magic of Myth*, which subsequently traveled to several art museums in the U.S. and Australia.[103] For many of these venues, this exhibition was the most popular (read lucrative) of all time, demonstrating that the real purpose was box office draw. Critics were quick to notice and comment on such commercial opportunism. Michael Kimmelman of the *New York Times* slammed the exhibition in its Brooklyn Museum iteration. For him, the "last straw" was the final gallery, where visitors could try on masks of characters in *Star Wars*, which led directly into the gift shop where the masks could be purchased. The show and the shop became "indistinguishable."[104] That art museums presented this exhibition was beyond shocking: the *Star Wars* theme was no more related to fine art than Versace's fashions. (The Brooklyn Museum did not learn from these missteps: during its 2008 solo exhibition of the work of Japanese artist Takashi Murakami, much to the chagrin of art critics, the museum sold Louis Vuitton bags designed by the artist from a shop located *within* the exhibition. The artist had sold out, but so had the museum.)

The Guggenheim was another frontrunner in presenting museums as populist places of entertainment—as is evident in its 1998 exhibition *The Art of the Motorcycle*, sponsored by BMW. That the Guggenheim chose to use the word "art" in the title, to justify its presentation in an art museum, was questionable. This was followed two years later by an exhibition of dresses by Giorgio Armani, for which Armani is said to have made a donation of $15 million to the museum, a gift referred to by critics as a "rental fee."[105] The donation was, of course, a quid pro quo.

Museums have justified this populist brand of exhibitions as necessary to offset financial pressures. They also talk about how populist shows help to broaden audiences, moving away from the elitism of high art museums, and inviting different constituencies through the front door. While that might all be true, it seems that these populist shows are primarily temporary attempts to make headlines, boost attendance, and generate revenue. While the drive to make cash may make sense for struggling museums, an institution like the Met has a generous endowment and support from the New York State government, and museums like the Whitney, the Brooklyn Museum, and the Guggenheim are also far from broke (despite their complaints to the contrary).

The question becomes: have blockbuster exhibitions actually broadened museum audiences? They might bring in a one-off influx of cash, as huge audiences commit to paying for higher-priced tickets. But once those visitors are inside the door, are they visiting the permanent collection or other exhibitions in the museum? Perhaps more importantly, will they return? This is an area that would benefit from further research. For now, it remains an open question.

It was in the wake of the *Sensation* controversy (which involved outside donations and sponsorship as a quid pro quo for an exhibition) that the AAMD, which represents 170 museums in the U.S., Canada, and Mexico, began a review of its professional practice guidelines on finances. Mimi Gaudieri, the then-AAMD director, said the review, which is meant to take place every ten years, noted that ethical oversight was pressing given that "it was a very different time."[106] In other words, from 1989 to 1999 there had been a radical shift in how museums were dealing with outside sponsors and donations. This period coincided with a huge dip in corporate funding, which, according to the Alliance for the Arts, declined by 30% between 1982 and 1998.[107] This decline in corporate funding forced museums to rely heavily on individual philanthropy, questionable corporate sponsorships, and populist marketing strategies. Despite the AAMD's recommendations to be more selective about who museums solicit sponsorship from, these types of exhibitions have become commonplace. What was once off-limits has now become the norm.[108] Indeed, brand-partnered exhibitions that would have been derided twenty-five years ago are now acclaimed to the extent that *The Art Newspaper* listed the Brooklyn Museum's Christian Dior show as a "must-see exhibition" in September 2021.[109]

It is no accident that many museums present populist exhibitions and look to major donors for naming opportunities during capital campaigns, when they are eager to renovate, expand, or construct new buildings. The "bigger is better" ethos—rooted in a consumer culture fixated on endless growth—manifests in the drive to build new mega-museums designed by starchitects, which have now become emblematic markers of corporatization.[110] This phenomenon is known as the "Bilbao effect"—that is, when glittering architectural projects transform cultural institutions into desirable tourist destinations, often with a stated intention of gentrifying the area, as with architect Frank Gehry's Guggenheim Museum in Bilbao, Spain, completed in 1997. Another example is Renzo Piano's Whitney Museum in New York's Meatpacking District in Lower Manhattan, completed in 2015.

This trend for showy, iconic museum architecture began in 1989 with the inauguration of the Pyramid at the Louvre, Paris, designed by architect I. M. Pei, a stunning, light-filled glass-and-metal structure, a feat of modern engineering that stands some 71 feet (22 m) high. Such buildings attract millions of people each year to locations worldwide. Countless museums are now contributing to what seems to have become a craze—expanding with new wings or entrances or building entirely new museums, mostly with the aim of increasing display spaces to accommodate bigger collections and increase attendance numbers—or adding cafés or retail spaces to drive revenue. Some notable U.S. examples will suffice: in 2025, the Frick Museum's $290 million expansion in 2025 increased its size by 10%, and in 2023 the Buffalo AKG Art Museum in New York tripled its footprint. Meanwhile, MoMA has more than doubled in size in the last twenty years. Its 2004 redevelopment increased the size of the museum by 30%; its latest project, with architectural firm Diller Scofidio + Renfro, was completed in October 2019 and increased exhibition space by an additional 30%.

But one needs to ask, did these museums really need to expand their footprints in order to serve their function as museums? Did the Whitney need a new building and MoMA a massive expansion? Where does it end? When is bigger big enough?

And why do museums like the Guggenheim and the Louvre feel compelled to establish corporate franchises around the world—other than, of course, for greed? In their quest to expand their brands globally many museums are seeking world domination of the culture industry. In 2007, for example, the United Arab Emirates signed a contract with France for $1.1 billion, which gave them the right to use the Louvre's name for thirty years, for a new museum in Abu Dhabi. Like colonialist enterprises, these museums conquer foreign lands, often where there has been a massive influx of wealth, and import their brand of culture. So greedy and expansionist is the Guggenheim that between 1997 and 2016 they had "branches" in Berlin (as the Deutsche Guggenheim, 1997–2013), Las Vegas (as Guggenheim Hermitage Museum in the

Venetian Resort Hotel Casino, designed by Rem Koolhaus, 2001–8), and were in the process of building other franchises in Rio de Janeiro (1999–2005), Taichung, Taiwan (2002–5), Guadalajara, Mexico (2004–8), Vilnius, Lithuania (2007–10), and Helsinki, Finland (2010–16).[111] Most of these cultural megaprojects were unrealized. However, the Guggenheim Abu Dhabi, currently under construction, is set to open in 2026.

Corporate-minded, profit-oriented board members fuel the relentless push to build, expand, and globalize. Uninterested in covering the everyday costs that keep an institution running, they eagerly bankroll capital projects. For these donors, bricks and mortar offer visible, name-plated results, making them far more appealing to fund than the unglamorous work of sustaining the museum's operations.[112] However, the drive to build creates a vicious cycle: bigger buildings lead to higher operating costs, necessitating more staff, requiring more art to fill the spaces, and ultimately demanding increased budgets to sustain them. All of this means increasing dependency on private philanthropy and corporate sponsorship, with no end in sight.

What would happen if the wealthiest museums eliminated 20% of their budget, the amount typically provided by board contributions? They would undoubtedly be a little less flush, but they may also learn that times of austerity call for austere measures, not continual growth. In other words, if museums had not been corporatized would we be perpetually seeking to build and grow? Would we learn to live within our economic means without compromising our ethics by whitewashing the reputations of our 1% patrons, presenting populist exhibitions, accepting money from heinous corporations? What if well-endowed museums reconfigured themselves to rely on the annualized distribution from their endowments or investments to cover all operating costs?

NATIONAL ACADEMY OF DESIGN

Perhaps this can only happen with a new or renewed institution in which this philosophy is embedded from the start. This is what I did as director of the National Academy of Design (NAD), an institution founded in 1825 that I helped bring back from the brink of bankruptcy between 2015 and 2018. The NAD had the opportunity to rebuild an old institution from scratch and to establish a financial plan that would secure the institution in perpetuity. The strategic plan I wrote and that our team implemented mandated that the NAD should *not* purchase a new building within five years of setting up the $65 million endowment that I'd helped them secure through the sale of their real estate assets, in order to allow for the principal to grow. The plan also recommended that the institution should not buy a building *larger than* could be operated by the annualized distribution of $65 million. At an estimated 4% annual distribution, this meant that the total operating expenses for the organization should not exceed $2.6 million. Otherwise, the institution would be wholly dependent on fundraising and commercialization to sustain itself into the future.

As of 2026, the NAD has not purchased a building. If and when they do purchase a building, it will be critical to ensure operational expenses require no more than $2.6 million annually to run. Otherwise, in due course it will find itself in the same financially precarious situation as in 2015.

Most institutions are not fortunate enough to be able to subsist on endowment proceeds alone. However, when museums complain of financial pressures, which they often do, they would be wise to remember that many of them were complicit in the corporate takeover in the 1980s. And those at the top (museum directors and senior management)—those who are paid the most within a corporate structure that favors individuals who hit or exceed targets—might be hesitant to give up their accumulated power and wealth. Would executive and senior staff take a substantive pay cut to ensure their staff are more adequately and fairly compensated?

Resistance to the corporatization of museums in the U.S. intensified with the election of Donald Trump in 2016. His push toward oligarchy highlighted issues like income inequality, racism, xenophobia, transphobia, and sexism. Since 2016, many of us have rediscovered the power of protest and community organizing. Whether through major, nationwide demonstrations drawing visibility to injustice, or open letters, petitions, or labor organizing in our communities, individuals and movements around the world are standing up to demand that those in power be held to account. In the case of museums, the disgruntled mobs—myself included—are holding museums accountable to a higher standard, demanding them to take an ethical stance on funding and sponsorship.

Today, many cultural institutions are selling out. The corporatization of museums, their for-profit mentalities, and ethically questionable patrons, is at the heart of the problem. The recent protests attest to this.

CONCLUSION

As a museum director, I understand the complexities of philanthropy. If the Sacklers offered me a gift of $5 million for my institution, would I accept it? What if my institution was suffering financially and needed cash fast? Given the widespread negative publicity surrounding the family, I would understand that in accepting the money I would be whitewashing their reputation or putting my museum's reputation at risk. In not taking the money, I would be jeopardizing my job, since the governing board would no doubt disagree with my decision. If Armani or BMW offered to foot the bill for an exhibition that could net millions for the museum, most board members would consider it a win-win situation. Or if BP sponsored an exhibition on climate change, they would argue that the end justifies the means—how would we present the exhibition without them? It is okay to "sleep with the enemy," as long as there is a profit involved. In sum, many for-profit boards can justify egregious actions if it affects the bottom line substantively. And if a board pushes for a new wing or a new museum, what director would say no?

Is there an alternative to the 1% boards? Can museums operate without their contributions? Again, private contributions account for, on average, 20% of an annual budget. In times of austerity, it's easy to imagine that percentage ballooning. To address budgetary shortages—such as those experienced by museums across the globe during the 2008 recession, and mass closures that resulted from the Covid-19 pandemic—the obvious but unlikely alternative in the U.S. would be to substantially increase public funding for the arts in general. This is not going to happen anytime soon, especially under the Trump administration where federal funding is drying up as the National Endowment for the Arts (NEA) and the National Endowment for the Humanities (NEH) are gutted. The director of the Moderna Museet in Stockholm does not have to raise money because the museum receives 100% government funding. Again, since this is not likely to happen in the U.S., what alternatives are there? There could be a pause on all capital projects, with an exclusive focus on the museum's current building maintenance. Bigger is not always better. Museums could streamline: the smaller the budget, the less fundraising is required and the less need there is for the 1%. If we could encourage museums to rethink their identities without oodles of money and to work with a budget that reflects fiscal responsibility, then we're moving in the right direction.

Directors could also promise not to sign deals with the devil—namely, stop accepting restricted gifts that legally bind a museum to its donor in perpetuity. In other words, eliminate restrictive naming opportunities and promises to exhibit a collection or artwork forever. Museum directors could encourage donations towards endowments, for long-term support of an institution, and gifts toward operating expenses (not just brick and mortar projects). This would help subsidize salaries, keep the lights on, ensure facility maintenance, and so on.

We could also reconceptualize museum boards. The artist Andrea Fraser calls for democratizing museums by abolishing financial barriers to board service and opening trusteeship to all stakeholders—artists, staff and community members alike.[113] So, board members would be brought in for their expertise, not their wallets. This would mean disentangling governance from funding, since there is no inherent reason that those who finance museums should also be the ones who govern them. Although, in my experience working with governing boards, it is the case that 1%s will not give to a museum (even board dues) unless they have control over distribution of the money. Let's contemplate it as a possibility, nonetheless—there must be a way to establish a more transparent, less oligarchic form of museum governance. Imagine museum boards comprised of artists, community leaders, educators, staff, and other cultural figures—none bound by fiduciary obligations. Museums would stand to gain enormously from their expertise, creativity, and perspectives.

Alternatively, what if these primarily "creative" boards had just a few business folks on them, invited and selected solely for their professional expertise? They could then serve, for example, on investment committees, providing guidance but *not* taking control? It would be a board that prioritized expertise over wealth. (This is the principle behind the new board I established at the NAD in 2017 to ensure its future financial viability; it comprises artists, architects, and a few CEO/bankers and investors.)

What if all board members were required to take a course on nonprofit governance to ensure that a for-profit mentality did not predominate the board and institution? We should not presume that artists, community leaders, and educators who join a board will have a not-for-profit mentality, as this is not always the case. A course in nonprofit governance would be helpful for all involved.

Just as there are acquisition and development committees, among others, on boards, there could be ethics committees tasked with reviewing the board's decisions and actions. The nominating committee on each board could work in tandem with the ethics committee to ensure stricter board-member vetting procedures. This would involve thoroughly examining a prospect's finances and researching the companies they work for and do business with. No prospective board member would be thrilled about this and no amount of forensic accounting can completely identify nefariousness in comingled investments, but it's certainly worth trying. The ethics committee could work to ensure that board members' and donors' personal and business activities are consistent with the museum's mission and values. Board-member bylaws and governance policies could also have mechanisms to remove trustees who fail to meet these criteria. With these policies in place, a Rebekah Mercer, a Sackler, a Leon Black, a Warren Kanders, and others, would never have made it onto museum boards. And let's not just stop at the board. Museums should have internal ethics committees that could also work with fundraising departments to ensure odious corporate sponsors such as BP or Shell are prohibited from contributing funds.

I don't know of any internal ethics committees in U.S. museums, but there are several in the U.K. Tate was the first British institution to set up a board ethics committee in 2007; following suit were the National Gallery in London, the V&A, the British Museum, and the National Portrait Gallery (NPG). Indeed, as a result of scrutiny from the NPG's Ethics Committee, established in 2018, which decides whether the promised money is "in conflict with the objectives and values of the gallery," the Sackler family withdrew a £1m donation in 2019.[114] The NPG Ethics Committee, comprised of two trustees and one external member, reviews any donations that may raise ethical concerns.[115]

We must de-corporatize museums. Until then, activists such as Nan Goldin, DTP, and BP or Not BP will continue agitating against museums accepting money from ecocidal art patrons, drug pushers, private-prison racketeers, sexual predators, and so on. These protests expose how art institutions, which profess to support socially progressive causes in their exhibitions and programs and commend themselves as champions of freedom of speech, often undermine these causes at leadership and governance levels. From where I sit in the U.S., increased government and direct public funding for the arts seems like a remote possibility. Perhaps what we need are more open letters, signed by art stars or luminaries, such as Nan Goldin and Ai Weiwei, stating that they will refuse to exhibit at museums unless the institutions cut ties with abhorrent funders.

It will require immense ethical courage and artistic integrity before we can witness substantive change. The artists and activists, the scholars, museum workers, and members of the public who repeatedly take it upon themselves to speak out against injustice, and who have made the museum a forum for the most important reckonings of our time, have demonstrated that there is power in resistance.

POSTSCRIPT: "UNDER HIS EYE"

The world has changed dramatically since the completion of this book's manuscript. Alt-right parties are increasingly on the rise—in Hungary, France, Germany, Bulgaria, Slovakia, Australia, the Netherlands, and the U.S., among other countries—and the impact on arts and culture is profound. Donald Trump's assumption of power in January 2025, for instance, had an immediate effect on cultural institutions across the U.S. His anti-DEI crusade, and the many executive orders associated with it, mandate an end to federally funded DEI programs, arguing that such initiatives are "illegal," "immoral," "radical," and "wasteful."[1] In Trump's government *all* DEI programs, defined broadly as those that support women, LGBTQ+, BIPOC, and disabled individuals, are perceived as discriminatory.

As the administration's lackies troll through institutional mission statements, university curricula, and grants associated with federally funded agencies, such as the National Institute for Health, the regime is policing words like "gender ideology," "minority," "biases," and even "women." Arwa Mahdawi writing for the *Guardian* explains that even NASA is "busy scrubbing mentions of terms related to women in leadership from public websites in an attempt to comply with Trump's executive orders."[2] The level of forensic analysis and deep diving into the goals and aspirations of federally funded agencies and institutions is terrifying. Indeed, the National Gallery of Art in Washington and the Smithsonian Institution (which oversees twenty-one museums across the U.S.), both of which are almost exclusively funded by the federal government, immediately fell in line with the new mandate, closing DEI offices, removing related language from their websites, and eliminating the acronym from their mission statements in favor of less inflammatory words like "welcoming" and "accessible." Less clear at first was how the executive order would affect exhibition programming and whether the two museums would self-censor moving forward. Within months, the Smithsonian had postponed "woke" exhibitions, citing funding woes, and museums across the U.S. began censoring exhibitions, including exhibitions featuring Black and queer artists at the Art Museum of the Americas in Washington, D.C., and an exhibition titled *transfeminisms* at the Scottsdale Museum of Contemporary Art that I co-curated (which perhaps comes as no surprise given that Arizona legislature had just introduced anti-transgender bills).[3] So oppressive is the Trump regime that it has called for a review of all future and current shows at Smithsonian museums, in order to gage their "alignment with American ideals."[4] If museums do not fall in line with his conservative agenda, Trump has threatened to revoke federal funding, as well institutions' tax-exempt statuses, which would be devastating. The effect of these threats on the museum sector at large is still to be seen, but directors are reeling and afraid, nonetheless.

Fear in the cultural sector was further exacerbated in February 2025 when Trump disbanded the President's Committee on Arts and Humanities (PCAH), an organization that partnered with the NEA, NEH, and the Institute of Museum and Library Services (IMLS) to advise the government's investments within the cultural sector. Indeed, there are ongoing concerns that Trump will eliminate these three arts organizations altogether, as he attempted to do during his first term.[5] In February 2025, in the face of anti-DEI scrutiny, the NEA reported that its grants for 2026 would no longer include a program for underserved communities and instead prioritize projects celebrating the 250th anniversary of the signing of the Declaration of Independence.[6]

While Trump appears proactively hostile to the arts, he also appears to want to control the industry, or at least one of its most prestigious culture centers. In February 2025, no doubt as a warning to the arts sector, he appointed himself chair of the John F. Kennedy Center for the Performing Arts and installed his ally, Richard Grenell, as its director, signaling that he can now dictate which artistic voices will be given a public platform at the Center.[7] Then, in December 2025, Trump renamed the organization: "The Donald J. Trump and The John F. Kennedy Memorial Center for the Performing Arts."

His so-called "enemies from within" are endless, a chilling reminder that Americans are now "Under His Eye," a reference to Margaret Atwood's *The Handmaid's Tale* in which the "Eyes" serve as the secret police of Gilead, enforcing the regime's laws and maintaining control through fear and intimidation. For the foreseeable future, the U.S. is without question the new Gilead. The future of museums under this authoritarian regime remains to be seen.

NOTES

Introduction

1 Rhiannon Mason, Alistair Robinson and Emma Coffield, "First Principles," *Museum and Gallery Studies: The Basics* (New York: Routledge, 2018); "TrendsWatch 2019: Confronting the Past: The long, hard work of decolonization," *Center for the Future of Museums Blog*, April 19, 2019, https://www.aam-us.org/2019/04/19/trendswatch-2019-confronting-the-past-the-long-hard-work-of-decolonization/.

2 Philip T. Hoffman, *Why Did Europe Conquer the World?* (Princeton, NJ: Princeton University Press, 2015): 2–3.

3 Clémentine Deliss quoted in Edward M. Gómez, "Shaking Up the Ethnographic Museum," *Hyperallergic*, July 18, 2020, https://hyperallergic.com/577138/shaking-up-the-ethnographic-museum/.

4 Rolando Vázquez, "The Museum, Decoloniality, and the End of the Contemporary," in *The Future of the New: Artistic Innovation in Times of Social Acceleration*, ed. Thijs Lijster (Amsterdam: Valiz, 2019): 181–95.

5 Some of the key texts associated with "new museology" include: Peter Vergo, *The New Museology* (Chicago: University of Chicago Press, 1989); Eilean Hooper-Greenhill, *Museums and the Shaping of Knowledge* (New York: Routledge, 1992); and Robert Sandell, *Museums, Society and Inequality* (London: Routledge, 2002).

6 ICOM quoted in Angelica Villa, "Industry Group Adds the Word 'Diversity' to Its Definition of Museums—But Some Say It's Not Enough," *ARTnews*, August 26, 2022, https://www.artnews.com/art-news/news/international-council-revises-definition-museum-1234637556/. See also Alex Marshall, "What Is a Museum? A Dispute Erupts over a New Definition," *New York Times*, August 6, 2020, https://www.nytimes.com/2020/08/06/arts/what-is-a-museum.html.

7 Villa, "Industry Group Adds the Word 'Diversity' to Its Definition of Museums."

8 Benjamin Sutton, "New Tool Tracks Incidents of Artistic Censorship Related to Israel-Hamas War," *The Art Newspaper*, May 23, 2024, https://www.theartnewspaper.com/2024/05/23/new-tool-tracks-incidents-of-artistic-censorship-related-to-israel-hamas-war.

9 Claire Moulène, "La démission fracassante de Sandra Hegedüs des Amis du Palais de Tokyo crée la polémique, sur fond de conflit israélo-palestinien," *Libération*, May 8, 2024, https://www.liberation.fr/culture/la-demission-de-sandra-hegedus-membre-des-amis-du-palais-de-tokyo-cree-la-polemique-sur-fond-de-conflit-israelo-palestinien-20240508_PL2ERJYU7ZCA7DONQEDZOUEWWE/.

10 Sara Herschander, "Nonprofits Are Taking a Stance on Gaza—and Paying the Price," *Chronicle of Philanthropy*, June 18, 2024, https://www.philanthropy.com/article/nonprofits-are-taking-a-stance-on-gaza-and-paying-the-price.

11 Chris Lehmann, "The Bipartisan War on Pro-Palestinian Activism," *Nation*, April 29, 2024, https://www.thenation.com/article/politics/nonprofits-palestine-congress/.

12 Lehmann, "Bipartisan War."

13 Geraldine Kendall Adams, "Government Interference in Heritage Threatens Freedom of Speech, Warn Historians," *Museums Association Journal*, March 24, 2021, https://www.museumsassociation.org/museums-journal/news/2021/03/government-interference-in-heritage-threatens-freedom-of-speech-warn-historians/. The open letter on the Royal Historical Society is reproduced in Henry Irving, "RHS Asks Government to Clarify Its Position on Historical Research," *Social History Society*, March 22, 2021, https://socialhistory.org.uk/2021/03/22/rhs-asks-government-to-clarify-its-position-on-historical-research/.

14 Geraldine Kendall Adams, "Arts Council to Clarify Guidance After NPO Censorship Row," *Museums Assocation Journal*, February 15, 2024, https://www.museumsassociation.org/museums-journal/news/2024/02/arts-council-responds-to-npo-censorship-row/. See also Geraldine Kendall Adams, "NPOs Must Support Freedom of Expression, Says Revised Arts Council Guidance," *Museums Association Journal*, February 29, 2024, https://www.museumsassociation.org/museums-journal/news/2024/02/npos-must-support-freedom-of-expression-says-revised-arts-council-guidance/.

15 Geraldine Kendall Adams, "Museum Governance 'Synonymous with Privileges for Politicians,'" *Museums Association Journal*, June 24, 2022, https://www.museumsassociation.org/museums-journal/news/2022/06/museum-governance-synonymous-with-privileges-for-politicians/. See also Ian King and Annick Schramme, "Museum Watch Governance Management Project" (Paris: ICOM, January 2022): 20, https://cimam.org/documents/192/Museum_Watch_Governance_Management_Project_INTERCOM-CIMAM.April2022.pdf.

16 Adams, "Museum Governance."

17 Julia Halperin and Charlotte Burns, "Museums Claim They're Paying More Attention to Female Artists. That's an Illusion," *Artnet*, September 19, 2019, https://news.artnet.com/womens-place-in-the-art-world/womens-place-art-world-museums-1654714; "The

Ongoing Gender Gap Report in Art Museum Directorships," report, Association of Art Museum Directors (AAMD), 2017; Chad Topaz et al., "Diversity of Artists in Major U.S. Museums," *PLOS One*, vol. 14, no. 3 (2019): 1–15; Charlotte Bonham-Carter, "Representation of Women Artists in the UK During 2021," report, Freelands Foundation, 2022.

18 Joe Ware, "'My Grandfather Would Be Horrified': Protests against National Trust's Links to Barclays Take Place across UK," *The Art Newspaper*, July 29, 2024, https://www.theartnewspaper.com/2024/07/29/horrified-that-the-national-trust-is-banking-with-barclays-climate-campaigners-begin-a-week-of-protests-at-historic-sites.

Chapter 1: DECOLONIZING MUSEUMS

1 Amy Lonetree, *Decolonizing Museums: Representing Native America in National and Tribal Museums* (Chapel Hill: University of North Caroline Press, 2012), 173; "TrendsWatch 2019: Confronting the Past: The long, hard work of decolonization," *Center for the Future of Museums Blog*, April 19, 2019, https://www.aam-us.org/2019/04/19/trendswatch-2019-confronting-the-past-the-long-hard-work-of-decolonization/.

2 See, for instance, Walter Mignolo (with Catherine Walsh), *On Decoloniality: Concepts, Analytics, Praxis* (Durham, NC: Duke University Press, 2018); Mignolo, "Delinking," *Cultural Studies*, vol. 21, no. 2 (2007): 449–514; Mignolo, "Epistemic Disobedience and the Decolonial Option: A Manifesto," *Transmodernity* (Fall 2011): 44–66; Aníbal Quijano, "Coloniality and Modernity/Rationality," *Cultural Studies*, vol. 21, nos. 2–3 (2007): 168–78; Quijano, "Coloniality of Power, Eurocentrism, and Latin America," *Nepantla: Views from the South*, vol. 1, no. 3 (2000): 533–80; María Lugones, "Heterosexualism and the Colonial/Modern Gender System," *Hypatia*, vol. 22, no. 1 (2007): 186–209; Lugones, "Towards a Decolonial Feminism," *Hypatia*, vol. 25, no. 4 (Fall 2010): 742–59; Rolando Vázquez, "Towards a Decolonial Critique of Modernity: Buen Vivir, Relationality and the Task of Listening," in *Capital, Poverty, Development*, ed. Raúl Fornet-Betancourt (Aachen: Wissenschaftsverlag Mainz, 2012): 241–52; Vázquez, "The Museum, Decoloniality and the End of the Contemporary," in *The Future of the New: Artistic Innovation in Times of Social Acceleration*, ed. Thijs Lijster (Amsterdam: Valiz, 2018): 181–95.

3 On the concept of "epistemic de-linking," see Mignolo, "Delinking."

4 Madina V. Tlostanova and Walter Mignolo, *Learning to Unlearn: Decolonial Reflections from Eurasia and the Americas* (Columbus: Ohio State University Press, 2012).

5 Walter Mignolo, *The Darker Side of Western Modernity: Global Futures, Decolonial Options* (Durham, NC: Duke University Press, 2011); Vázquez, "The Museum, Decoloniality and the End of the Contemporary," 191–92.

6 It is for this reason that Mignolo, in particular, argues for what he terms a "decolonial aesthesis." See Walter Mignolo and Rolando Vázquez, "Decolonial AestheSis: Colonial Wounds/Decolonial Healings," *Social Text*, July 15, 2013, as well as Ivan Muñiz-Reed, "Thoughts on Curatorial Practices in the Decolonial Turn," *On Curating*, no. 35 (December 2017).

7 Walter Mignolo, "Museums in the Colonial Horizon of Modernity: Fred Wilson's *Mining the Museum* (1992)," in *Globalization and Contemporary Art*, ed. Jonathan Harris (Hoboken, NJ: Blackwell Publishing, 2011): 71. See also Mignolo, "Delinking."

8 "Decolonization" is a term without a clear definition, or with many working definitions. See, for instance, Eve Tuck and K. Wayne Yang, "Decolonization Is Not a Metaphor," *Decolonization: Indigeneity, Education & Society*, vol. 1, no. 1 (2012): 1–40; Amy Lonetree, *Decolonizing Museums: Representing Native America in National and Tribal Museums* (Chapel Hill: University of North Caroline Press, 2012), and Linda Tuhiwai Smith, *Decolonizing Methodologies: Research and Indigenous Peoples* (London: Zed Books, 2012); Shaheen Kasmani, "How Can You Decolonise Museums?" film, *MuseumNext*, June 2, 2020; Wanda Nanibush in "Shared Authority," *Art in America*, October 1, 2017; Decolonize This Place, "Decolonial Operations Manual," https://decolonizethisplace.org/downloadable-materials. See also notes 3 and 7.

9 The "colonial matrix of power" is used repeatedly in Walter Mignolo's writings. See, for instance, Mignolo, "The Colonial Matrix of Power," in *Talking About Global Inequality: Personal Experiences and Historical Perspectives*, ed. Christian Olaf Christiansen et al. (Cham: Palgrave Macmillan, Springer International, 2023): 39–46.

10 "TrendsWatch 2019: Confronting the Past."

11 Clémentine Deliss, *The Metabolic Museum* (Berlin: Hatje Cantz, 2020). Hereafter, Deliss 2020; Coco Fusco, "Deaccessioning Empire," *New York Review*, February 25, 2021, https://www.nybooks.com/articles/2021/02/25/deaccessioning-empire/.

12 Deliss 2020, 99.

13 Clémentine Deliss quoted in Edward Gómez, "Shaking Up the Ethnographic Museum," *Hyperallergic*, July 18, 2020, https://hyperallergic.com/577138/shaking-up-the-ethnographic-museum/.

14 Deliss 2020, 60.

15 Gómez, "Shaking Up the Ethnographic Museum."

16 "To remediate the ethnographic collection is to engage with that mix of discomfort, doubt, and melancholia, the *caput mortuum* phase of alchemical regeneration, transforming these objects into a contemporary environment and thereby building additional interpretations onto their existing

set of references." Clémentine Deliss, "Collecting Life's Unknowns," *Decolonising Museums* (L'Internationale Online, 2015): 28, https://framerframed.nl/wp-content/uploads/2015/11/Decolonising-Museums.pdf.

17 Deliss 2020, 41–43.

18 Fusco, "Deaccessioning Empire."

19 Deliss 2020, 75.

20 Deliss 93. See also Fusco, "Deaccessioning Empire."

21 Deliss 2020, 33.

22 Tom McCarthy, *Satin Island* (London: Jonathan Cape, 2015); Deliss 2020, 83.

23 Deliss 2020, 24–25.

24 Deliss 84. See also Fusco, "Deaccessioning Empire."

25 Deliss, "Collecting Life's Unknowns," n.p. Deliss also curated exhibitions at the Weltkulturen Museum, including *Foreign Exchange* (2014–15). See Deliss 2020, 43.

26 "Introduction," in *Decolonising Museums* (L'Internationale Online, 2015), https://framerframed.nl/wp-content/uploads/2015/11/Decolonising-Museums.pdf.

27 Maximiliano Durón and Alex Greenberger, "The 10 Most Important Shows by Okwui Enwezor," *ARTnews*, March 29, 2021, https://www.artnews.com/list/art-news/artists/most-important-shows-okwui-enwezor-1234588006/postwar-art-between-pacific-and-atlantic-haus-der-kunst/.

28 Okwui Enwezor, Ulrich Wilmes, and Katie Seigel, eds., *Postwar: Art Between the Pacific and the Atlantic 1945–1965* (Munich: Haus der Kunst, 2016).

29 Durón and Greenberger, "The 10 Most Important Shows."

30 Durón and Greenberger, "10 Most Important Shows."

31 The concept of a global art history was also explored in the criticism of the much-maligned exhibition *Magiciens de la terre* (Centre Georges Pompidou/Grande halle de la Vilette, Paris, 1989). See Maura Reilly, *Curatorial Activism: Towards an Ethics of Curating* (London: Thames & Hudson, 2018): 106–11.

32 Joaquín Barriendos Rodríguez, "Geopolitics of Global Art: The Reinvention of Latin America as a Geo-Aesthetic Region," in *The Global Art World*, ed. Hans Belting and Andrea Buddensieg (Berlin: Hatje Cantz, 2009): 110.

33 "OnCurating: Decolonizing Art Institutions," *Notes on Curating* 35 (December 2017), https://www.on-curating.org/files/oc/dateiverwaltung/issue-34/PDF_to_Download/Oncurating_Decolonizing_Issue35.pdf.

34 Marie-Laure Allain Bonilla, "Some Theoretical and Empirical Aspects on the Decolonization of Western Collections," *Notes on Curating* 35 (December 2017): 129–39, https://www.on-curating.org/files/oc/dateiverwaltung/issue-34/PDF_to_Download/Oncurating_Decolonizing_Issue35.pdf.

35 Tim Barringer in Catherine Grant and Dorothy Price, eds., "Decolonizing Art History," *Art History*, vol. 43, no. 1 (2020): 7, https://doi.org/10.1111/1467-8365.12490.

36 Grant and Price, "Decolonizing Art History."

37 On the curatorial strategy of "exhibition-as-polylogue," see Reilly, *Curatorial Activism*, 30–33; and Reilly, "Draw Your Own Conclusion as a Writerly Text," in *Pas de besoin d'un dessin*, ed. Jean Hubert-Martin (Geneva: Museé d'Art et d'Histoire de la Ville de Genève, 2022), 32–39.

38 Sarah Farrar, "On the Internal Front Lines: Curatorial Activism and Collection Exhibitions" (Ph.D. diss., Monash University, Melbourne, 2018). As Te Papa's (former) Senior Curator of Art and the Lead Curator for the "Art Renewal" project, for eighteen months Sarah Farrar led an internal curatorial team to work specifically on this exhibition, which included Māori curator Megan Tamati-Quennell (Curator of Modern and Contemporary Māori and Indigenous Art, iwi affiliations: Te Ātiawa, Ngāti Mutunga, Ngāi Tahu, Kāti Māmoe), Tongan-New Zealand curator Nina Tonga (Curator of Pacific Art), Pākehā curator Rebecca Rice (Curator of Historical New Zealand Art), Māori curator Matariki Williams (Curator of Mātauranga Māori, iwi affiliations: Tūhoe, Te Ātiawa, Ngāti Whakaue, Ngāti Hauiti), and British curator Lizzie Baikie (Assistant Curator Art, Special Projects).

39 Reilly, *Curatorial Activism*, 30–33.

40 Farrar, "On the Internal Front Lines," 157.

41 Farrar, 153.

42 Farrar, 153

43 Farrar, 173.

44 Farrar, 173.

45 Farrar, 174.

46 Neil Prior, "Battle of Waterloo: Thomas Picton, the Hero and Villain," *BBC News*, June 18, 2015, https://www.bbc.com/news/uk-wales-33110128.

47 "*Reframing Picton*: New Artworks Go on Display at National Museum Cardiff Alongside Re-Interpreted Portrait of Thomas Picton," press release, Sub-Sahara Advisory Panel (SSAP), August 2, 2022, https://www.ssap.org.uk/blog/reframing-picton.

48 "*Reframing Picton*," press release.

49 "*Reframing Picton*."

50 "*Reframing Picton*."

51 "*Reframing Picton*."

52 "*Reframing Picton*."

53 Fadhili Maghiya, quoted in "*Reframing Picton*."

54 Awuor Onyango, "Absent Figures: The Difficult Questions Restitution Raises," *Contemporary And*, May 17, 2021, https://contemporaryand.com/magazines/absent-figures-the-difficult-questions-restitution-raises/.

55 Onyango, "Absent Figures."

56 Onyango.

57 Onyango.

58 Jaclynn Ashly, "A Kenyan Tribe's Search for Its Leader's Stolen Skull," *Al Jazeera*, June 23, 2024, https://www.aljazeera.com/features/longform/2024/6/23/a-kenyan-tribes-search-for-its-leaders-stolen-skull.

59 "Tsavo Lions," *Field Museum Blog*, February 10, 2018, https://www.fieldmuseum.org/blog/tsavo-lions.

60 Centre for the Study of the Legacies of British Slavery,

database, Department of History, University College London: https://www.ucl.ac.uk/lbs/.

61 Arielle Xena Alterwaite, "Slavery on Display," *Slavery & Abolition: A Journal of Slave and Post-Slave Studies* 44, no. 1 (2023): 210.

62 See also Katie Donington, "Slavery and the Bank of England: Exploitation on Display," Centre for the Study of the Legacies of British Slavery (blog), October 5, 2022, https://lbsatucl.wordpress.com/2022/10/05/slavery-and-the-bank-of-england-exploitation-on-display/.

63 Donington, "Slavery and the Bank of England."

64 Sarah Pruitt, "What Was the Royal African Company?" *History*, May 18, 2023, https://www.history.com/news/what-was-the-royal-african-company; Padraic Scanlan, "The Colonial Rebirth of British Anti-Slavery: The Liberated African Villages of Sierra Leone, 1815–1824," *American Historical Review* 121, no. 4 (October 2016): 1085–113.

65 Michael Taylor referenced in Jasper Jolly, "Bank of England Owned 599 Slaves in the 1770s, New Exhibition Reveals," *Guardian*, April 17, 2022, https://www.theguardian.com/world/2022/apr/15/bank-of-england-owned-599-slaves-in-1770s-new-exhibition-reveals. See also, Michael Taylor, *The Interest: How the British Establishment Resisted the Abolition of Slavery* (London: Bodley Head, 2020).

66 Taylor quoted in Jolly, "Bank of England."

67 Taylor quoted in Jolly, "Bank of England."

68 In his essay "Museums in the Colonial Horizon of Modernity," Walter Mignolo describes Wilson's intervention as "a move toward the decoloniality of being and of knowledge that, on the one hand, reveals the underlying assumptions in the institution itself and, on the other hand, uses the institution to reveal what has been hidden in colonial histories of slavery and also the consequences of racism."

69 Walter Mignolo, "Decolonial Aesthetics: Unlearning and Relearning the Museum Through Pedro Lasch's 'Black Mirror/Espejo Negro,'" in *Black Mirror/Expejo Negro*, ed. Pedro Lasch (Durham, NC: John Hope Franklin Humanities Institute/Nasher Museum of Art – Duke University, 2008): 102.

70 Pedro Lasch, "Black Mirror/Espejo Negro–Artist Statement," in Lasch, ed., *Black Mirror/Expejo Negro*, 10.

71 Mignolo, "Decolonial Aesthetics," 100.

72 See Amalia Mesa-Bains, "New World Wunderkammer," artist's website, 2013, https://amaliamesabains.com/exhibit/the-new-world-wunderkammer/. See also "New World Wunderkammer: A Project by Amalia Mesa-Bains," Fowler Museum at the University of California, Los Angeles, October 13, 2013, https://fowler.ucla.edu/exhibitions/new-world-wunderkammer-a-project-by-amalia-mesa-bains/.

73 Amalia Mesa-Bains, "The Latino Cabinet of Curiosities: A Postcolonial Reopening," *Museum and Curatorial Studies Review*, vol. 1, no. 1 (2013): 36.

74 "Fowler At Fifty", press release, Fowler Museum, UCLA, August 19, 2013, https://fowler.ucla.edu/wp-content/uploads/2021/06/FowlerAtFifty_PressRelease2_0.pdf. See also Amalia Mesa-Bains, *New World Wunderkammer*, exhibition handout (Los Angeles: The Fowler Museum at UCLA, 2013).

75 Mesa-Bains, "The Latino Cabinet of Curiosities," 49.

76 See the Museums Association's definition of decolonization here: https://www.museumsassociation.org/campaigns/decolonising-museums/.

77 For an in-depth description of the Pitt Rivers Museum's decolonization process, see "Critical Changes to Displays as Part of the Decolonization Process," Pitt Rivers Museum, University of Oxford, accessed June 3, 2023, https://www.prm.ox.ac.uk/critical-changes.

78 Laura Van Broekhoven quoted in "Critical Changes."

79 Broekhoven quoted in "Critical Changes."

80 Broekhoven quoted in "Critical Changes."

81 Laura Van Broekhoven, "On Decolonizing the Museum in Practice," *Journal of Museum Ethnography*, no. 32 (March 2019): 5.

82 Decolonize This Place quoted in MTL Collective, "From Institutional Critique to Institutional Liberation? A Decolonial Perspective on the Crises of Contemporary Art," *October*, no. 165 (Summer 2018): 205.

83 Just 4% of staffers in those positions were Black, 3% of them were Hispanic, and 6% were Asian. See Roger Schonfeld and Mariët Westermann, *The Andrew W. Mellon Foundation Art Museum Staff Demographic Survey* (New York: Andrew W. Mellon Foundation, 2015).

84 Steven Nelson quoted in Rachel Hatzipanagos, "The 'Decolonization' of the American Museum," *Washington Post*, October 11, 2018, https://www.washingtonpost.com/nation/2018/10/12/decolonization-american-museum/.

85 Email exchange with Lori Fogarty, Director of the Oakland Museum of California, April 5, 2021.

86 Tuck and Yang, "Decolonization," 7.

Chapter 2: "WE WERE HERE FIRST"

1 According to the NNKM director, Jérémie McGowan, the "X" had a number of different associations: as a reference to "No" signs, like "No parking," which he linked to "No museum"; and as an intersection marking the location of a place "where something happens, or might be found." See "How Sámi Dáiddamusea came to life," Sámi Dáiddamusea, April 3, 2017, https://www.sdmx.no/en/news/how-sámi-dáiddamusea-came-life.

2 There is a total of eleven Sámi languages stretching throughout

Sápmi. The North Sámi language is the largest of these and is spoken in the Sámi clan-based territories (*siida*), of which the city of Tromsø is a part.

3 Jérémie McGowan, interview (2019), quoted in Sarah Caulfield, "The Nordnorsk Kunstmuseum 2014–2020: Decolonisation in Practice" (Master's thesis in Indigenous Studies, University of Tromsø—The Artic University of Norway, 2021): 40, https://hdl.handle.net/10037/21794.

4 Maja Dunfjeld Aagård, "Tjaalehtjimmie: Form and Content in South Sámi Ornamentation," in *Duodji Reader: Guoktenuppelot Sámi čállosa duoji birra/Twelve Essays on Duodji by Sámi Writers*, ed. Harald Gaski and Gunvor Guttorm (Kárášjohka/Karasjok: Davvi Girjji, 2022): 164–73.

5 Harald Gaski, "Indigenous Aesthetics: Add Context to Context," in *Sámi Art and Aesthetics: Contemporary Perspectives*, ed. Svein Aamold, Elin Haugdal, and Ulla Angkjær Jørgensen (Aarhus: Aarhus University Press, 2017): 179–93.

6 Hanna Horsberg Hansen, "Constructing Sámi National Heritage: Encounters Between Tradition and Modernity in Sámi Art," *Konsthistorisk tidskrift*, vol. 85, no. 3 (2016): 240–55.

7 Liisa-Rávná Finbog, "Duodji," in Susanne Hætta, Liisa-Rávná Finbog, and Kimberley Moulton, *Mázejoavku: Indigenous Collectivity and Art*, ed. Katya García-Antón (Kautokeino: Office for Contemporary Art Norway, 2021): 30. Hereafter, Finbog 2021.

8 "There Is No," Sámi Dáiddamusea, February 15, 2017, https://www.sdmx.no/en/exhibitions/there-no.

9 Caulfield, "The Nordnorsk Kunstmuseum 2014–2020."

10 Liisa-Rávná Finbog, "Yul Brynner in Space is Life," *Contemporary Art Stavanger*, March 26, 2023, https://contemporaryartvanger.no/archive/yul-brynner-in-space-is-life.

11 Brook Garru Andrew, "Notes of a Journal IV" in *Galang 01*, ed. Andrew et al. (Melbourne: Garru Editions and Powerhouse Publishing, 2022): 120.

12 Anne May Olli, "Pesticider i samisk gjenstandsmateriale" (Master's thesis, University of Oslo, 2013), http://urn.nb.no/URN:NBN:no-37710.

13 Joar Nango quoted in Andreas Breivik, "Where Do We Go from Here?" *Nordic Art Review*, vol. 30, no. 6 (2020), https://kunstkritikk.com/where-do-we-go-from-here/.

14 Kimberley Moulton, "Sovereign Art and the Colonial Canon: Are We Lost Until We Are Found?" in *Sovereignty*, ed. Paola Bella and Max Delany (Melbourne: Australian Centre for Contemporary Art, 1995): 19.

15 Moulton, "Sovereign Art," 31.

16 Amy Lonetree, *Decolonizing Museums: Representing Native America in National and Tribal Museums* (Chapel Hill: University of North Carolina Press, 2012): 47.

17 Lonetree, *Decolonizing Museums*, 45.

18 Eve Tuck and K. Wayne Yang, "Decolonization Is Not a Metaphor," *Decolonization: Indigeneity, Education & Society*, vol. 1, no. 1 (2012): 1–40.

19 Walter Mignolo and Catherine Walsh, *On Decoloniality: Concepts, Analytics, Praxis* (Durham, NC: Duke University Press, 2018); Rauna Kuokkanen, *Restructuring Relations: Indigenous Self-Determination, Governance, and Gender* (New York: Oxford University Press, 2019); María Lugones, "The Coloniality of Gender," *Worlds & Knowledges Otherwise* (Spring 2008): 1–17; Bonita Lawrence, "Gender, Race, and the Regulation of Native Identity in Canada and the United States: An Overview," *Hypatia: A Journal of Feminist Philosophy*, vol. 18, no. 2 (2003): 3–31; Aníbal Quijano, "Coloniality and Modernity/Rationality," *Cultural Studies* vol. 21, nos. 2–3 (2007): 168–78; Rolando Vázquez, "The Museum, Decoloniality and the End of the Contemporary," in *The Future of the New: Artistic Innovation in Times of Social Acceleration*, ed. Thijs Lijster (Amsterdam: Valiz, 2018): 181–95.

20 Walter Mignolo, "Delinking," *Cultural Studies*, vol. 21, no. 2 (2007): 449–514.

21 Puwai Cairns, "Decolonisation: We Aren't Going to Save You," American Alliance of Museums. December 17, 2018, https://www.aam-us.org/2018/12/17/DECOLONISATION-WE-ARENT-GOING-TO-SAVE-YOU/.

22 Moana Jackson quoted in Cairns, "Decolonisation."

23 Puwai Cairns, "Decolonize or Indigenize: Moving Towards Sovereign Spaces and the Maorification of New Zealand Museology," *Museum of New Zealand Te Papa Tongarewa* (blog), February 10, 2020, https://blog.tepapa.govt.nz/2020/02/10/decolonise-or-indigenise-moving-towards-sovereign-spaces-and-the-maorification-of-new-zealand-museology/.

24 Lisa Hilli quoted in Andrew et al., "Yarns," *Galang 01*, 107.

25 Stephen Gilchrist in conversation with Henry F. Skerritt, "Awakening Objects and Indigenizing the Museum," *Contemporaneity: Historical Presence in Visual Culture*, vol. 5, no. 1 (2016): 111. Gilchrist's proposition dovetails nicely with Mignolo's argument that decolonization involves a "de-linking" or *unlearning* of Eurocentric knowledge production.

26 Stephen Gilchrist, "Belonging and Unbelonging: Indigenous Forms of Curation as Expressions of Sovereignty" (Ph.D. diss., University of Sydney, 2020): 9, https://hdl.handle.net/2123/22301.

27 Aile Aikio, "Balancing Between Two Contested Worlds: The Challenges and Benefits of Being an Indigenous Museum Professional," *Museum International*, vol. 70, nos. 3–4 (2018): 100–11; Liisa-Rávná Finbog, *It Speaks to You—Making Kin Through Stories, People, and Duodji in Sámi Museums* (Lewes, DE: Dio Press, 2023). Hereafter, Finbog 2023.

28 Vuokko Hirvonen and Kaija Anttonen, *Sámi Culture and the School: Reflections by Sámi Teachers and the Realization of the Sámi School; An Evaluation Study of Reform 97* (Kautokeino and Karasjok: Čálliid Lágádus, 2004).

29 Asta Balto and Liv Østmo, "Mánggakultuvrralašvuoda oahpu sámáidahttin Sámi allaskuvllas/ Indigenizing the Study of Multicultural Understanding at the Sámi University College," *Sámi dieđalaš áigecála*, nos. 1–2 (2009): 28.

30 Balto and Østmo, "Indigenizing the Study," 36.

31 Aile Aikio, "Sámification and Sámi Museums," in *Sámi Research in Transition: Knowledge, Politics and Social Change*, ed. Laura Junka-Aikio, Jukka Nyyssönen, and Veli-Pekka Lehtola (London: Routledge, 2021): 113.

32 Finbog 2023, 75.

33 Marie Battiste and James (Sákéj) Youngblood Henderson, *Protecting Indigenous Knowledge and Heritage: A Global Challenge* (Saskatoon: Purich, 2000): 30.

34 Cara Krmpotich, "Repatriation and the Generation of Material Culture," *Mortality: Promoting the Interdisciplinary Study of Death and Dying*, vol. 16, no. 2 (2011): 145–60; Laura Peers, Lotten Reinius, and Jennifer Shannon, "Introduction: Repatriation and Ritual, Repatriation as Ritual," *Museum Worlds: Advances in Research*, vol. 5 (2017): 1–8; Anne May Olli and Eeva-Kristina Harliin, "Repatriation: Political Will and Museum Facilities," in *Museums and Restitution: New Practices, New Approaches*, ed. Louise Tythacott and Kostas Arvanitis (Farnham: Ashgate, 2014): 55–70; Finbog 2021.

35 Richard Sandell, *Museums, Moralities and Human Rights* (New York: Routledge, 2017).

36 Lonetree, *Decolonizing Museums*; Felwine Sarr and Bénédicte Savoy, *The Restitution of African Cultural Heritage: Toward a New Relational Ethics* (Paris: Philippe Rey/Seuil, 2018), https://www.unimuseum.uni-tuebingen.de/fileadmin/content/05_Forschung_Lehre/Provenienz/sarr_savoy_en.pdf; Kimberly Moulton, "I Can Still Hear Them Calling. Echoes of My Ancestors," in *Sovereign Words: Indigenous Art, Curation and Criticism*, ed. Katya García-Antón (Oslo/Amsterdam: OCA/Valiz, 2018): 197–214; Outi Pieski and Eeva-Kristiina Harlin, *Ládjogahpir—Máttaráhkuid gábagahpir /The Ládjogahpir—The Foremothers' Hat of Pride* (Kárášjohka/Karasjok: Davvi Girji, 2020); Finbog 2021.

37 Sarr and Savoy, *Restitution*, 40.

38 Sarr and Savoy, 41.

39 Moulton, "I Can Still Hear," 200.

40 Moulton; Finbog 2023.

41 Sarr and Savoy, 34.

42 Lonetree, *Decolonizing Museums*, 192.

43 Pieski and Harlin, *Ládjogahpir*; Finbog 2023.

44 Robin R. R. Gray, "Rematriation: Ts'msyen Law, Rights of Relationality, and Protocols of Return," *Native American and Indigenous Studies*, vol. 9, no. 1 (2022): 1–27.

45 Finbog 2023, 232.

46 Rauna Kuokkanen, *Reshaping the University: Responsibility, Indigenous Epistemes, and the Logic of the Gift* (Vancouver: UBC Press, 2007); Kim Tallbear, "The US-Dakota War and Failed Settler Kinship," *Anthropology News*, vol. 57, no. 9 (2016).

47 Kuokkanen, *Reshaping the University*, 75.

48 Ailton Krenak, *Ideas to Postpone the End of the World* (Toronto: House of Anansi Press, 2019): 25.

49 Ann Fienup-Riordan, "From Consultation to Collaboration," in *Sharing Knowledge and Cultural Heritage: First Nations of the Americas. Studies in Collaboration with Indigenous Peoples from Greenland, North and South America*, ed. Laura Van Broekhoven, Cunera Buijs, and Pieter Hovens (Leiden: Sidestone Press, 2010): 4; Laura L. Peers, "'Ceremonies of Renewal': Visits, Relationships, and Healing in the Museum Space," *Museum Worlds*, vol. 1, no. 1 (2013): 146; Finbog 2023, 230.

50 Olli, "Pesticider," 87.

51 Steven Newcomb, "Perspectives: Healing, Restoration, and Rematriation," *American Indian Ritual Object Repatriation Foundation News & Notes*, Spring/ Summer 1995, 3.

52 Gray, "Rematriation," 15.

53 Aileen Moreton-Robinson, *The White Possessive: Property, Power and Indigenous Sovereignty* (Minneapolis: University of Minnesota Press, 2015): xi.

54 Outi Pieski in interview with Yuvinka Medina, Bonniers Konsthall website, accessed May 9, 2024, https://bonnierskonsthall.se/en/utstallning/outi-pieski-rematriation-of-a-ladjogahpir-return-to-mattarahkka%E2%80%AF/interview-with-outi-pieski/.

55 Pieski and Harlin, *Ládjogahpir*, 127.

56 F. Graeme Chalmers, "Cultural Colonialism and Art Education: Eurocentric and Racist Roots of Art Education," in *Art, Culture, and Pedagogy*, ed. Dustin Garnet and Anita Sinner (Leiden: Brill, 2019): 37.

57 Finbog 2023, 107.

58 Liisa-Rávná Finbog, "The *Duojár*: An Agent of the Symbolic Repatriation of Sámi Cultural Heritage," in *Research Journeys In/ To Multiple Ways of Knowing*, ed. Jennifer Markides and Laura Forsythe (Lewes, DE: Dio Press, 2019): 98.

59 Rosanna Raymond in conversation with Maura Reilly on July 15, 2021.

60 See note 59.

61 Miriam Clavir, *Preserving What Is Valued: Museums, Conservation, and First Nations* (Vancouver: UBC Press, 2002).

62 Jean Baudrillard, *Simulacra and Simulation* (Ann Arbor: University of Michigan Press, 1994): 15.

63 Larissa Behrendt, "Decolonizing Institutions and Assertive Self-Determination: Implications for Legal Practice," in *Decolonizing Research: Indigenous Storywork as Methodology*, ed. Jo-Ann Archibald, Jenny Lee-Morgan, and Jason De Santolo (London: ZED, 2019): 175, 177.

64 Lonetree, *Decolonizing Museums*, 47.
65 See the *Indigenous Roadmap* project outlined at the end of Chapter 2.
66 The exhibition design is shaped by the philosophy of Iver Jåks, who, together with Jon Ole Andersen, a pioneering *duojá* (practitioner of *duodji*), designed both the exhibition cases and arranged them within the main exhibition room. Jåks was one of the most important Sámi artists of the last century (1932–2007). He was particularly known for his ability to actualize his Sámi heritage through contemporary art. His work experimented with traditional and Western expressions of art, blending them beautifully with *duodji*.
67 Bjørnar Olsen, "Bilder fra fortida? Representasjoner av Samisk kultur i samiske museer," *Nordisk Museologi*, vol. 2 (2000): 13–30; Sharon Webb, "Contested Histories of Multiple Pasts? The Representation of the Archaeological Past in the Museum" (Ph.D. diss., University of Cambridge, 2001).
68 James Clifford, "Museums as Contact Zones," in *Routes: Travel and Translation in the Late 20th Century* (Cambridge, MA: Harvard University Press, 1997): 188–219.
69 In public conversation—for example, during a lecture at the 2022 edition of Documenta (Kassel, Germany)—artist Richard Bell regularly refers to the "ghettoization" of Indigenous art in museums into their own segregated area, which he calls a "darkies' corner."
70 Shannon O'Loughlin, quoted in: Gabriella Angeleti, "Native American Group Denounces Met's Exhibition of Indigenous Objects," *The Art Newspaper*, November 6, 2018, https://www.theartnewspaper.com/2018/11/06/native-american-group-denounces-mets-exhibition-of-indigenous-objects.
71 Angeleti, "Native American Group Denounces Met's Exhibition of Indigenous Objects."
72 Angeleti.
73 Sarah Bahr, "Met Hires Its First Full-Time Native American Curator," *New York Times*, September 9, 2020, https://www.nytimes.com/2020/09/09/arts/design/met-museum-native-american-curator.html.
74 TSP 2022—The Sámi Pavilion, press kit: https://drive.google.com/file/d/14NczIcuuDX2vpb1lNPD p5B8D tdDV79wt/view.
75 Finbog in communication with the author on April 27, 2022.
76 heather ahtone, "Opening Keynote: heather ahtone: Decolonizing the Museum: what does it mean to serve the community?" *MCN*, October 5, 2021, https://mcn.edu/resources/opening-keynote-heather-ahtone-decolonizing-the-museum-what-does-it-mean-to-serve-the-community/.
77 heather ahtone, "Opening Keynote."
78 Lonetree, *Decolonizing Museums*, 23.
79 Shawn Wilson, "What Is an Indigenous Research Methodology?" *Canadian Journal of Native Education*, vol. 25, no. 2 (2001): 176.
80 Lonetree, *Decolonizing Museums*, 22.
81 Trudy Nicks, "Introduction to 'Museums and Contact Work' Part 1," in *Museums and Source Communities: A Routledge Reader*, ed. Laura L. Peers and Alison K. Brown (New York: Routledge, 2003): 21.
82 Lonetree, *Decolonizing Museums*, 42. According to Amy Lonetree (*Decolonizing Museums*, 34), the concept of "survivance" was defined by scholar Gerlad Vizenor.
83 Lonetree, *Decolonizing Museums*, 90.
84 Cairns, "Decolonisation."
85 MTL Collective, "From Institutional Critique to Institutional Liberation? A Decolonial Perspective on the Crises of Contemporary Art," *October*, no. 165 (Summer 2018): 218.
86 The Abbe Museum's 2015 strategic plan is available on their website: https://abbemuseum.wordpress.com/the-plan/.
87 Terry Janke et al., *First Peoples: A Roadmap for Enhancing Indigenous Engagement in Museums and Galleries* (Canberra: Australian Museums and Galleries Association, 2018), https://www.amaga-indigenous.org.au/_files/ugd/f76062_c67539d5b2e2433181f66b15ec499d89.pdf; Frank Howarth, "Decolonizing the Museum Mind," American Alliance of Museums (blog), October 8, 2018, https://www.aam-us.org/2018/10/08/decolonizing-the-museum-mind/.
88 Frank Howarth, former director of the Australian Museum has explained that, as part of the *Indigenous Roadmap*, the museum has brought in leaders to review the collections. Notably, the Australian Museum invited Chief Jerry Taki, a Ni-Vanuatu leader, to review the Vanuatu collections and help the museum understand the diversity of arrowheads, knowledge of which they were unaware until then. See Howarth, "Decolonizing the Museum Mind."
89 Janke et al., *First Peoples*.

Chapter 3: "GIVE IT ALL BACK"

1 As Macron explained: "I cannot accept that a large part of the cultural heritage of several African countries should be in France.…Africa's heritage must be showcased in Paris, but also in Dakar, in Lagos, in Cotonou. This will be one of my priorities. Starting today, and in the next five years, I want to see the conditions put in place so as to allow for the temporary or definitive restitution of African cultural heritage to Africa." Macron quoted in Farah Nayer, "Museums in France Should Return African Treasures, Report Says," *New York Times*, November 21, 2018, https://www.nytimes.com/2018/1½1/arts/design/france-museums-africa-savoy-sarr-report.html.
2 Macron quoted in Patty Gerstenblith, "Historical Appropriations: Of Time and Reparative Justice," in *Cultural Objects and Reparative Justice:*

A Legal and Historical Analysis," (Oxford: Oxford University Press, 2023): 255.

3 Felwine Sarr and Bénédicte Savoy, *The Restitution of African Cultural Heritage: Toward a New Relational Ethics* (Paris: Philippe Rey/Seuil, 2018): 61, https://www.unimuseum.uni-tuebingen.de/fileadmin/content/05_Forschung_Lehre/Provenienz/sarr_savoy_en.pdf.

4 Sarr and Savoy, *Restitution*, 44.

5 Sally Price, *Paris Primitive: Jacques Chirac's Museum on the Quai Branly* (Chicago: Chicago University Press, 2007). See also, James Clifford, "Quai Branly in Process," *October*, 120 (2007): 8.

6 Sarr and Savoy, *Restitution*, 61; Tristram Hunt, "Should museums return their colonial artefacts?" *Guardian*, June 29, 2019, https://www.theguardian.com/culture/2019/jun/29/should-museums-return-their-colonial-artefacts?

7 Sarr and Savoy, *Restitution*, 16.

8 As defined in *Encyclopedia Britannica*, "Ordinance of Moulins," accessed May 1, 2024, https://www.britannica.com/topic/Ordinance-of-Moulins.

9 "Macron Orders Return of Looted Benin Thrones and Statues 'Without Delay,'" *Frieze*, November 26, 2018, https://www.frieze.com/article/macron-orders-return-looted-benin-thrones-and-statues-without-delay.

10 French Senate, "Retour de biens culturels au Bénin et au Sénègal," press release, Sénat.fr, December 17, 2020, https://www.senat.fr/salle-de-presse/202010/retour-de-biens-culturels-au-benin-et-au-senegal.html.

11 Bénédicte Savoy, "The Restitution Revolution Begins," *The Art Newspaper*, February 16, 2018, https://www.theartnewspaper.com/2018/02/16/the-restitution-revolution-begins.

12 Gareth Harris, "Nigeria's Hotly Anticipated Edo Museum of West African Art: Newly Appointed Curator Aindrea Emelife Discusses Her plans," *The Art Newspaper*, April 17, 2023, https://www.theartnewspaper.com/2023/04/17/nigerias-edo-museum-of-west-african-art-newly-appointed-curator-aindrea-emelife.

13 Dan Hicks, *The Brutish Museum: The Benin Bronzes, Colonial Violence and Cultural Restitution* (London: Pluto Press, 2020): 18.

14 In 2021, the Met repatriated 2 Benin Bronzes; it still has 163 objects from Benin in its collection. Alex Greenberger, "Metropolitan Museum of Art Returns Two Benin Bronzes," *ARTnews*, June 10, 2021, https://www.artnews.com/art-news/news/metropolitan-museum-of-art-returns-two-benin-bronzes-1234595399/.

15 In 2022, the Smithsonian (Washington, DC) repatriated twenty-nine Benin Bronzes to representatives of Nigeria's National Commission for Museums and Monuments. Matt Stevens, "Smithsonian to Return Most of Its Benin Bronze Collection to Nigeria," *New York Times*, March 8, 2022, https://www.nytimes.com/2022/03/08/arts/design/smithsonian-benin-bronze-nigeria.html.

16 On July 1, 2022, Germany restituted two Benin bronzes and "put more than 1,000 other items from its museums' collections into Nigeria's ownership." See Philip Oltermann, "Germany Hands over Two Benin Bronzes to Nigeria," *Guardian*, July 1, 2022, https://www.theguardian.com/world/2022/jul/01/germany-hands-over-two-benin-bronzes-to-nigeria. See also, "Historic Return of Bronzes to Nigeria," German Federal Foreign Office, July 1, 2022, https://www.auswaertiges-amt.de/en/aussenpolitik/themen/-/2540358.

17 See Oltermann, "Germany Hands over Two Benin Bronzes."

18 Oltermann.

19 Adam Kuper, "Who Owns the 'Victorious Youth'?" *New York Times*, June 30, 2024, https://www.nytimes.com/2024/06/30/opinion/museum-statue-looted-culture.html.

20 Kwame Opoku, "The Oba of Benin Owns the Benin Bronzes," *Modern Ghana*, May 24, 2023, https://www.modernghana.com/news/1232864/the-oba-of-benin-owns-the-benin-bronzes.html.

21 Daniel Cassidy, "Nigeria Works to Reclaim Benin Bronzes, With a Change of Custodian," *ARTnews*, February 26, 2025, https://www.artnews.com/art-news/news/nigeria-benin-bronzes-ncmm-oba-1234733527/.

22 MoMAA, "Cambridge Surrenders 116 Benin Bronzes to Nigeria—and the British Museum Has Nowhere Left to Hide," Museum of Modern African Art (MoMAA), February 16, 2026, https://momaa.org/cambridge-surrenders-116-benin-bronzes-to-nigeria-and-the-british-museum-has-nowhere-left-to-hide/; Geraldine Kendall Adams, "Cambridge University Transfers Ownership of 116 Benin Bronzes to Nigeria," *Museums Association Journal*, February 9, 2026, https://www.museumsassociation.org/museums-journal/news/2026/02/cambridge-university-transfers-ownership-of-116-benin-bronzes-to-nigeria/.

23 Such as the National Museum of Egyptian Civilization (NMEC) in Cairo, the Acropolis Museum in Athens, and the Museum of West African Art (MWAA) in Benin City.

24 Farah Nayeri, "Museums in France Should Return African Treasures, Report Says," *New York Times*, November 21, 2018, https://www.nytimes.com/2018/11/21/arts/design/france-museums-africa-savoy-sarr-report.html.

25 Bénédicte Savoy quoted in Farah Nayeri, "Museums in France Should Return African Treasures, Report Says."

26 See "History of the Collections," Musée du quai Branly, accessed September 5, 2023, https://www.quaibranly.fr/en/collections/all-collections/history-of-the-collections.

27 See the British Museum fact sheet here: https://www.britishmuseum.org/sites/default/files/2019-10/fact_sheet_bm_collection.pdf.

https://www.britishmuseum.org/search?search_api_fulltext=fact-sheet-bm.

28 Cassie Packard, "Dan Hicks on the Benin Bronzes and Ultraviolence of World Culture Museums," *Hyperallergic*, January 29, 2021, https://hyperallergic.com/613840/dan-hicks-the-brutish-museums/.

29 "Declaration on the Importance and Value of Universal Museums," press release, Cleveland Museum of Art, December 8, 2002, https://archive.org/details/cmapr4492.

30 See note 28.

31 Hunt, "Should museums return their colonial artefacts?"

32 Kanishk Tharoor, "Museums and Looted Art: The Ethical Dilemma of Preserving World Culture," *Guardian*, June 29, 2015, https://www.theguardian.com/culture/ 2015/jun/29/museums-looting-art-artefacts-world-culture.

33 Tess Davis quoted in Tharoor, "Museums and Looted Art: The Ethical Dilemma of Preserving World Culture."

34 Geoffrey Lewis, "The Universal Museum—a Special Case?" *ICOM News*, vol. 57, no. 1 (2004): 3–5.

35 As Isaac Kaplan has noted, "Highlighting this [white men] is not a criticism of their job performance, nor an attempt to dismiss them or the museums they govern." "Rather," he continues, "it speaks to the very realities of who in our society—which is rife with gender and racial inequity—is privileged enough to be in a position to define so-called universality." Isaac Kaplan, "The Case against the Universal Museum," *Artsy*, April 26, 2016, https://www.artsy.net/article/artsy-editorial-the-case-against-the-universal-museum.

36 David Gill, "Review of James Cuno, *Who Owns Antiquity? Museums and the Battle over Our Ancient Heritage* (Princeton University Press, 2008)," *American Journal of Archaeology*, vol. 113 (2009): 104; Kwame Opoku, "Declaration on the Importance and Value of Universal Museums: Singular Failure of an Arrogant Imperialist Project," *Modern Ghana*, January 27, 2013, https://www.modernghana.com/news/441891/declaration-on-the-importance-and-value-of-univers.html. Hereafter, Opoku 2013. Mark O'Neill, "Enlightenment Museums: Universal or Merely Global?" *Museum and Society*, vol. 2, no. 3 (2004): 190–202; Tom Flynn, "The Universal Museum: A Valid Model for the 21st Century?" (unpublished manuscript, 2010), typescript, https://www.academia.edu/20053839/The_Universal_Museum_A_Valid_Model_for_the_21st_Century.

37 David Gill quoted in Opoku 2013.

38 Opoku 2013.

39 George Abungu, "The Declaration: A Contested Issue," *ICOM News*, vol. 57, no. 1. (2004): 5, quoted in Opoku 2013. See interview of Dr. Abungu by Tom Flynn: "Georges Okello Abungu at Forum d'Avignon," https://www.modernghana.com/news/433206/georges-okello-abungu-at-forum-davignon.html. Cited in Opoku, 2013. See also Lewis, "The Universal Museum."

40 Opoku 2013.

41 Since the 2002 Declaration, countless institutions and nations have had to return objects to source communities. "France has restored Korean manuscripts looted in 1866; Yale University has returned Peruvian artefacts that had been in the USA since 1912; and Egypt has recovered over the last decade some 5,000 artefacts wrongfully taken from the country. Several American museums and universities have returned looted artefacts to Italy and to Greece. The Brooklyn Museum has returned some 4,500 pre-Columbian artefacts taken from Costa Rica a century ago even though Costa Rica had not asked for them. China, Egypt, Greece, Peru, Nigeria and other States have established a conference to press for cases of restitution and submitted lists of objects to be returned to their countries of origin. Turkey's recent efforts to recover its looted artefacts appear to be successful and the Germans have returned the Bogazkoy Sphinx which they had kept for several decades." (Opoku 2013.)

42 Jason Felch, "Getty Studies Its Antiquities," *Los Angeles Times*, January 19, 2013, https://www.latimes.com/archives/la-xpm-2013-jan-18-la-et-getty-ambers-20130119-story.html.

43 "Convention for the Protection of Cultural Property in the Event of Armed Conflict with Regulations for the Execution of the Convention," UNESCO, adopted May 14, 1954, 249 UNTS 240, https://www.unesco.org/en/legal-affairs/convention-protection-cultural-property-event-armed-conflict-regulations-execution-convention. For an overview of the 1954 Hague Convention, see also Patty Gerstenblith, "Destruction of Cultural Heritage: A Crime against Property or a Crime against People?" *The John Marshall Review of Intellectual Property Law*, vol. 15, no. 336 (2016): 346–51.

44 "Convention on the Means of Prohibiting and Preventing the Illicit Import, Export and Transfer of Ownership of Cultural Property," UNESCO, adopted November 14, 1970, 823 UNTS 231, https://www.unesco.org/en/legal-affairs/convention-means-prohibiting-and-preventing-illicit-import-export-and-transfer-ownership-cultural.

45 "Convention on the Means of Prohibiting."

46 Anny Shaw, "Black Lives Matter Movement Is Speeding Up Repatriation Efforts, Leading French Art Historian Says," *The Art Newspaper*, October 21, 2020, https://www.theartnewspaper.com/2020/10/21/black-lives-matter-movement-is-speeding-up-repatriation-efforts-leading-french-art-historian-says.

47 Savoy quoted in Shaw, "Black Lives Matter."

48 Shaw, "Black Lives Matter."

49 Shaw.

50 "UNIDROIT Convention on Stolen or Illegally Exported Cultural Objects," UNIDROIT (International Institute for the Unification of Private Law), June 24, 1995, https://www.unidroit.org/instruments/cultural-property/1995-convention/.
51 Laurent Carpentier, "French Museums Face a Cultural Change over Restitution of Colonial Objects," *Guardian*, November 3, 2014, https://www.theguardian.com/world/2014/nov/03/france-museums-restitution-colonial-objects.
52 Carpentier, "French Museums Face a Cultural Change."
53 "United Nations Declaration on the Rights of Indigenous Peoples," United Nations General Assembly, adopted September 13, 2007, A/RES/61/295, https://www.un.org/development/desa/indigenouspeoples/wp-content/uploads/sites/19/2018/11/UNDRIP_E_web.pdf.
54 Carpentier, "French Museums Face a Cultural Change."
55 "Guidelines on the Acquisition of Archaeological Material and Ancient Art," Association of Art Museum Directors (AAMD), 2004. This document is no longer available on the AAMD website. However, it has been incorporated into the 2013 revised guidelines, reproduced here in full, including the preamble: https://asia.si.edu/wp-content/uploads/2024/05/AAMD-Guidelines-2013.pdf.
56 "Guidelines on the Acquisition of Archaeological Material and Ancient Art (revised 2013)," Association of Art Museum Directors (AAMD), January 29, 2013; Pei-Lin Yu, Chen Shen, and George Smith (eds.), *Relevance and Application of Heritage in Contemporary Society* (New York: Routledge, 2018), https://www.taylorfrancis.com/books/edit/10.4324/9780203702277/relevance-application-heritage-contemporary-society-chen-shen-pei-lin-yu-george-smith.
57 "Restitution and Repatriation: A Practical Guide for Museums in England," Arts Council England, September, 2023, https://www.artscouncil.org.uk/supporting-arts-museums-and-libraries/supporting-collections-and-cultural-property/restitution-and-repatriation-practical-guide-museums-england. On the subject of human remains, ACE suggests readers refer to the DCMS *Guidance for the Care of Human Remains in Museums* (Department of Culture, Media and Sport, October 2005).
58 "Restitution and Repatriation," 17.
59 "Guidelines on Dealing with Collections from Colonial Contexts," German Museums Association, July 2018, https://www.museumsbund.de/wp-content/uploads/2019/10/dmb-guidelines-colonial-context.pdf.
60 "Guidelines on Dealing with Collections."
61 Tharoor, "Museums and Looted Art."
62 U.S. Congress, *Native American Graves Protection and Repatriation Act*, November 16, 1990. Pub. L. No. 101–601, H.R. 5237, 101st Cong., https://www.congress.gov/101/statute/STATUTE-104/STATUTE-104-Pg3048.pdf.
63 See "Repatriation of Ceremonial Objects, Ancestral Human Remains and Intangible Cultural Heritage under the United Nations Declaration on the Rights of Indigenous Peoples," UN Human Rights Council, Expert Mechanism on the Rights of Indigenous Peoples, July 21, 2020, A/HRC/45/35, https://documents.un.org/doc/undoc/gen/g20/187/65/pdf/g2018765.pdf.
64 Logan Jaffe, Mary Hudetz, Ash Ngu, *ProPublica*, and Graham Lee Brewer, *NBC News*, "America's Biggest Museums Fail to Return Native American Human Remains," *ProPublica*, January 11, 2023, https://www.propublica.org/article/repatriation-nagpra-museums-human-remains; and Jennifer Schuessler, "What Should Museums Do with the Bones of the Enslaved?" *New York Times*, April 20, 2021, https://www.nytimes.com/2021/04/20/arts/design/museums-bones-smithsonian.html.
65 Jaffe et al., "America's Biggest Museums."
66 "The Repatriation Database: Illinois State Museum," *ProPublica*, November 29, 2023, https://www.propublica.org/article/repatriation-nagpra-museums-human-remains.
67 Darrell Newell quoted in Mary Hudetz and Ash Ngu, "Tribes in Maine Spent Decades Fighting to Rebury Ancestral Remains. Harvard Resisted at Every Turn," *ProPublica*, December 4, 2023, https://www.propublica.org/article/inside-wabanaki-tribes-struggle-to-reclaim-ancestral-remains-from-harvard.
68 Kathleen Sharp, "Is the Metropolitan Museum of Art Displaying Objects That Belong to Native American Tribes?" *ProPublica*, April 25, 2023, https://www.propublica.org/article/the-met-museum-native-american-collections.
69 Julia Jacobs and Zachary Small, "Leading Museums Remove Native Displays amid New Federal Rules," *New York Times*, January 26, 2024, https://www.nytimes.com/2024/0½6/arts/design/american-museum-of-natural-history-nagpra.html?; Julia Jacobs, "Six Objects that Explain New Rules on Native Displays in Museums," *New York Times*, February 21, 2024, https://www.nytimes.com/2024/02/21/arts/design/native-displays-museums-law.html.
70 The concept of "free, prior, and informed consent" is explicated in the 2023 update to the law, accessed here: https://www.federalregister.gov/documents/2023/12/13/2023-27040/native-american-graves-protection-and-repatriation-act-systematic-processes-for-disposition-or; see also Elaine Velie, "American Museum of Natural History Closes Native Exhibition Halls," *Hyperallergic*, January 26, 2024, https://hyperallergic.com/868254/american-museum-of-natural-

history-closes-native-exhibition-halls-nagpra-regulations/.

71 "Field Museum Alters Cultural Galleries in Response to Updated Federal Regulations," Field Museum, press release, January 9, 2024, https://www.fieldmuseum.org/about/press/field-museum-alters-cultural-galleries-in-response-to-updated-federal-regulations.

72 Jacobs and Small, "Leading Museums Remove Native Displays."

73 Jaffe et al., "America's Biggest Museums."

74 Geraldine Kendall Adams, "Smithsonian Moves Towards 'Informed Consent' Principle for Human Remains," *Museums Association Journal*, March 12, 2024, https://www.museumsassociation.org/museums-journal/news/2024/03/smithsonian-moves-towards-informed-consent-principle-for-human-remains/.

75 Adams, "Smithsonian Moves Towards 'Informed Consent' Principle."

76 Adams.

77 On human remains and the bill proposed to the French Parliament in January 2023, see Elaine Velie, "Understanding France's New Restitution Guidelines," *Hyperallergic*, May 4, 2023, https://hyperallergic.com/819941/understanding-frances-new-restitution-guidelines/; Vincent Noce, "France Simplifies Law on Restitution of Human Remains," *The Art Newspaper*, December 20, 2023, https://www.theartnewspaper.com/2023/12/20/france-simplifies-law-on-restitution-of-human-remains. On Nazi-looted art and the bill proposed to the French Parliament in January 2023, see Tessa Solomon, "France Passes Law Allowing Museums to Restitute Nazi-Looted Artworks," *ARTnews*, July 3, 2023, https://www.artnews.com/art-news/news/france-passes-law-museums-restitute-nazi-looted-artworks-1234673197/.

78 Jean-Luc Martinez, "Universalité, restitutions et circulation des œuvres d'art," April 27, 2023. The link to the report can be accessed here: https://www.culture.gouv.fr/fr/Espace-documentation/Rapports/Remise-du-rapport-Patrimoine-partage-universalite-restitutions-et-circulation-des-aeuvres-d-art-de-Jean-Luc-Martinez.

79 Pierre Ouzoulias quoted in Roxana Azimi, "In France, Restitution of African Artifacts Is Subject to Conditions," *Le Monde*, May 5, 2023, https://www.lemonde.fr/en/culture/article/2023/05/05/in-france-restitution-of-african-artifacts-is-subject-to-conditions_6025556_30.html.

80 Roxana Azimi, "Le Conseil d'Etat relève un frien aux restitutions d'ouvres d'art acquise par la France dans des conditions abusives," *Le Monde*, March 26, 2024, https://www.lemonde.fr/culture/article/2024/03/26/le-conseil-d-etat-releve-un-frein-aux-restitutions-d-uvres-d-art-acquises-par-la-france-dans-des-conditions-abusives_6224262_3246.html.

81 Rachel Holmes, *The Hottentot Venus: The Life and Death of Saartjie Baartman* (London: Bloomsbury, 2007).

82 Dalya Alberge, "British Museum Is World's Largest Receiver of Stolen Goods," *Guardian*, November 4, 2019, https://www.theguardian.com/world/2019/nov/04/british-museum-is-worlds-largest-receiver-of-stolen-goods-says-qc.

83 See "Everything You Ever Wanted to Know About the Rosetta Stone," British Museum (blog), July 14, 2017, https://blog.britishmuseum.org/everything-you-ever-wanted-to-know-about-the-rosetta-stone/.

84 Paul Daley, "The Gweagal Shield and the Fight to Change the British Museum's Attitude to Seized Artefacts," *Guardian*, September 25, 2016, https://www.theguardian.com/australia-news/2016/sep/25/the-gweagal-shield-and-the-fight-to-change-the-british-museums-attitude-to-seized-artefacts; Naomi Polonsky, "Hundreds Attend Guerrilla, Activist-Led Tour of Looted Artifacts at the British Museum," *Hyperallergic*, December 10, 2018, https://hyperallergic.com/hundreds-attend-guerrilla-activist-led-tour-of-looted-artifacts-at-the-british-museum/.

85 Kelly quoted in Paul Daley, "The Gweagal Shield."

86 Calla Wahlquist, "Australian Senate Joins Push to Repatriate Indigenous Artefacts from British Museum," *Guardian*, October 11, 2016, https://www.theguardian.com/australia-news/2016/oct/11/australian-senate-joins-push-to-repatriate-indigenous-artefacts-from-british-museum.

87 See "Early Shield from New South Wales, Australia," entry, British Museum website, https://www.britishmuseum.org/about-us/british-museum-story/contested-objects-collection/early-shield-australia.

88 Alexander Herman, "Museums, Restitution and the New Charities Act," *Art, Antiquity and Law*, vol. 27, no. 3 (2022): 196.

89 U.K. National Heritage Act, 1983, Chapter 47, https://www.legislation.gov.uk/ukpga/1983/47/pdfs/ukpga_19830047_en.pdf. See also Hunt, "Should museums return their colonial artefacts?"

90 Geraldine Kendall Adams, "National Museums to Be Excluded from Law Enabling Restitution on Moral Grounds," *Museums Association Journal*, February 13, 2024, https://www.museumsassociation.org/museums-journal/news/2024/02/national-museums-to-be-excluded-from-law-enabling-restitution-on-moral-grounds/. Hereafter Adams 2024.

91 Adams 2024.

92 Adams 2024.

93 Adams 2024.

94 Adams 2024.

95 Kwame Opoku, "British Museum and Victoria and Albert Loan Looted Asante Artefacts to Asante," *Modern Ghana*,

February 28, 2024, https://www.modernghana.com/news/1295729/british-museum-and-victoria-and-albert-museum-loan.html. See also Simon Stephens, "V&A and British Museum to Loan Asante Gold to Ghana," *Museums Association Journal*, January 25, 2024, https://www.museumsassociation.org/museums-journal/news/2024/01/va-and-british-museum-to-loan-asante-gold-to-ghana/.

96 Ta-Nehisi Coates, "The Case for Reparations," *Atlantic*, June 2014.

97 Karen Warren, "A Philosophical Perspective on the Ethics and Resolution of Cultural Property Issues," *The Ethics of Collecting Cultural Property: Whose Culture? Whose Property?*, ed. Phyllis Mauch Messenger (Albuquerque: University of New Mexico Press, 1989): 1–26.

98 Isaac Kaplan, "The Case against the Universal Museum," *Artsy*, April 26, 2016, https://www.artsy.net/article/artsy-editorial-the-case-against-the-universal-museum.

99 Ariana Davis quoted in a "Stolen Goods" tour at the British Museum, organized by the activist group BP or Not BP. See "Hundreds Join Unofficial Tour to Challenge British Museum Stolen Items and BP Sponsorship," BP or Not BP website, December 10, 2018, https://bp-or-not-bp.org/2018/12/10/hundreds-join-unofficial-tour-to-challenge-british-museum-stolen-items-and-bp-sponsorship/.

100 As described by Antoaneta Roussi, "Kenya Demands Return of Man-Eating Tsavo Lions Hailed as 'First Resistance' against Colonial Rule," *Telegraph*, March 20, 2021, https://www.telegraph.co.uk/news/2021/03/20/kenya-demands-return-man-eating-tsova-lions-hailed-first-resistance/.

101 On July 25, 2022, President Uhuru Kenyatta officially opened the Mashujaa state-of-the-art Uhuru Gardens National Monument and Museum. Maureen Kinyanjui, "Inside the Iconic Museum at Uhuru Gardens," *Star*, July 27, 2022, https://www.the-star.co.ke/in-pictures/2022-07-27-photos-inside-the-iconic-museum-at-uhuru-gardens/.

102 Roussi, "Kenya Demands Return of Man-Eating Tsavo Lions."

103 The Great Zimbabwe birds (of which there are eight in total) date back to the 11th century. They are the national emblem of the nation, appearing on its flag, currency, and on stamps. Of the eight, seven have been repatriated to Zimbabwe. The only remaining bird not to have been returned is in the collection of the Groote Schuur Estate, Cape Town, which was the British colonialist Cecil Rhodes's home, and later served as the residence of the prime ministers of South Africa. The last bird is still located in what was Rhodes's bedroom. Many Zimbabweans believe that their country will never experience good fortune until its eight birds are reunited. "Great Zimbabwe Bird—One Still Remains," *Africa Global News*, April 20, 2020, https://africaglobalnews.com/great-zimbabwe-bird-one-still-remains/. The Nefertiti bust in the collection of the Neues Museum, Berlin, is a painted limestone bust of one of the most famous women of ancient Egypt that dates back to 1345 BCE. It was excavated by a German archaeological team in 1912, after which it has resided in several German museum collections. Since 1934, Egypt has been demanding its repatriation, arguing that it was smuggled out of the country illegally. Egypt also says that the statue was taken in breach of the rules for archaeological digs at the time, which stated that "exceptional antiquities" discovered by foreign excavation teams were to be handed over to Egypt, "while the remaining artifacts would be distributed among the party that discovered them and the Egyptian Museum in Cairo." Germany insists that the acquisition of the bust was lawful and refuses to lend it to Egypt because, they argue, it is too fragile for transport. See Ibrahim Ayyad, "Egypt Renews Demands to Retrieve Nefertiti Bust from Germany," *Al-Monitor*, October 1, 2020, https://www.al-monitor.com/originals/2020/10/egypt-germany-nefertiti-bust-claim-stolen-antiquities.html?; and "Seeking Nefertiti," *Deutsche Welle*, December 22, 2009, https://www.dw.com/en/germany-acquired-nefertiti-illegally-egyptian-official-says/a-5046115.

104 Warren, "A Philosophical Perspective," 13.

105 Hicks, *The Brutish Museum*, 243.

106 Robin Scher, "Better Safe Than Sorry: America Museums Take Measures Mindful of Repatriation of African Art," *ARTnews*, June 11, 2019, https://www.artnews.com/artnews/news/african-art-repatriation-american-museums-12750/?

107 Stuart Braun, "Calls Grow to Return Looted Colonial Art," *Deutsche Welle*, May 5, 2019, https://www.dw.com/en/looted-colonial-art-is-there-the-political-will-to-return-pilfered-artifacts/a-46961670.

108 Foley quoted in Braun, "Calls Grow to Return Looted Colonial Art."

109 Philip Oltermann, "'Inconvenient Truths': Berlin's Humboldt Forum Faces Up to Its Colonial Past," *Guardian*, September 19, 2022, https://www.theguardian.com/culture/2022/sep/19/inconvenient-truths-berlin-humboldt-forum-faces-up-to-its-colonial-past.

110 Scher, "Better Safe Than Sorry."

111 Artnet News, "The Prado Is Installing Replica Works by Goya, El Greco, and Other Old Masters from Its Collection All over Madrid," *Artnet*, May 30, 2021, https://news.artnet.com/art-world/art-in-the-streets-prado-museum-1974017.

112 See "Preserving Cultural Heritage: University of Chicago Replicates Warka Vase with PolyJet™ 3D Printing," Case study, Stratasys, July 5, 2023, https://www.stratasys.com/en/resources/case-studies/isac-museum-warka-vase-replica/.

113 Spencer Woodman, Malia Politzer, Delphine Reuter, and Namrata Sharma, "More than 1000 Artifacts in the Metropolitan Museum of Art Catalog Linked to Alleged Looting and Trafficking Figures," *International Consortium of Investigative Journalists*, March 20, 2023, https://www.icij.org/investigations/hidden-treasures/more-than-1000-artifacts-in-metropolitan-museum-of-art-catalog-linked-to-alleged-looting-and-trafficking-figures/.

114 Spencer Woodman, "In Response to Scandals and Stolen Art Seizures the Met Plans to Scour Its Collections for Looted Artifacts," *International Consortium of Investigative Journalists*, May 11, 2023, https://www.icij.org/investigations/hidden-treasures/in-response-to-scandals-and-stolen-art-seizures-the-met-plans-to-scour-its-own-collections-for-looted-artifacts/. See also Spencer Woodman and Malia Politzer, "Flurry of Seizures Intensify Pressure on the Met over Artifacts Linked to Accused Traffickers," *International Consortium of Investigative Journalists*, August 31, 2022, https://www.icij.org/investigations/hidden-treasures/flurry-of-seizures-intensify-pressure-on-the-met-over-artifacts-linked-to-accused-traffickers/.

115 Dan Hicks, "The British Museum is an anachronism – here's how to fix it," *Telegraph*, August 29, 2023, https://www.telegraph.co.uk/art/architecture/dan-hicks-how-to-fix-the-british-museum/.

116 Dan Hicks, "The Last Remaining Argument against Restitution Has Now Been Lost," *The Art Newspaper*, August 29, 2023, https://www.theartnewspaper.com/2023/08/29/the-last-remaining-argument-against-restitution-has-now-been-lost.

117 Kwame Okobu, "Can We Trust the British Museum with Our Cultural Treasures?" *Modern Ghana*, September 7, 2023, https://www.modernghana.com/news/1257371/can-we-trust-the-british-museum-with-our-cultural.html; "Chinese State Media Demands British Museum Return 23,000 Cultural Relics," *9 News*, August 29, 2023, https://www.9news.com.au/world/calls-for-british-museum-to-return-cultural-relics-to-china/.

118 Okobu, "Can We Trust the British Museum with Our Cultural Treasures?" See also: Sean Seddon, "British Museum recovers some of 2,000 stolen items," *BBC News*, August 26, 2023, https://www.bbc.com/news/entertainment-arts-66626619.

119 "British Museum Collection," factsheet, British Museum, https://www.britishmuseum.org/sites/default/files/2019-10/fact_sheet_bm_collection.pdf.

Chapter 4: WHOSE MUSEUM IS IT?

EDITORIAL NOTE:
Parts of this chapter incorporate material from articles written by the author and previously published in *ARTnews*. All texts are reproduced here with permission: "What Is Curatorial Activism?" November 7, 2017, https://www.artnews.com/art-news/news/what-is-curatorial-activism-9271/; "MoMA's Revisionism Is Piecemeal and Problem-Filled: Feminist Art Historian Maura Reilly on the Museum's Rehang," October 31, 2019, https://www.artnews.com/art-news/reviews/moma-rehang-art-historian-maura-reilly-13484/; "Misfired Canon: A Feminist Curator Finds the Rehang Seriously Lacking," Winter 2020, http://www.maurareilly.com/pdf/essays/2020-Reviews_MoMA_Reilly.pdf; and "With a Majority-Female 2022 Edition, the Venice Biennale Will Make History for Women Artists," February 10, 2022, https://www.artnews.com/art-news/news/venice-biennale-2022-women-artists-maura-reilly-1234618777/.

1 Julia Halperin and Charlotte Burns, "Museums Claim They're Paying More Attention to Female Artists. That's an Illusion," *Artnet*, September 19, 2019, https://news.artnet.com/womens-place-in-the-art-world/womens-place-art-world-museums-1654714.

2 Julia Halperin and Charlotte Burns, "Perceptions of Progress in the Art World Are Largely a Myth: Here Are the Facts," The Burns Halperin Report, *Artnet*, December 13, 2022, https://news.artnet.com/art-world/perceptions-of-progress-in-the-art-world-are-largely-a-myth-here-are-the-facts-2227941.

3 One of the infographics (Table 1) in the report computes that 76.4% of museums with annual budgets of $15 million or more are run by a male director. Another stat cited in the report gives a different figure, stating that "70% of museums with annual budgets of $15 million or more are run by a male director." See "The Ongoing Gender Gap in Art Museum Directorships," Association of Art Museum Directors (AAMD), 2017, https://aamd.org/our-members/from-the-field/gender-gap-report-2017#.

4 Linda Sweeney, Deirdre Harkins, Celeste Watkins-Hayes, and Dominique Adams-Santos, "The BTA 2022 Art Museum Trustee Survey," Ithaka S+R, November 16, 2022, https://sr.ithaka.org/publications/the-bta-2022-art-museum-trustee-survey/.

5 Adam Sage, "Female Art Was a Bargain—I Created the Gallery for the Price of One Male Artist," *The Times*, June 28, 2024, https://www.thetimes.com/world/europe/article/inside-the-female-artist-only-gallery-on-picassos-doorstep-wf6w5zbt7.

6 Christian Levett quoted in Sage, "Female Art Was a Bargain."

7 Jasmine Weber, "Artist Covertly Hangs #MeToo-Inspired Wall Labels at the Met Museum," *Hyperallergic*, November 7, 2018, https://hyperallergic.com/469996/artist-covertly-hangs-metoo-inspired-wall-labels-at-the-met-museum/. See also the artist's Instagram @michellehartneyart.

8 Cody Delistraty, "How Picasso Bled the Women in His Life for Art," *Paris Review*, November 9, 2017, https://www.theparisreview.org/blog/2017/11/09/how-picasso-bled-the-women-in-his-life-for-art/.

9 Erin Blakemore, "Rare Photographs Could Show Paul Gauguin in Tahiti," *Smithsonian Magazine*, February 13, 2017, https://www.smithsonianmag.com/smart-news/rare-photographs-show-paul-gaugin-in-tahiti-180962112/.

10 Peter Schjeldahl, "Moral Conundrums and Political Passions," *New Yorker*, December 25, 2017, https://www.newyorker.com/magazine/2018/01/01/moral-conundrums-and-political-passions.

11 Hannah Gadsby, *Nanette* (Netflix, 2018).

12 Roxane Gay, "Can I Enjoy the Art but Denounce the Artist?" *Marie Claire*, February 6, 2018, https://www.marieclaire.com/culture/a16105931/roxane-gay-on-predator-legacies/.

13 Gay, "Can I Enjoy the Art?"

14 In 2018, the Guerrilla Girls, in their response to the #MeToo movement, produced a poster titled *3 Ways to Write a Museum Wall Label when the Artist is a Sexual Predator* in which they used artist Chuck Close, who had been accused of sexual misconduct, to depict a three-tier option of portraying the artist and his accusations. https://www.guerrillagirls.com/2018-projects.

15 Cited in Nadja Sayej, "The Art World Tolerates Abuse: The Fight to Change Museum Wall Labels," *Guardian*, November 28, 2018, https://www.theguardian.com/artanddesign/2018/nov/28/the-art-world-tolerates-abuse-the-fight-to-change-museum-wall-labels.

16 Thanks to curator Christopher Riopelle (one of the curators of the exhibition *Gauguin Portraits* at the National Gallery, London) for sharing the exhibition's wall labels via email in April 30, 2020. He also shared the gallery brochure which included this information.

17 See note 16.

18 Gauguin's three "unofficial wives" included Teha'amana, Pau'ura, and Vaeoho Marie-Rose. He also had a wife back in Europe and five children, including a daughter named Aline who was approximately the same age as Teha'amana. Like Teha'amana, Aline died young. See Sarah Stewart-Kroeker, "'What Do We Do with the Art of Monstrous Men?' Betrayal and the Feminist Ethics of Aesthetic Involvement," *De Ethica: A Journal of Philosophical, Theological and Applied Ethics* 6, no. 1 (2020): 69.

19 Another work, a sculpture titled *Head of a Savage, Mask*, was displayed with a label explaining that the words "savage" and "barbarian," "considered offensive today, reflect attitudes common to Gauguin's time and place."

20 Caroline Vercoe quoted in the National Gallery's audio guide to *Gauguin Portraits*.

21 Farah Nayeri, "Is It Time Gauguin Got Cancelled?" *New York Times*, November 18, 2019, https://www.nytimes.com/2019/11/18/arts/design/gauguin-national-gallery-london.html. For an earlier article questioning the sharing of male artists' egregious behavior, like Schiele, see Jane Kallir, "Egon Schiele Was Not a Sex Offender," *The Art Newspaper*, June 1, 2018, https://www.theartnewspaper.com/2018/06/01/egon-schiele-was-not-a-sex-offender.

22 Nayeri, "Is It Time?"

23 Phil Helsel, "Stonewall Jackson Statue Down After Richmond Mayor Orders Removal of Confederate Monuments," *NBC News*, June 1, 2020, https://www.nbcnews.com/news/us-news/stonewall-jackson-statue-down-after-richmond-mayor-orders-removal-all-n1232732; Martin Farrer, "Who Was Edward Colston and Why Was His Bristol Statue Toppled?" *Guardian*, June 8, 2020, https://www.theguardian.com/uk-news/2020/jun/08/who-was-edward-colston-and-why-was-his-bristol-statue-toppled-slave-trader-black-lives-matter-protests.

24 Kurt Zindulka, "British Museum Removes Bust of Founder Sir Hans Sloane From Pedestal," *Breitbart*, August 26, 2020, https://www.breitbart.com/europe/2020/08/26/british-museum-removes-bust-of-founder-sir-hans-sloane-from-pedestal/. See also: PA Media, "British Museum Removes Statue of Slave-Owning Founder," *Guardian*, August 25, 2020, https://www.theguardian.com/culture/2020/aug/25/british-museum-removes-founder-hans-sloane-statue-over-slavery-links.

25 The wall text was provided to the author by the British Museum press office on July 9, 2021.

26 The author had an email exchange with the curator Neal Spencer on July 21, 2021, within which he made this statement. Similarly, Hartwig Fischer is quoted as saying that the murder of George Floyd "altered the awareness of everybody." See Alex Marshall, "The British Museum Reopens to a World That Has Changed," *New York Times*, August 27, 2020, https://www.nytimes.com/2020/08/27/arts/design/british-museum-reopening.html.

27 See British Museum, *Collecting and Empire* (blog), August 21, 2020, https://www.britishmuseum.org/blog/collecting-and-empire.

28 Quoted in Sayej, "The Art World Tolerates Abuse."

29 See note 28.

30 Nayeri, "Is It Time?"

31 Alfred Barr's narrative of modern art is a synchronic, linear progression of "isms" in which one (heterosexual, white) male "genius" from Europe or the U.S. influences a younger artist who inevitably must trump and subvert the previous master, thereby creating an avant-garde progression. See Maura Reilly, "Misfired Canon," *ARTnews*, Winter 2020, 110–13.

32 These statistics were provided by an insider at the Pompidou Center, who will remain anonymous.

33 The Pompidou owns nine works by Claude Cahun (none of which are illustrated in their database), two works by Gunta Stölzl (one is illustrated), but there are no works by Clausen or Moss.

34 Maura Reilly, "With a Majority-Female 2022 Edition, the Venice Biennale Will Make History for Women Artists."

35 Cecilia Alemani quoted in Charlotte Higgins, "Venice Biennale: Women Outnumber Male Artists in Main Halls for the First Time," *Guardian*, April 22, 2022, https://www.theguardian.com/artanddesign/2022/apr/22/venice-biennale-female-artists-outnumber-males-for-first-time.
36 Alemani, curatorial statement, La Biennale di Venezia website, 2022, https://www.labiennale.org/en/art/2022/statement-cecilia-alemani. Hereafter, Alemani 2022.
37 Alemani quoted in Vivienne Chow, "The Venice Biennale's Main Exhibition Will Challenge the Idea of 'Men as the Center of the Universe,'" *Artnet*, February 2, 2022, https://news.artnet.com/art-world/venice-biennale-challenge-white-men-2067142.
38 Alemani email to the author, July 21, 2023. See also Alemani 2022.
39 Madeline Weisburg, "Simone Leigh," La Biennale di Venezia website, 2022, https://www.labiennale.org/en/art/2022/milk-dreams/simone-leigh.
40 Alemani 2022.
41 Alemani 2022.
42 Okwui Enwezor's 2002 edition of Documenta was the first (and last, to date) to employ a postcolonial curatorial strategy. It's considered one of the most influential Euro-American exhibitions of the 21st century. See Maura Reilly, *Curatorial Activism: Towards an Ethics of Curating* (London: Thames & Hudson, 2018): 138–43.
43 Maurice Berger, "Are Art Museums Racist?" *Art in America*, September 1990, 70.
44 Berger, "Are Art Museums Racist?" 74.
45 See the Mellon Foundation's 2022 "Art Museum Staff Demographic Survey," https://assets.ctfassets.net/nslp74meuw3d/6gnnNJOBeDbYImaDPNnyT9/3221a846b1706bd73c552b2eb5931b5e/art_museum_staff_dem_survey_2022.pdf. For the Art Fund's findings, read their 2022 report titled "It's About Handing over Power: The Impact of Ethnic Diversity Initiatives on Curatorial Roles in the UK Arts and Heritage Sector, 1998–2021," https://bibli.artfund.org/m/53e933cf196387c3/original/Art-Fund-Curatorial-Diversity-report.pdf. See also Victoria L. Valentine, "Mellon Foundation Issues Report on Art Museum Diversity, Findings Show Significant Progress for African American Curators," *Culture Type*, February 1, 2019.
46 Chad Topaz et al., "Diversity of Artists in Major U.S. Museums," *PLOS One*, vol. 14, no. 3 (2019): 1–15. Crucially, the 13% female representation in museums combines women of *all* ethnicities, defined in the survey as white, Black, Latinx, and Asian. Of that 13%, Black women artists comprise just 2.2% of U.S. museum collections. This is an appalling statistic. The four largest groups represented across all eighteen museums in terms of gender and ethnicity are—in order of majority—white men (75.7%), white women (10.8%), Asian men (7.5%), and Hispanic/Latinx men (2.6%). All other groups, including Native Americans, are represented in proportions less than 1%.
47 Halperin and Burns, "Perceptions of Progress."
48 Halperin and Burns, "Perceptions of Progress." There is only one study I could find that specifically addressed representation of women artists of color: Hrag Vartanian, "Study Claims 80.5% of Artists Represented by NYC's Top 45 Galleries Are White," *Hyperallergic*, June 1, 2017, https://hyperallergic.com/382547/study-claims-80-5-of-artists-represented-by-nycs-top-45-galleries-are-white/. This article concludes that in 2017, just 5.6% of artists represented in a cross section of galleries in New York City were BIPOC women.
49 Liam Sweeney, Deirdre Harkins, and Joanna Dressel, *Art Museum Staff Demographic Survey 2022* (New York: Ithaka S+R, 2022), https://doi.org/10.18665/sr.317927; and a 2018 report from the Mellon Foundation titled "Art Museum Staff Demographic Survey" (see note 45), also made this abundantly clear.
50 Kenzie Grogan, "Austin's Museums and Galleries in the Age of Black Lives Matter" (Honors Thesis, The University of Texas at Austin, 2021), http://dx.doi.org/10.26153/tsw/13810.
51 Calculations based on the exhibition checklist accessed from the LACMA page dedicated to this 1976 exhibition: https://www.lacma.org/sites/default/files/icon-upload/date%3Acustom%3AY%5D-04/TwoCenturiesChecklist.pdf.
52 For additional information on the exhibition *The Decade Show*, see Reilly, *Curatorial Activism*, 112–17.
53 Robin Progrebin, "Curators Urge Guggenheim to Fix Culture that 'Enables Racism,'" *New York Times*, June 22, 2020, https://www.nytimes.com/2020/06/22/arts/design/guggenheim-curators-racism-sexism.html?
54 Aaron Randle, "'We Were Tired of Asking': Why Open Letters Have Become Many Activists' Tool of Choice for Exposing Racism at Museums," *Artnet*, July 14, 2020, https://news.artnet.com/art-world/museum-open-letters-activism-1894150.
55 Randle, "'We Were Tired of Asking.'"
56 For more information on the scandal surrounding the Baltimore Museum of Art's attempt to deaccession artworks, see Alex Greenberger, "Baltimore Museum Deaccessioning Controversy Explained," *ARTnews*, October 28, 2020, https://www.artnews.com/art-news/news/baltimore-museum-deaccessioning-controversy-explained-1234575222/.
57 However, in countries in the Asia Pacific region, such as Australia and New Zealand, there is far greater exposure for Indigenous artists. There are many more solo and group exhibitions dedicated to Aboriginal, Māori, Pacific Islander, and Torres Strait Islander artists than anywhere else in the world.
58 Amy Lonetree, *Decolonizing Museums: Representing Native America in National and Tribal Museums* (Chapel Hill: University

of North Caroline Press, 2012), 42. According to Lonetree (*Decolonizing Museums*, 34), the concept of "survivance" was defined by the scholar Gerlad Vizenor.

59 Sarah Bahr, "The Met Hires Its First Full-Time Native American Curator," *New York Times*, September 9, 2020, https://www.nytimes.com/2020/09/09/arts/design/met-museum-native-american-curator.html.

60 "'Most of These Items Are Not Art': Native American Advocacy Group Protests Met Show," *Frieze*, November 7, 2018, https://www.frieze.com/article/most-these-items-are-not-art-native-american-advocacy-group-protests-met-show. See press release from the Association on American Indian Affairs, dated October 29, 2018: https://www.indian-affairs.org/uploads/8/7/3/8/87380358/2018-10-29_met_pr.pdf.

61 Farah Nayeri, "A Museum Pivots to Become an 'Empathy Machine,'" *New York Times*, February 17, 2023, https://www.nytimes.com/2023/02/17/arts/design/manchester-museum-reopening-diversity.html; Safi Bugel, "Reopened Manchester Museum Gives Voice to South Asian Diaspora," *Guardian*, February 16, 2023, https://www.theguardian.com/uk-news/2023/feb/16/reopened-manchester-museum-gives-voice-to-south-asian-diaspora; Mark Brown, "Manchester Museum to Reopen with Ordinary Folk Co-Curating New Gallery," *Guardian*, October 31, 2022, https://www.theguardian.com/uk-news/2022/oct/31/manchester-museum-to-reopen-with-ordinary-folk-co-curating-new-gallery.

62 Esme Ward quoted in Brown, "Manchester Museum."

63 Nayeri, "A Museum Pivots to Become an 'Empathy Machine.'"

64 Richard Sandell quoted in Alex Marshall, "Is This the World's Most Accessible Museum?" *New York Times*, September 11, 2019, https://www.nytimes.com/2019/09/06/arts/design/disabled-access-wellcome-collection.html.

65 "Disability," World Health Organization, accessed March 7, 2023, https://www.who.int/news-room/fact-sheets/detail/disability-and-health.

66 Geraldine Kendall Adams, "Workforce Diversity Remains Static at Museums in England," *Museums Association Journal*, February 19, 2019, https://www.museumsassociation.org/museums-journal/news/2019/02/19022019-museums-workforce-diversity-static/.

67 Philippa Kelly, "Groundbreaking UK Exhibition Spotlights Work of Disabled D/deaf and Neurodivergent Artists," *The Art Newspaper*, July 19, 2024, https://www.theartnewspaper.com/2024/07/19/groundbreaking-uk-exhibition-spotlights-work-of-disabled-ddeaf-and-neurodivergent-artists.

68 National Endowment for the Arts, "New NEA Research on Arts Participation Among People with Disabilities," July 1, 2015, https://www.arts.gov/news/press-releases/2015/new-nea-research-arts-participation-among-people-disabilities.

69 Anny Shaw, "Wheelchair User Blasts Olafur Eliasson Show at Tate Modern over Rampless Work," *The Art Newspaper*, August 12, 2019, https://www.theartnewspaper.com/2019/08/12/wheelchair-user-blasts-olafur-eliasson-show-at-tate-modern-over-rampless-work. O'Connor continues to document her experiences via X (Twitter): @Cioconnor.

70 See note 69.

71 See note 69.

72 Ciara O'Connor quoted in Zachary Small, "Wheelchair User Criticizes Tate Modern for Inaccessibility Issues at Olafur Eliasson Exhibition," *Hyperallergic*, August 12, 2019, https://hyperallergic.com/513173/wheelchair-user-criticizes-tate-modern-for-at-olafur-eliasson/.

73 Robert R. Janes and Richard Sandell, eds., *Museum Activism* (London: Routledge, 2019): 113. See also Jocelyn Dodd, Ceri Jones, Debbie Jolly, and Richard Sandell, "Disability Reframed: Challenging Visitor Perceptions in Museums," in *Re-Presenting Disability: Activism and Agency in the Museum*, ed. Richard Sanell, Jocelyn Dodd and Rosemaire Garland-Thomson (London: Routledge, 2010): 92–111.

74 Marshall, "Is This the World's Most Accessible Museum?"

75 Clare Barlow, "Rejecting Normal: Curating Queer British Art, 1861–1967 at Tate Britain and Being Human at Wellcome Collection, London," *Garage Journal: Studies in Art, Museums & Culture*, no. 1 (2020): 274.

76 Barlow, "Rejecting Normal," 274.

77 Barlow, 276.

78 Marshall, "Is This the World's Most Accessible Museum?"

79 See note 78.

80 Claire Voon, "Museums Are Finally Taking Accessibility for Visitors with Disabilities Seriously," *Artsy*, October 14, 2019, https://www.artsy.net/article/artsy-editorial-museums-finally-accessibility-visitors-disabilities-seriously.

81 Voon, "Museums Are Finally Taking Accessibility for Visitors with Disabilities Seriously."

82 Marshall, "Is This the World's Most Accessible Museum?"

83 Sandell quoted in Marshall, "Is This the World's Most Accessible Museum?"

84 See the Zimmerli Art Museum website for *Smoke & Mirrors*: https://zimmerli.rutgers.edu/art/exhibition/smoke-mirrors. The exhibition paid homage to the figure of the "fugitive" in Black studies as a specific condition of Black life in the aftermath of slavery, as espoused by Fred Moten. As curator Amanda Cachia explained in the exhibition proposal for *Smoke & Mirrors*: "For Moten, fugitivity is 'a category of the irregular that escapes easy representations and predications,' and which can 'undiscipline... histories in productive ways.' Fugitivity is also a critical key word in Indigenous studies, where it is posited between the politics of

movement and place, and intersections with settler-colonialism. Scholars Jarrett Martineau and Eric Ritskes write, 'That which is fugitive proposes an insurgent force of dissident visibility; it is the hidden that reveals itself in motion.'" See also Martha Feldman, "Fugitive Voice," *Representations*, vol. 154, no. 1 (2021): 10–22; Jarrett Martineau and Eric Ritskes, "Fugitive Indigeneity: Reclaiming the Terrain of Decolonial Struggle Through Indigenous Art," *Decolonization: Indigeneity, Education & Society*, vol. 3, no. 1 (2014): i–xii.

85 This quote comes from Amanda Cachia's exhibition proposal for *Smoke & Mirrors*, dated September 1, 2023.

86 Izabel Galliera et al., eds., *Pedagogical Art in Activist and Curatorial Practices* (New York: Routledge, 2025), https://www.taylorfrancis.com/books/edit/10.4324/9781003473800/pedagogical-art-activist-curatorial-practices-noni-brynjolson-izabel-galliera.

87 "Smoke & Mirrors", Zimmerli Art Museum website.

88 Adams, "Workforce Diversity"; Voon, "Museums Are Finally Taking Accessibility for Visitors with Disabilities Seriously."

89 See the ARCHES website for details: https://www.arches-project.eu.

90 See note 89.

91 Arts House and City of Melbourne, "Arts House Disability Inclusion Action Plan, 2019–21," http://www.artshouse.com.au/wp-content/uploads/2020/11/Arts_House_DIAP_2019-2021_Accessible_PDF.pdf.

92 "Arts House Disability Inclusion Action Plan, 2019–21."

Chapter 5: PRIZING OPEN THE MUSEUM'S CLOSETS

1 James Saslow, "Closets and the Museum: Homophobia and Art History," in *Lavender Culture*, ed. K. Jay and A. Young (New York: New York University Press, 1978): 226.

2 The 2015 glossary compiled by the Van Abbemuseum compares the acronym LGBTQ+ to alternatives, like LGBTQQIP2SAA, "which includes a second Q for questioning (i.e., people currently questioning their sexual orientation), P for pansexual people, a second A for (straight) allies and 2S for two spirit people. 2S refers to Native Americans, whose culture believes that a masculine and feminine spirit can be present in one person simultaneously. However, it is legitimate to question whether inclusivity can be obtained through acronyms. When would this stretching and adding become meaningless, and even laughable or useless." See Alice Venir and Olle Lundin, *A Queer Glossary* (Eindhoven: Van Abbemuseum, 2015): 13. Throughout this essay, I have chosen the acronym LGBTQ+ as an all-inclusive term for any and all non-heteronormative sexualities, believing the "+" to accommodate all identities. I agree with the Van Abbemuseum's argument that to continue to add letters to LGBTQ+ is "meaningless, and even laughable or useless."

3 See David Gaimster, "Sex and Sensibility at the British Museum," *History Today*, vol. 50, no. 9 (September 2000): 10–15.

4 See Renaud Chantraine and Bruno Brulon Soares, "Introduction," *Museum International*, vol. 72, nos. 3–4 (2020): 5.

5 Michael Petry, "Hidden Histories: The Experience of Curating a Male Same-Sex Exhibition and the Problems Encountered," in *Gender, Sexuality and Museums: A Routledge Reader*, ed. Amy K. Levin (London and New York: Routledge, 2010): 153–54.

6 Petry, "Hidden Histories," 153–54.

7 Nikki Sullivan, *A Critical Introduction to Queer Theory* (New York: New York University Press, 2003): vi.

8 James H. Sanders, "Queering the Museums," *Culture Work: A Periodic Broadside for Arts and Culture Workers*, no. 1 (2007): 3. Sanders argues that queering a museum is not just about putting marginalized sexual subjects into the focus of the curator. Rather, the aim of queering a museum collection should be: "to disrupt those socio-sexual assumptions that have been thoughtlessly reenacted. Through this repeated practice of queerly (un)naming and opening history and artworks to multiple readings, one may reinvest in the museum as an institution and its objects' ongoing (re)production, relevancy and vitality."

9 Elizabeth Freeman, *Time Binds: Queer Temporalities, Queer Histories* (Durham, NC: Duke University Press, 2010): xxi.

10 More canonical queer exhibitions around the world: *Don't Leave Me This Way: Art in the Age of AIDS* (National Gallery of Australia, Canberra, 1994–95), *In a Different Light* (University of California, Berkeley Art Museum and Pacific Film Archive, 1995), *Pride and Prejudice: Lesbian and Gay London* (Museum of London, 1999), *Hidden Histories* (The New Art Gallery, Walsall, 2004); *En todas partes* (Galician Center of Contemporary Art, Santiago de Compostela, 2009), *Gay Icons* (National Portrait Gallery, London, 2009), *Homosexuality_ies* (Deutsches Historisches Museum and Schwules Museum, Berlin, 2015), *Queer California: Untold Stories* (Oakland Museum of California, 2019), *Art After Stonewall* (Columbus Museum of Art, Ohio, 2019), *Queer* (National Gallery of Victoria, Melbourne, 2022).

11 Jo Darbyshire, *The Gay Museum: An Exhibition Exploring the History of Lesbian and Gay Presence in Western Australia* (Perth: Western Australian Museum, 2003).

12 Darbyshire, email to the author, April 22, 2021. See also Josephine Wilson, "The Gay Museum—a History of Lesbian and Gay Presence in Western Australia," *Artlink* 23, no. 2 (June 2003), https://www.artlink.com.au/articles/2464/the-gay-museum-

E28093-a-history-of-lesbian-and-gay-pres/.
13 Wilson, "The Gay Museum."
14 Darbyshire, email to the author, April 22, 2021.
15 Bec Dean, "The Gay Museum," *RealTime*, no. 54 (April–May 2003): 30.
16 Wilson, "The Gay Museum."
17 Marek Bartelak, "Ars Homo Erotica," *Artforum* 49, no. 2 (October 2010), https://www.artforum.com/events/ars-homo-erotica-196429/.
18 Paweł Leszkowicz, *Ars Homo Erotica* (Warsaw: National Museum in Warsaw, 2010): 8–16.
19 Paweł Leszkowicz, "The Power of Queer Curating in Eastern Europe," in *Working with Feminism: Curating and Exhibitions in Eastern Europe*, ed. Katrin Kivimaa (Tallinn: Tallinn University Press, 2012): 125.
20 Leszkowicz, "Power of Queer Curating," 119.
21 Bartelak, "Ars Homo Erotica."
22 Leszkowicz, *Ars Homo Erotica*, 162.
23 Rafal Kiepuszewski, "Gay Art," *Deutsche Welle*, June 22, 2010, https://www.dw.com/en/warsaws-exhibition-of-homoerotic-art-stirs-protest/a-5716488.
24 Leszkowicz, email to the author, March 15, 2021.
25 MP Stanisław Pięta quoted in Rafal Kiepuszewski, "Gay Art," *Deutsche Welle*, June 22, 2010. On the controversy surrounding the exhibition, see Julia Michalska, "Poland's National Museum Champions Gay Rights: Critics up in Arms," *The Art Newspaper*, May 31, 2010, https://www.theartnewspaper.com/2010/06/01/polands-national-museum-champions-gay-rights-critics-up-in-arms.
26 Matt Smith, "Queering the Museum," in "Museos, género y sexualidad," *ICOM España*, no. 8 (2013): 86. Incidentally, Matt Smith has performed other museum interventions, including at the Fitzwilliam Museum in Cambridge, U.K., in 2018 in an exhibition titled *Flux: Parian Unpacked*, in which he worked with the museum's extensive collection of Glynn parian busts.
27 Smith, "Queering the Museum," 88.
28 Matt Smith, "Making Things Perfectly Queer: Art's Use of Craft to Signify LGBT Identities" (Ph.D. diss., University of Brighton, 2015): 107.
29 Smith, "Making Things Perfectly Queer," 97.
30 Stuart Frost, "Queering the Museum: Birmingham Museum and Art Gallery," *Social History in Museums 35* (2011): 59–61, https://shcg.org.uk/domains/shcg.org.uk/local/media/downloads/Journal_035.pdf.
31 Matt Smith, "Queering the Pitch," in *Queering the Museum* (Birmingham: Birmingham Museum & Art Gallery, 2010).
32 Smith, "Queering the Museum," 88.
33 For more on Fred Wilson's *Mining the Museum*, see Maura Reilly, *Curatorial Activism: Towards an Ethics of Curating* (London: Thames & Hudson, 2018): 120–23.
34 Kerr Houston, "How Mining the Museum Changed the Art World," *BmoreArt*, May 3, 2017.
35 Smith, "Queering the Pitch."
36 Frost, "Queering the Museum."
37 Smith, "Queering the Pitch."
38 See note 35.
39 See note 35.
40 Frost, "Queering the Museum."
41 Robert Mills, "Theorizing the Queer Museum," *Museum & Social Issues*, vol. 3, no. 1 (2008): 50.
42 Anna Conlan, "Representing Possibility: Morning, Memorial, and Queer Museology," in *Gender, Sexuality and Museums: A Routledge Reader*, ed. Amy K. Levin (London and New York: Routledge, 2010): 257.
43 The full label copy from the Metropolitan Museum of Art reads as follows: "A. M. Cassandre's famous poster plays with the name of the aperitif: Dubo (du beau, 'beautiful'), Dubon (du bon, 'good'), Dubonnet. The solitary woman is as oblivious to this jaunty refrain as she is to the inviting smile of the top-hatted fellow at her shoulder. Kertész saw these inapposite conjunctions and in the same instant knew that the pedestrian departing the poignant scene should not be allowed to make his getaway." See https://www.metmuseum.org/art/collection/search/265597.
44 Peter Ackroyd, *Queer City: Gay London from the Romans to the Present Day* (London: Chatto & Windus, 2017): 35.
45 Ackroyd, *Queer City*, 35.
46 As cited in Randy P. Conner et al., *Cassell's Encyclopedia of Queer Myth, Symbol, and Spirit* (London: Cassell, 1997): 128.
47 Judith Butler, "Imitation and Gender Insubordination" in *Inside/ Out: Lesbian Theories, Gay Theories*, ed. Diana Fuss (New York: Routledge, 1991): 20.
48 Clare Barlow, "Rejecting Normal: Curating Queer British Art, 1861–1967 at Tate Britain and Being Human at Wellcome Collection, London," *Garage Journal: Studies in Art, Museums & Culture*, no. 1 (2020): 272.
49 Barlow, "Rejecting Normal," 272.
50 Carolyn Dinshaw, "Got Medieval?" *Journal of the History of Sexuality*, vol. 10, no. 2 (2001): 204.
51 Gloria Anzaldúa has advised that "even when we shelter under [the term queer], we must not forget that it homogenizes, erases our differences." Gloria Anzaldúa, *The Gloria Anzaldúa Reader* (Durham, NC: Duke University Press, 2009): 164.
52 Mills, "Theorizing the Queer Museum," 48.
53 "Jasper Johns: Mind/Mirror," Whitney Museum of American Art, September 2021, https://whitney.org/exhibitions/jasper-johns.

Chapter 6: HOW BLOODY IS TOO BLOODY?

1 Rhonda Lieberman, "Painting over the Dirty Truth," *New Republic*, September 23, 2019. Hereafter, Lieberman 2019.
2 Robin Pobrebin, "How Do You Raise $3.47 Billion? Ask These Guys," *New York Times*, October 9, 2015, https://www.nytimes.com/interactive/2015/10/11/arts/the-big-ask.html.

3 Rain Embuscado, "The Whitney Museum Is Now Officially the Leonard A. Lauder Building," *Artnet*, April 6, 2016, https://news.artnet.com/art-world/leonard-lauder-building-whitney-museum-467309.

4 For examples of growing statistics see, "Understanding the Opioid Overdose Epidemic," Centers for Disease Control and Prevention, April 5, 2024, https://www.cdc.gov/overdose-prevention/about/understanding-the-opioid-overdose-epidemic.html.

5 Masha Gessen, "Nan Goldin Leads a Protest at the Guggenheim against the Sackler Family," *New Yorker*, February 10, 2019, https://www.newyorker.com/news/our-columnists/nan-goldin-leads-a-protest-at-the-guggenheim-against-the-sackler-family.

6 Richard Sackler has also been quoted as saying: "The launch of OxyContin tablets will be followed by a blizzard of prescriptions that will bury the competition. The prescription blizzard will be so deep, dense, and white." See Gessen, "Nan Goldin"; see also Joanna Walters, "OxyContin Maker Expected a 'Blizzard of Prescriptions' Following Drug's Launch," *Guardian*, January 16, 2019, https://www.theguardian.com/us-news/2019/jan/15/oxycontin-purdue-pharma-massachusetts-opioid-crisis?utm_source=chatgpt.com.

7 The $600 million is confirmed here: Abbie VanSickle, "Supreme Court Appears Split over Opioid Settlement for Purdue Pharma," *New York Times*, December 4, 2023, https://www.nytimes.com/2023/12/04/us/politics/supreme-court-purdue-pharma.html.

8 Patrick Radden Keefe, *Empire of Pain: The Secret History of the Sackler Dynasty* (New York: Doubleday, 2021).

9 The $11 billion is confirmed here: Antoinette Radford, "Sackler Family Wins Immunity from Opioid Lawsuits," *BBC News*, May 31, 2023, https://www.bbc.com/news/world-us-canada-65764307. See also: Congress. gov, "H. Rept. 117-699—Activities of the Committee On Oversight and Reform One Hundred Seventeenth Congress December 31, 2022 Pursuant to House rule XI, I(d)(1)," September 12, 2024, https://www.congress.gov/congressional-report/117th-congress/house-report/699/1.

10 VanSickle, "Supreme Court Appears Split."

11 Daniel Cassady, "Supreme Court Rules Against Civil Liability Protections for the Sackler Family," *ArtNews*, June 27, 2024; Abbie VanSickle, "Supreme Court Rejects Liability Shield at Center of Purdue Pharma Settlement," *New York Times*, June 27, 20.

12 Jan Hoffman, "Judge to Approve Purdue Pharma Bankruptcy, Releasing Billions for Opioid Plaintiffs," *New York Times*, November 14, 2025.

13 Hoffman, "Judge to Approve Purdue Pharma Bankruptcy."

14 Hoffman.

15 In addition to their philanthropy, the extended family members have served in board governance at the V&A, the Met, the Brooklyn Museum, and many others.

16 Rhonda Lieberman, "Painting Over Dirty Truth", *New Republic*, September 23, 2019, https://newrepublic.com/article/154991/rich-art-museum-donors-exploit-identity-politics-launder-reputations-philanthropy.

17 Julia Michalska and Hannah McGivern, "'Like Being Married to a Serial Killer': Hito Steyerl Denounces Sackler Sponsorship of Museums," *The Art Newspaper*, April 10, 2019, https://www.theartnewspaper.com/2019/04/10/like-being-married-to-a-serial-killer-hito-steyerl-denounces-sackler-sponsorship-of-museums.

18 Anand Giridharadas, "When Your Money Is So Tainted Museums Don't Want It," *New York Times*, May 16, 2019, https://www.nytimes.com/2019/05/16/opinion/sunday/met-sackler.html.

19 Arthur M. Sackler, who died in 1987, did not benefit from the sale of OxyContin. Nonetheless, he has been implicated by association with Purdue Pharma. Some have argued that it was Arthur M. Sackler who revolutionized the marketing of Valium in the 1970s. Valium was one of the top-selling drugs in the U.S. for decades and Sackler amassed a fortune from sales. See Christopher Rowland, "The Other Sackler: Inside a Widow's Campaign to Protect Her Husband's Name from the Opioid Addiction Epidemic," *Washington Post*, November 27, 2019, https://www.washingtonpost.com/business/economy/the-other-sackler-inside-a-widows-campaign-to-protect-her-husbands-name-from-the-opioid-addiction-epidemic/2019/1½6/013e5c9e-f4db-11e9-8cf0-4cc99f74d127_story.html; Petula Dvorak, "Washington Worried About the Sackler Drug Tactics Years Before Opioids," *Washington Post*, June 1, 2023, https://www.washingtonpost.com/dc-md-va/2023/06/01/sackler-opioids-valium-smithsonian/.

20 Robin Pogrebin, "Trustee Who Funds Climate Change Deniers Leaves Natural History Board," *New York Times*, February 27, 2020, https://www.nytimes.com/2020/02/27/arts/design/natural-history-trustee-mercer-out.html.

21 These figures are from a 2018 report by the AAMD looking at museums' average revenue streams. See Association of Art Museum Directors (AAMD), "Art Museums by the Numbers," 2018.

22 Robin Pogrebin, Elizabeth Harris, and Graham Bowley, "New Scrutiny of Museum Boards Takes Aim at World of Wealth and Status," *New York Times*, October 2, 2019, https://www.nytimes.com/2019/10/02/arts/design/whitney-art-museums-trustees.html. Hereafter, Pogrebin et al. 2019.

23 Pogrebin et al. 2019.

24 Max Anderson with Steve Schindler and Katie Wilson-Milner, "Museum Controversies:

Reputational Concerns and 'Offensive' Art," *Art Law Podcast*, September 4, 2019.
25 David Allyn, "Nonprofits Shouldn't Be So Quick to Reject Funds from Tainted Donors," *Washington Post*, April 26, 2019, https://www.washingtonpost.com/opinions/nonprofits-shoudnt-be-so-quick-to-reject-funds-from-tainted-donors/2019/04/26/9fbaa8ba-62db-11e9-bfad-36a7eb36cb60_story.html.
26 Giridharadas, "When Your Money Is So Tainted."
27 Whitney Mallett and Katy Schneider, "Ranking New York's Most Toxic Museum Boards," *Vulture*, August 7, 2019, https://www.vulture.com/2019/08/new-york-most-toxic-museum-boards.html.
28 Zachary Small, "Activists Demand MoMA Divest from Private Prisons and Weapons Manufacturers," *Hyperallergic*, March 7, 2019, https://hyperallergic.com/activists-demand-moma-divest-from-private-prisons-and-weapons-manufacturers/.
29 Rhonda Lieberman, "Painting Over Dirty Truth."
30 Small, "Activists Demand MoMA Divest."
31 Hakim Bishara, "'Strike MoMA' Protest Attracts 300+, NYPD Tackles and Arrests Protester Who Waved Palestinian Flag," *Hyperallergic*, May 16, 2021, https://hyperallergic.com/646300/strike-moma-protest-palestine-nypd-tackles-protester-arrested/.
32 For current MoMA trustees, visit: https://www.moma.org/about/trustees.
33 Karen K. Ho, "Hundreds of Pro-Palestine Protestors Stage Events at MoMA and Brooklyn Museum," *ARTnews*, February 11, 2024, https://www.artnews.com/art-news/news/pro-palestine-protestors-moma-brooklyn-museum-1234695962/.
34 Hakim Bishara, "Guerrilla Girls Target MoMA Trustee with Ties to Jeffrey Epstein in an Ad Takeover," *Hyperallergic*, November 12, 2019, https://hyperallergic.com/527973/guerrilla-girls-target-moma-trustees-with-ties-to-jeffrey-epstein-in-an-ad-takeover/.
35 Hakim Bishara, "Behind the Scenes of MoMa PS-1 Exhibition, Artists Confronted Leadership over Chairman's Implication in Iraq War," *Hyperallergic*, March 18, 2021, https://hyperallergic.com/620499/moma-ps1-gulf-wars-exhibition-conflict/.
36 Hakim Bishara, "MoMA Trustee Leon Black Accused of Rape, Again," *Hyperallergic*, November 29, 2022, https://hyperallergic.com/784129/moma-trustee-leon-black-accused-of-rape-again/.
37 Hakim Bishara, "Over 150 Artists Call for Leon Black's Removal from MoMA's Board over Jeffrey Epstein's Financial Ties," *Hyperallergic*, February 4, 2021, https://hyperallergic.com/619709/artists-call-for-leon-blacks-removal-moma-jeffrey-epstein/.
38 Artnet News, "Climate Activists Called for MoMA to Drop Its Board Chair in a Demonstration Outside the Museum's Annual Fundraiser," *Artnet*, June 7, 2023, https://news.artnet.com/art-world-archives/climate-activists-protest-moma-fundraiser-drop-kravis-2317095.
39 Elaine Velie, "Protesters Crash MoMA Gala over Board Chair's Fossil Fuel Ties," *Hyperallergic*, June 6, 2023, https://hyperallergic.com/826458/protesters-crash-moma-gala-over-board-chairs-fossil-fuel-ties/.
40 CodePink quoted in Lieberman 2019.
41 The full Strike MoMA letter is reproduced in Hakim Bishara, "In a Letter to MoMA's Director, Activists Declare Plan to Protest Inside Museum," *Hyperallergic*, April 25, 2021, https://hyperallergic.com/640625/in-a-letter-to-momas-director-activists-declare-plan-to-protest-inside-museum/.
42 Bishara, "In a Letter to MoMA's Director."
43 Sam Biddle, "Ousted Whitney Museum Board Member Still Selling Tear Gas Despite Divestment Claim," *Intercept*, June 5, 2022, https://theintercept.com/2022/06/05/tear-gas-whitney-museum-safariland-warren-kanders/. See also Jasmine Weber, "A Whitney Museum Vice Chairman Owns a Manufacturer Supplying Tear Gas at the Border," *Hyperallergic*, November 27, 2018, https://hyperallergic.com/472964/a-whitney-museum-vice-chairman-owns-a-manufacturer-supplying-tear-gas-at-the-border/.
44 The full letter from the Whitney staff is reproduced in Hrag Vartanian, Zachary Small and Jasmine Weber, "Whitney Museum Staffers Demand Answers After Vice Chair's Relationship to Tear Gas Manufacturer Is Revealed," *Hyperallergic*, November 30, 2018, https://hyperallergic.com/473702/whitney-tear-gas-manufacturer-is-revealed/.
45 Jerry Saltz, "A True Protest Biennial," *Vulture*, July 22, 2019, https://www.vulture.com/2019/07/artists-withdrawing-from-whitney-biennial-over-kanders.html.
46 Adam Weinberg quoted in Alex Greenberger, "'We Truly Live in Difficult Times': Whitney Director Responds to Demands for Action against Vice Board Chair," *ARTnews*, December 3, 2018, https://www.artnews.com/art-news/news/truly-live-difficult-times-whitney-museum-director-responds-demands-action-vice-board-chair-11442/.
47 See note 46.
48 See note 46.
49 Deniz Çam, "Meet the Safariland Multimillionaire Getting Rich Off Tear Gas and More in the Defense Industry," *Forbes*, December 6, 2018, https://www.forbes.com/sites/denizcam/2018/12/06/meet-the-safariland-multimillionaire-getting-rich-off-tear-gas-and-more-in-the-defense-industry/.
50 Pogrebin et al. 2019.
51 DTP quoted in Rhonda Lieberman 2019, and as summarized in Pogrebin et al. 2019.

52 Hannah Black, Tobi Haslett, and Ciarán Finlayson, "The Tear Gas Biennial," *Artforum*, July 17, 2019, https://www.artforum.com/columns/a-statement-from-hannah-black-ciaran-finlayson-and-tobi-haslett-regarding-warren-kanders-and-the-2019-whitney-biennial-244098/.

53 The artists as quoted in Eileen Kinsella, "Eight Artists Withdraw Their Work from the Whitney Biennial as Protest of Warren Kanders Spreads to the Museum's Marquee Show," *Artnet*, July 19, 2019, https://news.artnet.com/art-world-archives/artists-withdraw-whitney-biennial-1605475; see also Victoria Stapley-Brown, "Four Artists Withdraw Their Work from the Whitney Biennial," *The Art Newspaper*, July 19, 2019, https://www.theartnewspaper.com/2019/07/19/artists-withdraw-their-work-from-the-whitney-biennial.

54 "The targeted campaign of attacks against me and my company that has been waged these past several months has threatened to undermine the important work of the Whitney. I joined this board to help the museum prosper. I do not wish to play a role, however inadvertent, in its demise." Warren Kanders quoted in Robin Pogrebin and Elizabeth Harris, "Warren Kanders Quits Whitney Board After Tear Gas Protests," *New York Times*, July 25, 2019, https://www.nytimes.com/2019/07/25/arts/whitney-warren-kanders-resigns.html. Adam Weinberg, the Whitney's director, said in a statement, "Warren and Allison Kanders have been unwavering in their commitment to this institution, including a generous lead gift towards the Museum's building project. The Whitney's groundbreaking Warhol exhibition and the past exhibitions of the works of Laura Owens, Jeff Koons and Wade Guyton, among others, were in part made possible thanks to their support. As Director, I am very grateful." (Kanders's wife also resigned from a subcommittee of the board.) See Pogrebin and Harris, "Warren Kanders Quits."

55 Kanders quoted in Pogrebin and Harris.

56 Hours after Kanders resigned, his fellow trustee Kenneth Griffin, a wealthy hedge fund manager, quit in protest. "By the end of the day, Griffin had changed his mind. But according to people privy to the events, he did so only after Leonard Lauder, the cosmetics titan and the museum's powerful chairman emeritus, phoned Griffin from [his *luxury yacht*] to coax him back." See Pogrebin et al. 2019.

57 Pogrebin et al. 2019.

58 PharmaVoice, "Philanthropy: Beyond the Numbers," *PharmaVoice*, May 1, 2017, https://www.pharmavoice.com/news/2017-5-philanthropy/612782/.

59 John List and Fatemeh Momeni, "When Corporate Social Responsibility Backfires: Theory and Evidence from a Natural Field Experiment," *National Bureau of Economic Research*, December 2017, https://www.nber.org/papers/w24169; "Does Doing Good Give You License to Be Bad?" *Freakonomics Radio*, Episode 335, May 16, 2018, https://freakonomics.com/podcast/does-doing-good-give-you-license-to-be-bad/.

60 Marianne Bertrand et al., "Tax Exempt Lobbying: Corporate Philanthropy as a Tool of Political Influence," *American Economic Review* 110, no. 7 (July 2020): 2065–102; Stephen J. Dubner, 'The Most Vilified Industry in America Is Also the Most Charitable', *Freakonomics Radio*, May 23, 2018, https://freakonomics.com/podcast/the-most-vilified-industry-in-america-is-also-the-most-charitable/.

61 Mel Evans, *Artwash: Big Oil and the Arts* (London: Pluto Press, 2015): 6.

62 Suzanne Goldenberg, "Just 90 Companies Caused Two-Thirds of Man-Made Global Warming Emissions," *Guardian*, November 20, 2013, https://www.theguardian.com/environment/2013/nov/20/90-companies-man-made-global-warming-emissions-climate-change.

63 Rebecca Speare-Cole, "Shell and BP Among Oil Firms Accused of Greenwashing over Renewable Energy," *Independent*, August 23, 2023, https://www.independent.co.uk/climate-change/news/shell-bp-oil-greenwashing-greanpeace-climate-b2397689.html.

64 Benjamin Sutton, "The British Museum and BP's Sponsorship Deal Will End After 27 Years," *The Art Newspaper*, June 2, 2023, https://www.theartnewspaper.com/2023/06/02/british-museum-bp-sponsorship-ends-27-years-protests-global-warming. See also Ron Bousso, Shadia Nasralla, and Sarah Mcfarlane, "Insight: Inside BP's Plan to Reset Renewables as Oil and Gas Boom," *Reuters*, March 7, 2023, https://www.reuters.com/business/sustainable-business/inside-bps-plan-reset-renewables-oil-gas-boom-2023-03-07/.

65 Joe Ware, "British Museum and Science Museum under increasing pressure to scrap BP sponsorship after oil giant drops climate targets," *The Art Newspaper*, February 28, 2025, https://www.theartnewspaper.com/2025/02/28/british-museum-science-museum-under-increasing-pressure-to-scrap-bp-sponsorship-after-oil-giant-drops-climate-targets.

66 Ron Bousso and Shadia Nasralla, "BP Makes Record Profit in 2022, Slows Shift from Oil," *Reuters*, February 7, 2023, https://www.reuters.com/business/energy/bp-profits-soar-record-28-bln-dividend-increased-2023-02-07/.

67 Rhea Nayyar, "British Museum Announces $63M Partnership with Oil Giant," *Hyperallergic*, December 19, 2023, https://hyperallergic.com/862948/british-museum-announces-63m-partnership-with-oil-giant-bp/.

68 Nayyar, "British Museum Announces."

69 Rhea Nayyar, "British Museum Pledges 'Net-Zero Carbon' Despite

Big Oil Funding", *Hyperallergic*, January 1, 2023, https://hyperallergic.com/790610/british-museum-pledges-net-zero-carbon-despite-big-oil-funding/?; Geraldine Kendall Adams, "British Museum Gears up for Radical Modernisation Project," *Museums Association Journal*, February 15, 2022, https://www.museumsassociation.org/museums-journal/news/2022/02/british-museum-gears-up-for-radical-modernisation-project/.

70 Nayyar, "British Museum Pledges 'Net-Zero Carbon.'"

71 George Osbourne quoted in Nayyar, "British Museum Announces."

72 Hartwig Fischer quoted in Gareth Harris, "British Museum Director Endorses Controversial Sponsor as Part of Future Vision," *The Art Newspaper*, July 8, 2019, https://www.theartnewspaper.com/2019/07/08/british-museum-director-endorses-controversial-sponsor-bp-as-part-of-future-vision. See also Claire Selvin, "British Museum Director Endorses BP as Sponsor as Calls for Divestment Grow Louder", *ARTnews*, July 10, 2019, https://www.artnews.com/art-news/news/british-museum-bp-sponsorship-endorsement-12951/.

73 Douglas Parr quoted in Geraldine Kendall Adams, "Deputy Chair Quit Before British Museum Announced £50m BP Deal," *Museums Association Journal*, December 20, 2023, https://www.museumsassociation.org/museums-journal/news/2023/12/deputy-chair-quit-ahead-of-british-museums-announcement-of-bp-deal/.

74 "The Science Museum to Open UK's first Major Exhibition on Carbon Capture and Storage on 19 May", press release, Science Museum, April 15, 2021, https://www.sciencemuseum.org.uk/about-us/press-office/science-museum-open-uks-first-major-exhibition-carbon-capture-and-storage-19.

75 Bill McGuire quoted in Valentina Di Liscia, "London's Science Museum Faces Backlash over Oil-Sponsored Climate Exhibition," *Hyperallergic*, April 19, 2021, https://hyperallergic.com/639027/the-science-museum-in-london-faces-backlash-over-oil-sponsored-climate-exhibition/.

76 Geraldine Kendall Adams, "Coal Giant Adani to Sponsor Science Museum's Green Energy Gallery," *Museums Association Journal*, October 19, 2021, https://www.museumsassociation.org/museums-journal/news/2021/10/coal-giant-adani-to-sponsor-science-museums-green-energy-gallery/.

77 See Science Museum's website for a description of the Energy Revolution: The Adani Green Energy Gallery, https://www.sciencemuseum.org.uk/see-and-do/energy-revolution-adani-green-energy-gallery.

78 The Atmosphere Gallery closed permanently on March 20, 2022. See https://www.sciencemuseum.org.uk/see-and-do/atmosphere.

79 Damian Carrington, "Science Museum Chooses Fossil Fuel Company as New Climate Show Sponsor," *Guardian*, October 19, 2021, https://www.theguardian.com/environment/2021/oct/19/science-museum-chooses-fossil-fuel-company-as-new-climate-show-sponsor.

80 Fossil Free Science Museum, *Science Museum Group: An Unravelling Tragedy*, March 2023, https://cultureunstained.org/wp-content/uploads/2023/03/adani-unravelling-tragedy.pdf.

81 See Joe Ware, "'Don't Fudge the Facts': Campaigners Call On Science Museum to Go Further After Cutting Ties with Oil Giant Equinor," *The Art Newspaper*, July 16, 2024, https://www.theartnewspaper.com/2024/07/16/dont-fudge-the-facts-campaigners-call-on-science-museum-to-go-further-after-cutting-ties-with-oil-giant-equinor. See also Geraldine Kendall Adams, "Opposition to Philanthropy is 'Imagined', Say Climate Campaigners," *Museums Association Journal*, June 10, 2025, https://www.museumsassociation.org/museums-journal/news/2025/06/opposition-to-philanthropy-is-imagined-say-climate-campaigners/?

82 "Go to Bed with a Smile, Spend the Night with Mona Lisa" (blog), *The Art Newspaper*, April 3, 2019, https://www.theartnewspaper.com/2019/04/03/go-to-bed-with-a-smilespend-the-night-with-mona-lisa.

83 "Go to Bed with a Smile" (blog).

84 "Ian Brossat dénonce la 'privatisation' du Louvre par Airbnb," *Le Point*, September 12, 2019 (quote trans. M. Reilly), https://www.lepoint.fr/societe/paris-ian-brossat-denonce-la-privatisation-du-louvre-par-airbnb-11-09-2019-2335246_23.php#11.

85 Ian Brossat quoted in Christine Henry, "Ian Brossat, "Il faut interdire les locations Airbnb dans le centre de Paris," *Le Parisien*, September 6, 2018 (quote trans. M. Reilly), https://www.leparisien.fr/paris-75/ian-brossat-il-faut-interdire-les-locations-airbnb-dans-le-centre-de-paris-05-09-2018-7877826.php.

86 Brossat quoted in Henry, "Ian Brossat."

87 Lieberman 2019.

88 Association of Art Museum Directors, "Art Museums by the Numbers."

89 As Rhonda Lieberman explains: "Philip Morris donated to Helms (an ultraconservative senator from North Carolina), and gave even more to vulnerable arts organizations, resulting in such cozy arrangements as a branch of the Whitney inside the corporate headquarters of Philip Morris." See Lieberman 2019.

90 Nizan Shaked, "Splitting the Public and Private Uses of Art," *Counterpunch*, February 20, 2015, https://www.counterpunch.org/2015/02/20/splitting-the-public-and-private-uses-of-art/.

91 Shaked, "Splitting the Public and Private Uses of Art."

92 Shaked.

93 Isabelle Graw, *High Price: Art Between the Market and Celebrity Culture* (Berlin: Sternberg Press, 2009): 101.
94 Angela Davic, "The US Museum Directors Salary Data," *Collector*, August 26, 2023, https://www.thecollector.com/the-us-museum-directors-salary-data/. See also Hakim Bishara, "Spreadsheet Highlights Major Income Disparities at Cultural Institutions," *Hyperallergic*, April 29, 2020, https://hyperallergic.com/560132/spreadsheet-highlights-major-income-disparities-at-cultural-institutions/.
95 Quoted in Lieberman 2019.
96 Alex Greenberger, "'It's Helpful to Know All Scales': Online Spreadsheet Discloses Museum Workers' Salaries," *ARTnews*, May 31, 2019, https://www.artnews.com/art-news/news/google-spreadsheet-museum-workers-disclose-salaries-12670/.
97 Tessa Solomon, "Louvre to Hike Admission Price Ahead of 2024 Summer Olympics," *ARTnews*, December 11, 2023, https://www.artnews.com/art-news/news/louvre-to-hike-admission-price-ahead-of-2024-summer-olympics-1234689342/.
98 Pogrebin et al. 2019.
99 Author's conversations with employees at the Kalamazoo Institute of Arts (via email, October 16, 2023), and the Columbus Museum of Art (via email, November 5, 2023), on the condition of anonymity.
100 *Museum Board Leadership 2017: A National Report* issued by the American Alliance of Museums and BoardSource found that 46% of museum boards are all white. Board members tend to be older and from wealthier populations, and their social networks also tend to be majority-white, https://www.aam-us.org/wp-content/uploads/2018/01/eyizzp-download-the-report.pdf.
101 Liam Sweeney, Deirdre Harkins, Celeste Watkins-Hayes, and Dominique Adams-Santos, "The BTA 2022 Art Museum Trustee Survey: The Characteristics, Roles, and Experiences of Black Trustees," Ithaka S+R, November 16, 2022, https://doi.org/10.18665/sr.317881.
102 Carol Vogel, "Armani Gift to the Guggenheim Revives Issue of Art and Commerce," *New York Times*, December 15, 1999, https://www.nytimes.com/1999/12/15/arts/armani-gift-to-the-guggenheim-revives-issue-of-art-and-commerce.html?
103 After the National Air and Space Museum, *Star Wars: The Magic of Myth* traveled to seven museums: San Diego Museum of Art, Minneapolis Institute of Art, Museum of Fine Arts, Houston, Toledo Museum of Art, and Brooklyn Museum of Art. It also traveled to the Field Museum of Natural History in Chicago and the Powerhouse Museum in Sydney, Australia. See "Marketing Exhibitions: Will They Come?" Smithsonian Institution, June 13–14, 2002, https://www.si.edu/content/opanda/docs/rpts2002/02.06.marketingexhibitions.final.pdf.
104 Michael Kimmelman, "The 'Star Wars' Effect, and the Part That's Art," *New York Times*, April 5, 2002, https://www.nytimes.com/2002/04/05/movies/art-review-the-star-wars-effect-and-the-part-that-s-art.html. In this article, Kimmelman refers to museum director Arnold Lehman as a "showman-director."
105 The motorcycle exhibition attracted some of the largest crowds in the museum's history. See Peter Plagens and Gordon Devin, "Rumble on the Ramps," *Newsweek*, vol. 132, no. 10, September 7, 1998, 80. For the quote regarding "rental fee," see "When Merchants Enter the Temple," *The Economist*, vol. 359, no. 8218 (April 21, 2001): 64–66.
106 Mimi Gaudieri quoted in Vogel, "Armani Gift to the Guggenheim Revives Issue of Art and Commerce."
107 "When Merchants Enter the Temple."
108 I find it interesting that the AAMD website does not offer access to this report, despite having made accessible reports that predate 1999 and postdate it.
109 Gabriella Angeleti, Wallace Ludel, Nancy Kenney, and Ruth Lopez, "The Top Five Museum Shows to See During Armory Week," *The Art Newspaper*, September 6, 2021, https://www.theartnewspaper.com/2021/09/06/the-top-five-museum-shows-to-see-during-armory-week.
110 Artist Andrea Fraser stated it perfectly in 2006: "I would say that museums have entered into a 'vicious' growth cycle of ever-expanding costs and expenditures. They need bigger shows to raise more money to have bigger shows. They need more staff to raise more money to hire more staff. They need to raise more money to build more space to have more fundraisers. They need to build bigger spaces to show bigger art that draws bigger audiences and justifies building bigger spaces. And so on. The logic is not only about money, but it is a market logic. Art for the sake of art has been discredited, but its replacement appears to be art for the sake of growth. Or growth for the sake of growth. Or growth for the sake of competition within a field increasingly defined by expanding and consolidating economies of scale, where more is always more and bigger is always better." Andrea Fraser, "A Museum Is Not a Business. It Is Run In a Business-Like Fashion," in *Art and Its Institutions: Current Conflicts, Critique, and Collaborations*, ed. Nina Möntmann (London: Black Dog Publishing, 2006): 89.
111 Hannah McGivern, "In Pictures: Six Global Guggenheim Museums That Never Happened," *The Art Newspaper*, November 24, 2017, https://www.theartnewspaper.com/gallery/six-global-guggenheim-museums-that-never-happened.
112 As John Wetenhall explains, "The funding of new museum

starchitecture is an enterprise almost guaranteed to go over budget, and the prudently estimated funds for operational endowment are almost never raised and may get consumed in cost overruns. The operational requirements of climate control and security are rarely included in the endowment components of building campaigns. And the need for more mission-critical staff will always (and I mean always) come last and are usually deferred." John Wetenhall, "Why Not to Run Your Museum 'More Like a Business,'" *Museum* (May–June 2017): 36–42.

113 Andrea Fraser, *2016 in Museums, Money, and Politics* (San Francisco, CA; Cambridge, MA: CCA Wattis Institute for Contemporary Arts; The MIT Press, 2018).

114 Martin Bailey, "London's National Portrait Gallery and Sackler Trust to 'Not Proceed' with £1m Grant," *The Art Newspaper*, March 19, 2019, https://www.theartnewspaper.com/news/london-s-national-portrait-gallery-rejects-gbp1m-grant-from-sackler-trust.

115 Bailey, "London's National Portrait Gallery."

Postscript: "UNDER HIS EYE"

1 Exec. Order No. 14151, "Ending Radical and Wasteful Government DEI Programs and Preferencing," 90 F.R. 8339 (2025), https://www.whitehouse.gov/presidential-actions/2025/01/ending-radical-and-wasteful-government-dei-programs-and-preferencing/. See also Fernanda Figueroa, Ayanna Alexander, and Corey Williams, "Trump Order Ending Federal DEI Programs Leaves Agencies and Stakeholders on Uncertain Ground," *Associated Press*, January 23, 2025, https://apnews.com/article/trump-dei-executive-order-diversity-inclusion-f67ea86032986084dd71c5aa0c6b8d1d

2 Arwa Mahdawi, "Saying 'Women' Is Not Allowed, but 'Men' and 'White' Are OK?" *Guardian*, February 15, 2025, https://www.theguardian.com/commentisfree/2025/feb/15/trump-banning-words-women.

3 In May of 2025, the Smithsonian National Museum of African Art postponed a LGBTQ+ art exhibition. On *transfeminisms*, see "Are an Arizona Museum's Changes to Transfeminisms Exhibition 'Violent' or Pragmatic?" *Southwest Contemporary*, March 13, 2025, https://southwestcontemporary.com/transfeminisms/.

4 Graham Bowley, Jennifer Schuessler, and Robin Pogrebin, "White House Announces Comprehensive Review of Smithsonian Exhibitions," *New York Times*, August 12, 2025, https://www.nytimes.com/2025/08/12/arts/design/smithsonian-exhibitions-review-white-house-trump.html.

5 Travis M. Andrews, "Behind the Right's Loathing of the NEA: Two 'Despicable' Exhibits Almost 30 Years Ago," *Washington Post*, March 20, 2017, https://www.washingtonpost.com/news/morning-mix/wp/2017/03/20/behind-the-loathing-of-the-national-endowment-for-the-arts-a-pair-of-despicable-exhibits-almost-30-years-ago/.

6 Sophia Nguyen, "NEA Nixes Grant Program for 'Underserved Communities,' Shifting Priorities," *Washington Post*, February 6, 2025, https://www.washingtonpost.com/entertainment/art/2025/02/06/nea-grants-canceled/.

7 So egregious was this maneuver that Philip Kennicott from the *Washington Post* explained: "The idea that the president of the United States, who has criticized the [Kennedy] Center for presenting drag shows, might involve himself with programming at the nation's cultural center is without precedent in the United States, and most if not all democratic countries." Philip Kennicott, "How Trump's Kennedy Center Takeover Could Change the Arts," *Washington Post*, February 10, 2025, https://www.washingtonpost.com/entertainment/2025/02/10/trump-plan-for-arts-humanities/.

SELECT BIBLIOGRAPHY

Introduction

Association of Art Museum Directors (AAMD). "The Ongoing Gender Gap Report in Art Museum Directorships." Report, 2017, https://aamd.org/our-members/from-the-field/gender-gap-report-2017#

Halperin, Julia, and Charlotte Burns. "Museums Claim They're Paying More Attention to Female Artists. That's an Illusion." *Artnet*, September 19, 2019, https://news.artnet.com/womens-place-in-the-art-world/womens-place-art-world-museums-1654714

Hooper-Greenhill, Eilean. *Museums and the Shaping of Knowledge*. New York: Routledge, 1992

Mason, Rhiannon, Alistair Robinson, and Emma Coffield. *Museum and Gallery Studies: The Basics*. New York: Routledge, 2018

Sandell, Richard. *Museums, Society and Inequality*. London: Routledge, 2002

Topaz, Chad, Bernhard Klingenberg, Daniel Turek, et al. "Diversity of Artists in Major U.S. Museums." *PLOS One*, vol. 14, no. 3 (2019)

"TrendsWatch 2019: Confronting the Past: The long, hard work of decolonization." *Center for the Future of Museums Blog*, April 19, 2019, https://www.aam-us.org/2019/04/19/trendswatch-2019-confronting-the-past-the-long-hard-work-of-decolonization/

Vázquez, Rolando. "The Museum, Decoloniality, and the End of the Contemporary." In *The Future of the New: Artistic Innovation in Times of Social Acceleration*, edited by Thijs Lijster. Amsterdam: Valiz, 2019

Vergo, Peter. *The New Museology*. Chicago: University of Chicago Press, 1989

Chapter 1: DECOLONIZING MUSEUMS

Alterwaite, Arielle Xena. "Slavery on Display." *Slavery & Abolition: A Journal of Slave and Post-Slave Studies* 44, no. 1 (2023)

Centre for the Study of the Legacies of British Slavery. Database, Department of History, University College London, https://www.ucl.ac.uk/lbs/

Decolonising Museums. L'Internationale Online, 2015, https://framerframed.nl/wp-content/uploads/2015/11/Decolonising-Museums.pdf.

Deliss, Clémentine. *The Metabolic Museum*. Berlin: Hatje Cantz, 2020

Enwezor, Okwui, Ulrich Wilmes, and Katie Seigel, eds. *Postwar: Art Between the Pacific and the Atlantic 1945–1965*. Munich: Haus der Kunst, 2016

Farrar, Sarah. "On the Internal Front Lines: Curatorial Activism and Collection Exhibitions." Ph.D. diss., Monash University, Melbourne, 2018

Fusco, Coco. "Deaccessioning Empire." *New York Review*, February 25, 2021, https://www.nybooks.com/articles/2021/02/25/deaccessioning-empire/

Grant, Catherine, and Dorothy Price. "Decolonizing Art History." *Wiley Online Library*, January 22, 2020, https://doi.org/10.1111/1467-8365.12490

Lasch, Pedro, ed. *Black Mirror/Expejo Negro*. Durham, NC: John Hope Franklin Humanities Institute/Nasher Museum of Art – Duke University, 2008

Lijster, Thijs, ed. *The Future of the New: Artistic Innovation in Times of Social Acceleration*. Amsterdam: Valiz, 2019

Lonetree, Amy. *Decolonizing Museums: Representing Native America in National and Tribal Museums*. Chapel Hill: The University of North Carolina Press, 2012

Mesa-Bains, Amalia. *New World Wunderkammer*. Exhibition handout. Los Angeles: The Fowler Museum at UCLA, 2013

Mignolo, Walter. *The Darker Side of Western Modernity: Global Futures, Decolonial Options*. Durham, NC: Duke University Press, 2011

Mignolo, Walter. "Delinking." *Cultural Studies*, vol. 21, no. 2 (2007)

Mignolo, Walter. "Museums in the Colonial Horizon of Modernity: Fred Wilson's *Mining the Museum* (1992)." In *Globalization and Contemporary Art*, edited by Jonathan Harris. Hoboken, NJ: Blackwell Publishing, 2011

Mignolo, Walter, and Rolando Vázquez. "Decolonial AestheSis: Colonial Wounds/Decolonial Healings." *Social Text*, July 15, 2013

Mignolo, Walter, and Catherine Walsh. *On Decoloniality: Concepts, Analytics, Praxis*. Durham, NC: Duke University Press, 2018

"OnCurating: Decolonizing Art Institutions." *Notes on Curating* 35 (December 2017), https://www.on-curating.org/files/oc/dateiverwaltung/issue-34/PDF_to_Download/Oncurating_Decolonizing_Issue35.pdf

Onyango, Awuor. "Absent Figures: The Difficult Questions Restitution Raises." *Contemporary And*, May 17, 2021, https://contemporaryand.com/magazines/absent-figures-the-difficult-questions-restitution-raises/

Pitt Rivers Museum, University of Oxford. "Critical Changes to Displays as Part of the Decolonization Process." Accessed June 3, 2023, https://www.prm.ox.ac.uk/critical-changes

Reilly, Maura. *Curatorial Activism: Towards an Ethics of Curating*. London: Thames & Hudson, 2018

Scanlan, Padraic. "The Colonial Rebirth of British Anti-Slavery: The Liberated African Villages of Sierra Leone, 1815–1824." *American Historical Review* 121, no. 4 (October, 2016)

Sub-Sahara Advisory Panel (SSAP). "*Reframing Picton*: New Artworks go on display at National Museum Cardiff Alongside Re-Interpreted Portrait of Thomas Picton." Press release, August 2, 2022, https://www.ssap.org.uk/blog/reframing-picton

Taylor, Michael. *The Interest: How the British Establishment Resisted the*

Abolition of Slavery. London: Bodley Head, 2020
Tuck, Eve, and K. Wayne Yang. "Decolonization Is Not a Metaphor." *Decolonization: Indigeneity, Education & Society*, vol. 1, no. 1 (2012)

Chapter 2: "WE WERE HERE FIRST"

Aikio, Aile. "Sámification and Sámi Museums." *Sámi Research in Transition: Knowledge, Politics and Social Change*, edited by Laura Junka-Aikio, Jukka Nyyssönen, and Veli-Pekka Lehtola. London: Routledge, 2021
Andrew, Brook Garru, Léuli Eshraghi, Liisa-Rávná Finbog, et al. *Galang 01*. Melbourne: Garru Editions and Powerhouse Publishing, 2022
Caulfield, Sarah. "The Nordnorsk Kunstmuseum 2014–2020: Decolonisation in Practice." Master's thesis in Indigenous Studies, University of Tromsø—The Artic University of Norway, 2021
Clavir, Miriam. *Preserving What Is Valued: Museums, Conservation, and First Nations*. Vancouver: UBC Press, 2002
Finbog, Liisa-Rávná. "Duodji." In Susanne Hætta, Liisa-Rávná Finbog, and Kimberley Moulton. *Mázejoavku: Indigenous Collectivity and Art*, edited by Katya García-Antón. Kautokeino: Office for Contemporary Art Norway, 2021
Finbog, Liisa-Rávná. *It Speaks to You—Making Kin Through Stories, People, and Duodji in Sámi Museums*. Lewes, DE: Dio Press, 2023
Finbog, Liisa-Rávná. "Yul Brynner in Space is Life." *Contemporary Art Stavanger*, March 26, 2023, https://contemporaryartvanger.no/archive/yul-brynner-in-space-is-life
Kuokkanen, Rauna. *Reshaping the University: Responsibility, Indigenous Epistemes, and the Logic of the Gift*. Vancouver: UBC Press, 2007
Lonetree, Amy. *Decolonizing Museums: Representing Native America in National and Tribal Museums*. Chapel Hill: University of North Carolina Press, 2012
Mignolo, Walter. "Delinking." 2007
Moreton-Robinson, Aileen. *The White Possessive: Property, Power and Indigenous Sovereignty*. Minneapolis: University of Minnesota Press, 2015
Moulton, Kimberly. "I Can Still Hear Them Calling. Echoes of My Ancestors." In *Sovereign Words: Indigenous Art, Curation and Criticism*, edited by Katya García-Antón. Oslo/Amsterdam: OCA/Valiz, 2018
Moulton, Kimberley. "Sovereign Art and the Colonial Canon: Are We Lost Until We Are Found?" In *Sovereignty*, edited by Paola Bella and Max Delany. Melbourne: Australian Centre for Contemporary Art, 1995
Sandell, Richard. *Museums, Moralities and Human Rights*. New York: Routledge, 2017
Sarr, Felwine, and Bénédicte Savoy. *The Restitution of African Cultural Heritage: Toward a New Relational Ethics*. Paris: Philippe Rey/Seuil, 2018
Tuck, Eve, and K. Wayne Yang. "Decolonization Is Not a Metaphor." 2012

Chapter 3: "GIVE IT ALL BACK"

Alberge, Dalya. "British Museum Is World's Largest Receiver of Stolen Goods." *Guardian*, November 4, 2019, https://www.theguardian.com/world/2019/nov/04/british-museum-is-worlds-largest-receiver-of-stolen-goods-says-qc
Arts Council England. "Restitution and Repatriation: A Practical Guide for Museums in England." September, 2023, https://www.artscouncil.org.uk/supporting-arts-museums-and-libraries/supporting-collections-and-cultural-property/restitution-and-repatriation-practical-guide-museums-england
Association of Art Museum Directors (AAMD). "Guidelines on the Acquisition of Archaeological Material and Ancient Art (revised 2013)." January 29, 2013, https://asia.si.edu/wp-content/uploads/2024/05/AAMD-Guidelines-2013.pdf
Cleveland Museum of Art. "Declaration on the Importance and Value of Universal Museums." Press release. December 8, 2002, https://archive.org/details/cmapr4492
German Museums Association. "Guidelines on Dealing with Collections from Colonial Contexts." July 2018, https://www.museumsbund.de/wp-content/uploads/2019/10/dmb-guidelines-colonial-context.pdf
Hicks, Dan. *The Brutish Museum: The Benin Bronzes, Colonial Violence and Cultural Restitution*. London: Pluto Press, 2020
Holmes, Rachel. *The Hottentot Venus: The Life and Death of Saartjie Baartman*. London: Bloomsbury, 2007
Jacobs, Julia, and Zachary Small. "Leading Museums Remove Native Displays amid New Federal Rules." *New York Times*, January 26, 2024, https://www.nytimes.com/2024/01/26/arts/design/american-museum-of-natural-history-nagpra.html
Oltermann, Philip. "Germany Hands Over Two Benin Bronzes to Nigeria." *Guardian*, July 1, 2022, https://www.theguardian.com/world/2022/jul/01/germany-hands-over-two-benin-bronzes-to-nigeria
Opoku, Kwame. "Declaration on the Importance and Value of Universal Museums: Singular Failure of an Arrogant Imperialist Project." *Modern Ghana*, January 27, 2013, https://www.modernghana.com/news/441891/declaration-on-the-importance-and-value-of-univers.html
Price, Sally. *Paris Primitive: Jacques Chirac's Museum on the Quai Branly*. Chicago: Chicago University Press, 2007
Sarr, Felwine, and Bénédicte Savoy. *The Restitution of African Cultural Heritage*.
UNESCO. "Convention for the Protection of Cultural Property in the Event of Armed Conflict with Regulations for the Execution of the Convention." Adopted May 14, 1954, 249 UNTS 240, https://www.unesco.org/en/legal-affairs/convention-protection-cultural-property-event-armed-conflict-regulations-execution-convention
UNESCO. "Convention on the Means of Prohibiting and Preventing the

Illicit Import, Export and Transfer of Ownership of Cultural Property." Adopted November 14, 1970, 823 UNTS 231, https://www.unesco.org/en/legal-affairs/convention-means-prohibiting-and-preventing-illicit-import-export-and-transfer-ownership-cultural

UNIDROIT (International Institute for the Unification of Private Law). "UNIDROIT Convention on Stolen or Illegally Exported Cultural Objects." June 24, 1995, https://www.unidroit.org/instruments/cultural-property/1995-convention/

United Nations General Assembly. "United Nations Declaration on the Rights of Indigenous Peoples." Adopted September 13, 2007, A/RES/61/295, https://www.un.org/development/desa/indigenouspeoples/wp-content/uploads/sites/19/2018/11/UNDRIP_E_web.pdf

United Nations Human Rights Council, Expert Mechanism on the Rights of Indigenous Peoples. "Repatriation of Ceremonial Objects, Ancestral Human Remains and Intangible Cultural Heritage Under the United Nations Declaration on the Rights of Indigenous Peoples." July 21, 2020, A/HRC/45/35, https://documents.un.org/doc/undoc/gen/g20/187/65/pdf/g2018765.pdf

Warren, Karen. "A Philosophical Perspective on the Ethics and Resolution of Cultural Property Issues." In *The Ethics of Collecting Cultural Property: Whose Culture? Whose Property?*, edited by Phyllis Mauch Messenger. Albuquerque: University of New Mexico Press, 1989

Yu, Pei-Lin, Chen Shen, and George Smith, eds. *Relevance and Application of Heritage in Contemporary Society*. New York: Routledge, 2018

Chapter 4: WHOSE MUSEUM IS IT?

Alemani, Cecilia. Curatorial statement. La Biennale di Venezia website, 2022, https://www.labiennale.org/en/art/2022/statement-cecilia-alemani

Association of Art Museum Directors. "The Ongoing Gender Gap in Art Museum Directorships." 2017

Barlow, Clare. "Rejecting Normal: Curating Queer British Art, 1861–1967 at Tate Britain and Being Human at Wellcome Collection, London." *Garage Journal: Studies in Art, Museums & Culture*, no. 1 (2020)

Berger, Maurice. "Are Art Museums Racist?" *Art in America*, September 1990.

British Museum. *Collecting and Empire* (blog), https://www.britishmuseum.org/blog/collecting-and-empire

Dodd, Jocelyn, Ceri Jones, Debbie Jolly, and Richard Sandell. "Disability Reframed: Challenging Visitor Perceptions in Museums." In *Re-Presenting Disability: Activism and Agency in the Museum*, edited by Richard Sanell, Jocelyn Dodd, and Rosemaire Garland-Thomson. London: Routledge, 2010

Galliera, Izabel, et al., eds. *Pedagogical Art in Activist and Curatorial Practices*. New York: Routledge, 2025

Gay, Roxane. "Can I Enjoy the Art but Denounce the Artist?" *Marie Claire*, February 6, 2018, https://www.marieclaire.com/culture/a16105931/roxane-gay-on-predator-legacies/

Grogan, Kenzie. "Austin's Museums and Galleries in the Age of Black Lives Matter." Honors thesis, The University of Texas at Austin, 2021, http://dx.doi.org/10.26153/tsw/13810.

Halperin and Burns. "Museums Claim They're Paying More Attention to Female Artists. That's an Illusion." 2019

Halperin, Julie, and Charlotte Burns. "Perceptions of Progress in the Art World Are Largely a Myth: Here Are the Facts." The Burns Halperin Report. *Artnet*, December 13, 2022, https://news.artnet.com/art-world/perceptions-of-progress-in-the-art-world-are-largely-a-myth-here-are-the-facts-2227941

Janes, Robert R., and Richard Sandell, eds. *Museum Activism*. London: Routledge, 2019

Kelly, Philippa. "Groundbreaking UK Exhibition Spotlights Work of Disabled D/deaf and Neurodivergent Artists." *The Art Newspaper*, July 19, 2024, https://www.theartnewspaper.com/2024/07/19/groundbreaking-uk-exhibition-spotlights-work-of-disabled-ddeaf-and-neurodivergent-artists#

Marshall, Alex. "Is This the World's Most Accessible Museum?" *New York Times*, September 11, 2019, https://www.nytimes.com/2019/09/06/arts/design/disabled-access-wellcome-collection.html

National Endowment for the Arts. "New NEA Research on Arts Participation among People with Disabilities." July 1, 2015, https://www.arts.gov/news/press-releases/2015/new-nea-research-arts-participation-among-people-disabilities

Nayeri, Farah. "Is It Time Gauguin Got Cancelled?" *New York Times*, November 18, 2019, https://www.nytimes.com/2019/11/18/arts/design/gauguin-national-gallery-london.html

Pogrebin, Robin. "Curators Urge Guggenheim to Fix Culture that 'Enables Racism.'" *New York Times*, June 22, 2020, https://www.nytimes.com/2020/06/22/arts/design/guggenheim-curators-racism-sexism.html?

Reilly, Maura. *Curatorial Activism*. 2018

Reilly, Maura. "Misfired Canon." *ARTNews*, Winter 2020, http://www.maurareilly.com/pdf/essays/2020-Reviews_MoMA_Reilly.pdf

Reilly, Maura. "MoMA's Revisionism Is Piecemeal and Problem-Filled: Feminist Art Historian Maura Reilly on the Museum's Rehang," *ARTNews*, October 31, 2019, https://www.artnews.com/art-news/reviews/moma-rehang-art-historian-maura-reilly-13484/

Reilly, Maura. "What Is Curatorial Activism?" *ARTnews*, November 7, 2017, https://www.artnews.com/art-news/news/what-is-curatorial-activism-9271/

Reilly, Maura. "With a Majority-Female 2022 Edition, the Venice Biennale Will Make History for Women Artists." *ARTnews*, February 10, 2022, https://www.artnews.com/art-news/news/venice-biennale-2022-women-artists-maura-reilly-1234618777/

Stewart-Kroeker, Sarah. "'What Do We Do with the Art of Monstrous Men?' Betrayal and the Feminist Ethics

of Aesthetic Involvement." *De Ethica: A Journal of Philosophical, Theological and Applied Ethics*, vol. 6, no. 1 (2020)
Sweeney, Liam, Deirdre Harkins and Joanna Dressel. *Art Museum Staff Demographic Survey 2022*. New York: Ithaka S+R, 2022, https://doi.org/10.18665/sr.317927c
Sweeney, Linda, Deirdre Harkins, Celeste Watkins-Hayes, and Dominique Adams-Santos. "The BTA 2022 Art Museum Trustee Survey." Ithaka S+R, November 16, 2022, https://sr.ithaka.org/publications/the-bta-2022-art-museum-trustee-survey/
Topaz, Klingenberg, Turek, et al. "Diversity of Artists in Major U.S. Museums." 2019
Voon, Claire. "Museums Are Finally Taking Accessibility for Visitors with Disabilities Seriously." *Artsy*, October 14, 2019, https://www.artsy.net/article/artsy-editorial-museums-finally-accessibility-visitors-disabilities-seriously

Chapter 5: PRIZING OPEN THE MUSEUM'S CLOSETS

Ackroyd, Peter. *Queer City: Gay London from the Romans to the Present Day*. London: Chatto & Windus, 2017
Barlow, Clare. "Rejecting Normal: Curating Queer British Art, 1861–1967 at Tate Britain and Being Human at Wellcome Collection, London." 2020
Butler, Judith. "Imitation and Gender Insubordination." In *Inside/Out: Lesbian Theories, Gay Theories*, edited by Diana Fuss. New York: Routledge, 1991
Conlan, Anna. "Representing Possibility: Morning, Memorial, and Queer Museology." In *Gender, Sexuality and Museums: A Routledge Reader*, edited by Amy K. Levin. London and New York: Routledge, 2010
Darbyshire, Jo. *The Gay Museum: An Exhibition Exploring the History of Lesbian and Gay Presence in Western Australia*. Perth: Western Australian Museum, 2003
Frost, Stuart. "Queering the Museum: Birmingham Museum and Art Gallery." *Social History in Museums* 35 (2011): 59–61
Leszkowicz, Paweł. *Ars Homo Erotica*. Warsaw: National Museum in Warsaw, 2010
Leszkowicz, Paweł. "The Power of Queer Curating in Eastern Europe." In *Working with Feminism: Curating and Exhibitions in Eastern Europe*, edited by Katrin Kivimaa. Tallinn: Tallinn University Press, 2012
Mills, Robert. "Theorizing the Queer Museum." *Museum & Social Issues*, vol. 3, no. 1 (2008)
Petry, Michael. "Hidden Histories: The Experience of Curating a Male Same-Sex Exhibition and the Problems Encountered." In *Gender, Sexuality and Museums: A Routledge Reader*, edited by Amy K. Levin. London and New York: Routledge, 2010
Reilly, Maura. *Curatorial Activism*. 2018
Sanders, James H. "Queering the Museums." *Culture Work: A Periodic Broadside for Arts and Culture Workers*, no. 1 (2007)
Saslow, James. "Closets and the Museum: Homophobia and Art History." In *Lavender Culture*, edited by K. Jay and A. Young. New York: New York University Press, 1978
Smith, Matt. "Making Things Perfectly Queer: Art's Use of Craft to Signify LGBT Identities." Ph.D. diss., University of Brighton, 2015
Smith, Matt. "Queering the Pitch." In *Queering the Museum*. Birmingham: Birmingham Museum & Art Gallery, 2010
Venir, Alice, and Olle Lundin. *A Queer Glossary*. Eindhoven: Van Abbemuseum, 2015
Wilson, Josephine. "The Gay Museum—a History of Lesbian and Gay Presence in Western Australia." *Artlink* 23, no. 2 (June 2003), https://www.artlink.com.au/articles/2464/the-gay-museum-E28093-a-history-of-lesbian-and-gay-pres/

Chapter 6: HOW BLOODY IS TOO BLOODY?

American Alliance of Museums and BoardSource. *Museum Board Leadership 2017: A National Report*. Washington, DC: BoardSource, 2017, https://www.aam-us.org/wp-content/uploads/2018/01/eyizzp-download-the-report.pdf
Association of Art Museum Directors (AAMD). "Art Museums by the Numbers." 2018
Bailey, Martin. "London's National Portrait Gallery and Sackler Trust to 'Not Proceed' with £1m Grant." *The Art Newspaper*, March 19, 2019, https://www.theartnewspaper.com/news/london-s-national-portrait-gallery-rejects-gbp1m-grant-from-sackler-trust
Bishara, Hakim. "In a Letter to MoMA's Director, Activists Declare Plan to Protest Inside Museum." *Hyperallergic*, April 25, 2021, https://hyperallergic.com/640625/in-a-letter-to-momas-director-activists-declare-plan-to-protest-inside-museum/
Bishara, Hakim. "Over 150 Artists Call for Leon Black's Removal from MoMA's Board over Jeffrey Epstein's Financial Ties." *Hyperallergic*, February 4, 2021, https://hyperallergic.com/619709/artists-call-for-leon-blacks-removal-moma-jeffrey-epstein/
Davic, Angela. "The US Museum Directors Salary Data." *Collector*, August 26, 2023, https://www.thecollector.com/the-us-museum-directors-salary-data/
Embuscado, Rain. "The Whitney Museum Is Now Officially the Leonard A. Lauder Building." *ARTnet*, April 6, 2016, https://news.artnet.com/art-world/leonard-lauder-building-whitney-museum-467309
Evans, Mel. *Artwash: Big Oil and the Arts*. London: Pluto Press, 2015
Fossil Free Science Museum. *Science Museum Group: An Unravelling Tragedy*. March 2023, https://cultureunstained.org/wp-content/uploads/2023/03/adani-unravelling-tragedy.pdf
Fraser, Andrea. *2016 in Museums, Money, and Politics*. San Francisco, CA; Cambridge, MA: CCA Wattis Institute for Contemporary Arts; The MIT Press, 2018
Fraser, Andrea. "A Museum Is Not a Business. It Is Run In a Business-Like Fashion." In *Art and Its Institutions: Current Conflicts, Critique, and Collaborations*, edited

by Nina Möntmann. London: Black Dog Publishing, 2006
Gessen, Masha. "Nan Goldin Leads a Protest at the Guggenheim against the Sackler Family." *New Yorker*, February 10, 2019, https://www.newyorker.com/news/our-columnists/nan-goldin-leads-a-protest-at-the-guggenheim-against-the-sackler-family
Giridharadas, Anand. "When Your Money Is So Tainted Museums Don't Want It." *New York Times*, May 16, 2019, https://www.nytimes.com/2019/05/16/opinion/sunday/met-sackler.html
Graw, Isabelle. *High Price: Art Between the Market and Celebrity Culture*. Berlin: Sternberg Press, 2009
Greenberger, Alex. "'It's Helpful to Know All Scales': Online Spreadsheet Discloses Museum Workers' Salaries." *ARTnews*, May 31, 2019, https://www.artnews.com/art-news/news/google-spreadsheet-museum-workers-disclose-salaries-12670/
Keefe, Patrick Radden. *Empire of Pain: The Secret History of the Sackler Dynasty*. New York: Doubleday, 2021
Kimmelman, Michael. "The 'Star Wars' Effect, and the Part That's Art." *New York Times*, April 5, 2002, https://www.nytimes.com/2002/04/05/movies/art-review-the-star-wars-effect-and-the-part-that-s-art.html
Lieberman, Rhonda. "Painting Over the Dirty Truth." *New Republic*, September 23, 2019
Mallett, Whitney, and Katy Schneider. "Ranking New York's Most Toxic Museum Boards." *Vulture*, August 7, 2019, https://www.vulture.com/2019/08/new-york-most-toxic-museum-boards.html
Michalska, Julia, and Hannah McGivern. "'Like Being Married to a Serial Killer': Hito Steyerl Denounces Sackler Sponsorship of Museums." *The Art Newspaper*, April 10, 2019, https://www.theartnewspaper.com/2019/04/10/like-being-married-to-a-serial-killer-hito-steyerl-denounces-sackler-sponsorship-of-museums
Nayyar, Rhea. "British Museum Announces $63M Partnership with Oil Giant." *Hyperallergic*, December 19, 2023, https://hyperallergic.com/862948/british-museum-announces-63m-partnership-with-oil-giant-bp/#
Pogrebin, Robin, and Elizabeth Harris. "Warren Kanders Quits Whitney Board After Tear Gas Protests." *New York Times*, July 25, 2019, https://www.nytimes.com/2019/07/25/arts/whitney-warren-kanders-resigns.html
Pogrebin, Robin, Elizabeth Harris, and Graham Bowley. "New Scrutiny of Museum Boards Takes Aim at World of Wealth and Status." *New York Times*, October 2, 2019, https://www.nytimes.com/2019/10/02/arts/design/whitney-art-museums-trustees.html
Shaked, Nizan. "Splitting the Public and Private Uses of Art." *Counterpunch*, February 20, 2015, https://www.counterpunch.org/2015/02/20/splitting-the-public-and-private-uses-of-art/
Small, Zachary. "Activists Demand MoMA Divest from Private Prisons and Weapons Manufacturers." *Hyperallergic*, March 7, 2019, https://hyperallergic.com/488435/activists-demand-moma-divest-from-private-prisons-and-weapons-manufacturers/
Sweeney, Harkins, Watkins-Hayes, and Adams-Santos. "The BTA 2022 Art Museum Trustee Survey." 2022
Vartanian, Hrag, Zachary Small, and Jasmine Weber. "Whitney Museum Staffers Demand Answers After Vice Chair's Relationship to Tear Gas Manufacturer Is Revealed." *Hyperallergic*, November 30, 2018, https://hyperallergic.com/473702/whitney-tear-gas-manufacturer-is-revealed/
Wetenhall, John. "Why Not to Run Your Museum 'More Like a Business.'" *Museum*, May/June 2017

Postscript: "Under His Eye"

Andrews, Travis M. "Behind the Right's Loathing of the NEA: Two 'Despicable' Exhibits Almost 30 Years Ago." *Washington Post*, March 20, 2017, https://www.washingtonpost.com/news/morning-mix/wp/2017/03/20/behind-the-loathing-of-the-national-endowment-for-the-arts-a-pair-of-despicable-exhibits-almost-30-years-ago/
Figueroa, Fernanda, Ayanna Alexander, and Corey Williams. "Trump Order Ending Federal DEI Programs Leaves Agencies and Stakeholders on Uncertain Ground." *Associated Press*, January 23, 2025, https://apnews.com/article/trump-dei-executive-order-diversity-inclusion-f67ea86032986084dd71c5aa0c6b8d1d
Kennicott, Philip. "How Trump's Kennedy Center Takeover Could Change the Arts." *Washington Post*, February 10, 2025, https://www.washingtonpost.com/entertainment/2025/02/10/trump-plan-for-arts-humanities/

PICTURE CREDITS

1 *Slavery and the Bank*, 2022–24. Exhibition installation. © Bank of England Museum
2 Amalia Mesa-Bains, *New World Wunderkammer*, 2013–14. "Cabinet of Curiosities" installation. Various materials, 3 × 9.1 × 1.5 m (10 × 30 × 5 ft). © Amalia Mesa-Bains. Photo: Joshua White/JW Pictures
3 Pedro Lasch, *Coatlicue and Las Meninas,* from the *Black Mirror/ Espejo Negro* series, 2007–present. Simulation of installation at Museo Nacional del Prado, Madrid, and Museo Nacional de Antropología, Mexico City. Courtesy of the artist
4 Richard Bell, *We Were Here First*, 2007. Acrylic on canvas, 2 parts, 243.8 × 365.8 cm (96 × 144 in.). Courtesy of the artist and Milani Gallery, Meeanjin/Brisbane
5 Outi Pieski, *Ovdavázzit—Forewalkers*, 2019. Wood, reindeer horn, metal, lace, reindeer moss, and peat. Variable dimensions. Alvar Aalto Pavilion at the 58th Venice Biennale, 2019. Courtesy of the artist. Photo: Ugo Carmeni
6 Tablet made of birch panels and sinews, crafted by the curatorial collective, artists, and other helpers associated with the Sámi Pavilion at the 59th Venice Biennale, 2022. The panel obscures from view the words "Finland," "Norway," and "Sweden." Photo © Maura Reilly
7 Richard Bell, *Whole Lot*, 2002. Acrylic on canvas, 160 × 120 cm (63 × 47¼ in.). Courtesy of the artist and Milani Gallery, Meeanjin/ Brisbane
8 Commemorative head of an Oba (king). Lost-wax cast in brass, 1550–1650, Benin City. 28 × 21 × 20 cm (11⅛ × 8⅜ × 7⅞ in.). © The Trustees of the British Museum
9 Pussy Galore, *Manhattan Boycott Guide*, 2025. © 2025 Pussy Galore
10 *Being Human*, 2019–present. Exhibition installation. Photo: Wellcome Collection/Steven Pocock
11 JJJJJerome Ellis, *Impediment Is Information*, 2021. Single-channel video. Courtesy of the artist
12 Carrie Mae Weems, *Guggenheim Bilbao*, 2008. Pigment print. © Carrie Mae Weems. Courtesy of the artist and Gladstone Gallery, New York, Fraenkel Gallery, San Francisco, and Galerie Barbara Thumm, Berlin
13 "Time of Struggle" section in the exhibition *Ars Homo Erotica*, National Museum in Warsaw, 2010. Artwork in foreground: David Černý, *Entropa: The Polish Panel*, 2009. Installation on the wall in the background: photograph of a copy of *Tyrannicide Monument (Harmodius and Arystogeiton)* by Kritios and Nesiotes, from the collection of The National Museum, Poland. Curated by Paweł Leszkowicz, National Museum, Warsaw. Photo © Paweł Leszkowicz
14 Jo Darbyshire, "GAY" neon artwork, for *The Gay Museum* exhibition, 2003, Western Australian Museum. Photo: Suzi Wild
15 Matt Smith, *The Ladies of Llangollen*, 2010. White earthenware, enamels, and transfers. Height 15.3 cm (6⅛ in.). From the exhibition *Queering the Museum* at Birmingham Museum & Art Gallery, 2010. Photo © Birmingham Museums Trust
16 André Kertész, *On the Boulevards, Paris (Dubonnet)*, 1934. Gelatin silver print. © The Estate of André Kertész/Courtesy Stephen Bulger Gallery
17 William Powhida, *Collectors (Halloween)*, 2019. Watercolor and acrylic on paper, 38 × 38 cm (15 × 15 in.). Courtesy of the artist and Postmasters Gallery
18 Decolonize This Place, Crisis of the Whitney, December 2018. Photo courtesy Decolonize This Place

INDEX

Numbers in *italics* refer to illustration plate numbers.

AUTHOR BIOGRAPHIES

MAURA REILLY is Director of the Zimmerli Art Museum and Professor of Art History at Rutgers University. She has held several leadership positions in the arts, including Executive Director of the National Academy of Design, New York City, and Senior Curator at the American Federation of Arts. Reilly is the Founding Curator of the Elizabeth A. Sackler Center for Feminist Art at the Brooklyn Museum, where she developed and launched the U.S.'s first exhibition and public programming space devoted entirely to feminist art. While there, she organized several landmark exhibitions, including the permanent installation of Judy Chicago's *The Dinner Party* and the blockbuster *Global Feminisms* (co-curated with Linda Nochlin), among others. Reilly has curated over two dozen exhibitions with a focus on underrepresented artists and social justice concerns, including *transfeminisms* (2024–25), *Michelle Agins: Storyteller* (2024), *Judy Watson: shadow bone* (2024), and *Wandamba yalungka/ Winds change direction* (2021). She has also organized international exhibitions on contemporary Indigenous art, LGBTQIA+ art, and feminist art, as well as retrospectives of Ghada Amer, Carolee Schneemann, Nayland Blake, Richard Bell, and Miriam Schapiro. Reilly has written extensively on curatorial practice and is the author of several books, including *Curatorial Activism: Towards an Ethics of Curating* (Thames & Hudson, 2018), which was listed as one of *The New York Times*'s "Best Art Books of 2018." Reilly has held academic teaching positions at Tufts University; Queensland College of Art and Design, Griffith University; Sydney College of the Arts, University of Sydney; and Arizona State University, and received her M.A. and Ph.D. in art history from the Institute of Fine Arts, New York University.

LIISA-RÁVNÁ FINBOG is a Sámi Indigenous scholar, *duojár*, and curator from Oslo, Vaapste, and Skánit in the Norwegian part of Sápmi. She is a founding member of Bárru Academic Collective, an equitable and collective gathering of Arctic Indigenous scholars and thinkers, and co-curated the first-ever Sámi Pavilion at the Venice Biennale in 2022. A prolific writer, Finbog has contributed to collective works such as *Research Journeys In/To Multiple Ways of Knowing*, published articles for platforms such as *Nordic Museology* and *Action Stories*, penned essays for multiple exhibition catalogues, and authored *It Speaks to You—Making Kin Through People, Stories, and Duodji in Sámi Museums*.

ACKNOWLEDGMENTS

To Roger Thorp, Editorial Director at Thames & Hudson, thank you for believing in this project from the start. Thank you also to the amazing Thames & Hudson colleagues who shepherded this book through to completion, especially Mohara Gill, Editorial Manager, as well as my editor extraordinaire, Elizabeth Keene. Thanks also to Rowena Alsey, Celia Falconer, Diana Loxley, Callin Mackintosh, and Matt Watson Young. To the many curators, writers, artists, and museum professionals cited throughout this book, I am greatly indebted. Those who have had an exceptional influence on this book's development include, among others, Cecilia Alemani, Clare Barlow, Maurice Berger, Puwai Cairns, Clémentine Deliss, Okwui Enwezor, Anand Giridharadas, the Guerrilla Girls, Dan Hicks, Rhonda Lieberman, Amy Lonetree, Walter Mignolo, Robert Mills, Kwame Opoku, Richard Sandell, Felwine Sarr, and Bénédicte Savoy. Special thanks are due to Sámi Indigenous scholar Liisa-Rávná Finbog, who co-authored the chapter on indigenizing museums. Finally, I thank the many colleagues and friends who have provided unwavering support as I was writing this book, including, but not limited to, my incredible partner, Rochelle Sanders. This book is dedicated to my sister Caitlin Reilly, who has been and continues to be a daily source of inspiration and joy.